Interpretive Quantification

Countering the divide between positivists who embrace quantitative, numerical approaches and postpositivist scholars who favor qualitative, interpretive approaches, J. Samuel Barkin and Laura Sjoberg argue that methods are more widely adaptable than is commonly assumed by either camp. In this volume, ten highly regarded scholars in the field of international relations apply quantitative methods and formal models to specific constructivist and critical research questions. In this way, each chapter serves not only as evidence that methods can productively be applied across paradigms but also as a guide to how this may be done. In sum, the contributors make a compelling case that when researchers cordon off particular methods for ideological reasons, they circumscribe their own paradigms and hinder their own research agendas.

J. Samuel Barkin is Professor of Global Governance and Human Security at the McCormack Graduate School of Policy and Global Studies at the University of Massachusetts Boston.

Laura Sjoberg is Associate Professor of Political Science at the University of Florida, with an affiliation with the Center for Women's Studies and Gender Research.

Interpretive Quantification

Methodological Explorations for Critical and Constructivist IR

J. Samuel Barkin and Laura Sjoberg, Editors

University of Michigan Press
Ann Arbor

Published in the United States of America by the
University of Michigan Press
Manufactured in the United States of America
♾ Printed on acid-free paper

2020 2019 2018 2017 4 3 2 1

A CIP catalog record for this book is available from the British Library.

Library of Congress Cataloging-in-Publication data has been applied for.

ISBN: 978-0-472-07339-9 (hardback)
ISBN: 978-0-472-05339-1 (paperback)
ISBN: 978-0-472-12265-3 (e-book)

To those we have lost along the way

Contents

Illustrations

Acknowledgments

The inspiration for this book was a long time in the making. Laura started talking about math in political science at the Institute for Qualitative Research Methods in 2002 as a second-year graduate student and has played with the idea off and on since—in draft articles never submitted or never published, in conversations with the late Hayward Alker, in comments and questions at conference panels, and in a variety of other ways under the surface. For decades, Sammy has been doing rational choice and constructivist work and thinking and writing about how they might fit together.

But the ideas in this book can be difficult to find an intellectual home for. Earlier work of ours along these lines got countless reviews that really got under our skin and helped to inspire this volume as a project, such as "I even ran a Google search on feminist mathematics and got nothing" and "unlike the author, I read the stated goal of the journal on its website." Our absolute favorite is the query "are you sure this is not a put-on?" Nope, and we're still not sure, because being sure requires a sort of ontological certainty that we do not have and that we worry about when we see expressed. But we hope that this volume starts a conversation in which critical theory and mathematical/quantitative/computational methods can be paired fruitfully—or at least in which such a pairing is not discarded *a priori.*

We are grateful to the University of Florida Department of Political Science, Michael Bernhard (the Raymond and Miriam Ehrlich Chair in Political Science), Larry Dodd (the Manning J. Dauer Chair in Political Science), and Paul D'Anieri (then dean of the College of Liberal Arts and Sciences) for sponsoring the Spring 2010 conference on epistemology and methodology in international relations that eventually inspired our engagement in this project. At that conference, Badredine Arfi, Nick Onuf, Harry Gould, Mauro Caraccioli, Phil Steinberg, Audie Klotz, Aida Hozic, and Patrick

Thaddeus Jackson provided both energy and feedback for the project. Audiences at ISA, ISA-West, ISA-Northeast, the University of Alabama, the Norwegian Institute of International Affairs, and the 2014 Millennium Conference on Method, Methodology, and Innovation were helpful as we worked out the framework presented in this book and how it relates to our other views on epistemology and method. To those ends, we are particularly grateful for comments from Ole Jacob Sending, Eric Blanchard, Sandra Harding, David Lake, and Daniel Levine. Portions of Chapter 1 are reprinted from our article, "Calculating Critique," *Millennium Journal of International Studies* 43(3) (2015): 852-871. Melody Herr from the University of Michigan Press turned this project from an idea we had toyed with and wanted to do someday to something we pursued. A Venture Workshop Grant from the International Studies Association (with Annette Freyberg-Inan, Ewan Harrison, and Patrick James) made pursuing this project possible, and its contributors produced an amazing two full days of discussion at the workshop. Jennifer Sterling-Folker, Colin Wight, Torbjorn Kutsen, Fred Chernoff, Sara Mitchell, Pat James, Annette Freyberg-Inan, and Ole Jacob Sending, as well as all of the chapter contributors, served as discussants who helped to make this project stronger and more coherent. At the end of the day, a project like this does not come together without an army of amazing contributors, a great editor at the press, and a lot of support. We had all of those things and cannot even begin to express our gratitude for them.

A number of the thoughts included herein developed in conversation with Hayward Alker, Nick Onuf, David Collier, and Kevin Knudson. An undergraduate of Laura's, Jeff Horowitz, had the desire to make a game-theoretic model of economic sanctions that accounted for ontological security—a project that inspired Laura to revisit the argument for traditional "quantitative" methods in critical theorizing. A statistical project with a former graduate student of both editors, Jessica Peet, pushed further in that direction. Beth DeSombre provided both moral support and an invaluable sounding board. Thanks as well, of course, to family and friends, as well as three Chihuahuas and a mutt named Max, April, Gizmo, and Zöe.

CHAPTER I

Introduction

Why Quantitative Methods for Constructivist and Critical Theorizing?

J. SAMUEL BARKIN AND LAURA SJOBERG

This is a book about broadening our thinking about research in international relations (IR).[1] Our goal is practical: showing the variety of ways in which scholars can design research that will produce useful analysis of social and political life. We focus on international relations as a discipline, but our argument applies across the social sciences and complements discussion to be found in other fields, such as psychology. After laying out an argument that IR research has largely misinterpreted the relationships among epistemology, inference, methodology, and method, this introductory chapter suggests a reinterpretation that breaks down the traditional, assumed pairings of research paradigms, philosophies of science, and particular methods in the discipline. It then suggests that a pairing of quantitative methods and critical and/or constructivist IR research has payoffs both in terms of the quality of research done and the ways that epistemology and method are thought about in the field.

To explore these arguments, we start with a question that scholars have asked countless times: what tools of research, what methods, are available to scholars of social science working in different theoretical and epistemological traditions? While this question has been asked over and over, the standard answers from within the disciplinary tradition of IR tend to offer a limited range of methodological possibilities and an even more limited palate of methods to go with any given research program. For example, it is often assumed that quantitative models are the best method for neopositivist causal analysis, and critical feminist theory is often understood to benefit most from methods like ethnography and discourse analysis. These traditional associations confuse method with methodology and homologize epistemology and research design. We argue here that these associations are limiting and are counterproductive to good methodology. Scholars should be drawing on a much broader palate of methodological possibilities in research designs than most currently do. Methods are tools—they have individual strengths and weaknesses but can nonetheless be used for a variety of tasks. To illustrate this argument, we focus on a set of methodological combinations that is particularly underutilized in the discipline: the use of quantitative, formal, and computational methods in critical and constructivist IR research programs.

Methods texts often teach that the divide between "quantitative" and "qualitative" maps onto the epistemological divide between "scientific" research and "post-positivist" research in IR.[2] Still, "qualitative" work has been successfully appropriated for "scientific" analysis,[3] and some scholars have argued that there are interpretive, theoretical uses for "quantitative" methods. These categories themselves, we believe, need to be questioned for these purposes, given that different tools put in the "quantitative" and "qualitative" toolboxes have different methodological uses (and are compatible with different epistemologies). We argue that the binaries often used to construct "research design" in IR are logically unsustainable and that the traditions they support therefore need to be reevaluated.

This book takes a particular approach to that reevaluation. Rather than opting for a specific epistemological perspective and matching a method to it, we start with a question about the knowledge uses of methods. What knowledge can we get from formal models, from statistics, or from theoretical mathematics? Asking this question removes the *a priori* assumption that these methods are only useful for "positivist" ends, and exploring the answers to these questions finds a wider spectrum of applicability.

Looking from this different perspective suggests that the discipline of IR has *wrongly* come to see "quantitative" methods as mapping one-to-one to what Patrick Thaddeus Jackson calls "neopositivist social science."[4] The perspective that pairs (increasingly sophisticated) quantitative methods and normal social science often places normative value on the pairing, suggesting that the best social science is large-*n* data analysis. An extension of this pairing is the tendency of social scientists to associate any piece of research that has numbers or equations with positivist social science. We think this is an incomplete representation of what tools like statistics, mathematics, and formal modeling have to offer, especially for perspectives that fall outside of the traditional boundaries of positivist social science, substantively or epistemologically. We contend that the surface-level tension between "objective" social science and "interested" critical research can be navigated and negotiated in different ways, including, but not limited to, the use of increasingly sophisticated techniques that account for subjectivity and even intersubjectivity, the heuristic use of formal models, agent-based modeling, constitutive uses of statistical methods, and the like. Further, we argue that the limitation of certain methods to "objective" knowledge uses represents an incomplete understanding of the potential contributions of those methods.

The goal of this project, then, is to explore methods' potential and thus begin rethinking the unsustainable assumptions underlying the epistemological and methodological practices of IR research. Particularly, this book looks at the potential uses of quantitative methods, broadly defined, for research trajectories for which they are rarely used and perhaps even more rarely recognized as proper tools. By "broadly defined," we mean that we use the term "quantitative methods" not to denote a narrow reference to statistical approaches but to describe statistical, mathematical, and computational tools that use numerical or mathematical notation. This book argues, theoretically and through examples, that the match between quantitative and neopositivist that is traditionally assumed in IR is nowhere near as close or as exclusive as the discipline is accustomed to seeing it. It contends that "quantitative methods" and "constructivist/critical theorizing," previously understood as not only distinct but mutually exclusive, can benefit from a dialogue *without* either misusing quantitative methods or changing the basic epistemological assumptions associated with constructivist and critical theorizing.

To be clear, we are not arguing for a takeover of quantitative methods by, or the dominance of quantitative methods in, critical or constructivist theorizing, or for an understanding of the utility of quantitative methods that demands a positivist epistemology. Nor are we arguing that it is necessary to operationalize or quantify concepts traditionally employed in critical IR. To argue that quantitative methods *can* be useful to constructivists and critical theorists is by no means to argue that they should be the only or even the primary methods used.

We *are* arguing that there are several ways that these methods can help to make a substantive contribution to critical and constructivist IR. We suggest as well that revealing the utility of quantitative methods for critical and constructivist IR demonstrates that the ideas of "method-driven" and "theory-driven" research are based on fundamental misconceptions of the relationships between method and theory. That quantitative (traditionally positivist) methods can be usefully paired with critical (traditionally post-positivist) theorizing is damning for the quantitative/qualitative and positivist/post-positivist divides, as well as the traditional ways we train students in methodology and practice methods in the field. In other words, discussing quantitative methods in the context of constructivist and critical research in IR is both an intellectually important intervention in itself and an exemplar of broader correctives necessary in the discipline and in the social sciences more broadly.

Epistemology and Method

To begin with the basics, we define both "research" and "international relations" broadly and consider neither the primary subject matter of this book. The authors in this book share an ontological interest in global politics and a disciplinary home in either political science or international relations, but in this conversation, they are leveraging those commonalities to explore the potential of methods traditionally not utilized for constructivist and critical research. By "IR research," we mean empirical analysis, theory building, theory testing, concept exploration, and other work seeking knowledge (broadly conceived) about the constitution, working, and/or functions of global politics.

By "method," we mean specific techniques and processes for gathering and/or analyzing information. For example, membership categorization device analysis (a form of critical discourse analysis) is a method,[5] as is a Cox proportional hazards regression model.[6] Methodology is the strategy by which methods are selected, given research questions. We suggest that methodology be understood as a bridge that links research questions, epistemology, and method. Particularly, by "methodology," we mean the way in which scholars (either in the context of a particular research project or more generally) think about the relationship between methods and research questions. Discussions of methodology have used broad-based categories like "quantitative" and "qualitative" incorrectly.[7] Other discussions have characterized methodology as the narrator of the processes of search and research.[8] This latter understanding more closely represents the one used in this book: methodology is the analysis of what methods are chosen and why, given certain assumptions.

Because of our adoption of this view, we characterize this book as centered around methodologies. That said, it is important to note that we do not see the predicates of the book's title—constructivism and critical theory—as methodologies. As we discuss below, we see constructivism as an assumption of where we should be looking for the source of outcomes in international politics (at the level of the intersubjective and the co-constitution of agent and structure), and we see critical theory as a claim about the relationships between knower and known, theory and practice. For both constructivism and critical theory, there are sets of methods that are appropriate to the assumptions of each and sets of methods that are less so. We argue that, to this point, the methodologies that have identified these sets of methods have been limited by both directional and utility assumptions that apply the quantitative/qualitative divide to the selection of methods. The mistaken assumption that there are "qualitative" and "quantitative" *methodologies*, built on the mistaken assumption of the epistemological unity of the category of "quantitative" methods, has reverberated across the field. It has produced an oversimplified mapping of the methods relevant to constructivist and critical research in IR.

Discussions of different ways of doing research in IR, mirroring discussions in the social sciences more broadly, tend to happen either at the level of epistemology or at the level of method. Rarely do these discussions look at the relationships among epistemology, methodology, and method, and when they do, they tend to start at the more abstract level of epistemology and then discuss different methods that fit in. Particularly, we often assume that it is appropriate first to determine the epistemological commitments of our work and then to match the appropriate method or methods to those epistemological commitments. For example, on the one hand, scholars who approach research from a feminist perspective often locate their epistemological understanding of the discipline in the grouping broadly identified as post-positivist, understanding knowledge as perspectival and regarding scholarship as political.[9] Many scholars derive from those epistemological commitments that the appropriate methods of feminist scholarship should be things like ethnography, discourse and dispositive analysis, searching for silences, and other tools.[10] On the other hand, scholars interested in the relationship between institutional design and institutional efficiency often express epistemological commitments to causal and predictive analysis.[11] Many scholars derive from those epistemological commitments that the appropriate methods for their work include predictive formal models and large-*n* regression analysis of empirical observations.[12] Even arguments purporting to broaden the discipline's use of method often begin by assuming a narrow epistemological perspective.[13]

We propose that it is fruitful to look at this conversation from the other direction. IR scholars, whatever their epistemological convictions, tend to receive their primary research training in methods already deemed appropriate for their particular epistemological perspectives. "Postivists" focus on mastering quantitative methods of various stripes, supplemented by the occasional hypothesis-testing case study.[14] "Post-positivists" focus on learning a class of methods often understood as "interpretive,"[15] which share perspectival and experience-near orientations.[16] We are instead interested in thinking about what our research specifically and the discipline generally would look like if we critically interrogated the directional relationship between method and epistemology.

Particularly, we are interested in whether choices of method constrain us or enable us as we think about our subject matter. Are there broader epistemological applications of certain methods than the field generally recognizes? Are more methods available to certain theoretical/epistemological approaches than their researchers routinely employ? What can we learn about the relationship between method and epistemology from exploring these questions?

While we are not interested in contributing to or feeding a trend of "method-driven" research (where scholars emphasize technique within particular methods and apply it to substantive questions rather than looking for appropriate tools to evaluate those questions), we think there is something to be gained from thought experiments that start with the potential of a "tool," rather than assuming that the conventional use of particular tools is the only appropriate application and that the tools available for certain research programs are only the ones that have previously been used as such. Particularly, we think that such an approach has profound implications for the presumed "unity" of "science" discussed in most methods texts, both qualitative and quantitative, in IR specifically and the social sciences generally.[17]

Inference and Method

Perhaps the best-known methods text within IR and political science more broadly is *Designing Social Inquiry* by King, Keohane, and Verba (henceforth KKV).[18] Its authors argue that the demands of good research design in the social sciences are similar across methods. They define the goal of scientific research as inference[19] and argue that the rules of inference developed in the context of statistical analysis can be applied to qualitative methods, broadly defined. Like so many of the terms used in the discussion of method, methodology, and epistemology, however, the term *inference* can be understood in a variety of ways. At its core, inference is learning about something from observing something else. Understood broadly, this definition covers almost all of what scholars might do across the social sciences. Postmodern scholarly analysis, for example, infers meaning from text, which is interpretable in various ways. This work is inference broadly speaking, if not either descriptive or causal in KKV's terms.[20]

But KKV use the concept of inference in a narrower and more statistical way. They speak of inference from empirical observations, which, in turn, they treat unproblematically as "facts." This epistemological approach draws on the supposition that "valid knowledge must in the end be related to some sort of accurate correspondence between empirical and theoretical propositions on the one hand and the actual character of a mind-independent world on the other,"[21] which is how we are generally taught to think of theory in the natural sciences. KKV, then, are in effect assuming that social science is no different in kind from the natural sciences, that the natural sciences can be studied in an entirely objective way, and that theory in both can be understood as adjudicable by empirical observation.

To the extent that social science research happens within a neopositivist epistemology, much of the advice that KKV give about research design is both logically sound and internally consistent. Their book remains an excellent guide to how to go about making inferential claims from empirical evidence, whether that evidence comes in quantified or nonquantified form; our task here is not to take issue with their effort to provide clear rules for research designs that do not rely on quantified empirics but that make inferential claims.[22] But we do take issue with their *ex ante* assumptions that the sort of inference they provide rules for defines and delimits what counts as science; that the natural sciences are adequate as a model for the social sciences and, by extension, IR; and that "science" in any form is the ultimate goal of *all* IR research (and therefore the standard for judgment of the utility of method). In other words, while KKV argue for the *unity* of science, we argue for its *disunity*.

A number of arguments found in the philosophy of science suggest that the scientific enterprise cannot be understood as the simple accumulation of empirical facts. Perhaps the best-known such argument in the context of the natural sciences is Thomas Kuhn's concept of paradigms.[23] Patrick Thaddeus Jackson,[24] speaking in the context of IR but with reference to questions of philosophy of science that span the social and natural sciences, notes a variety of ways in which accepted scientific and social-scientific practices draw on ontological and epistemological bases broader than KKV's neopositivism. Jackson suggests two axes on which to think about research in IR: (1)

mind-world monism versus dualism (where the former sees the "world" as endogenous to the practices of knowledge production, while the latter sees the possibility for the separation of researcher and research subject) and (2) phenomenalism versus transfactualism (where the former suggests that it is impossible to transcend experience, while the latter holds out the possibility of going beyond facts to grasp the deeper processes and factors underneath). From these two dichotomies, Jackson suggests four ideal types of social science: neopositivism (dualist, phenomenalist), critical realism (dualist, transfactualist), analyticism (monist, phenomenalist), and reflexivity (monist, transfactualist). Recognizing that "associations between particular substantive theories and particular methodological perspectives do not arise for compelling logical or intellectual reasons, but because of sociological developments," Jackson argues that these associations deprive the field of potentially "important intellectual gains."[25]

This line of argumentation suggests that KKV's assumptions about science and method do not define the limits of possibility in scientific research, whether natural or social. But IR, as is the case with much of social science, is also different in kind from natural science, in a way that places further demands on methodology than those to be found in the natural sciences. Social sciences are recursive, meaning that theory not only organizes observations about the object of study but actually changes that object. This insight underlies all critical and postmodern approaches to IR specifically and social science more broadly. IR theory, whether empirical or normative, changes not only the knowledge base of the objects of study but also the normative and discursive contexts within which the objects of study interact. IR theory, as a form of social theory, is, in this sense, inherently political.

Texts on epistemology, methodology, and method in constructivist and critical theorizing in IR often grasp this notion that theory is political, but they often draw from it the implication that method must be interpretive and therefore qualitative. As Lene Hansen explains, "the modernist belief in our ability to rationally perceive and theorize the world is in poststructuralism replaced by dis-belief in unproblematic notions of modernity, enlightenment, truth, science, and reason."[26] This leads, in Hansen's words (citing Jef Huysmans), to scholarship by genealogy, which "does not look for a continuous history, but for discontinuity and forgotten meanings; it does not look for an origin, indeed, it is assumed one cannot be found; and it does not, finally, focus on the 'object of genealogy' itself, but on the conditions, discourses, and interpretations surrounding it."[27] This look at the conditions, discourses, and interpretations surrounding the object is necessarily both *perspectival* and political and is incorporated into the methodological outlooks of post-structuralist research.

This is also true in feminist research. As Brooke Ackerly, Maria Stern, and Jacqui True have argued, "feminist IR scholars have developed not just a toolkit of methods but ways of incorporating ontological and epistemological reflections into methodological choices that lead them to rethink the boundaries of the IR discipline."[28] The key to this critical reflection, in the authors' understanding, is "reflexivity, which encourages the researcher to re-interrogate critically her own scholarship."[29]

In describing potential methodological choices for constructivist research, Audie Klotz and Cecilia Lynch suggest that "researchers' own normative views" will be influential both in shaping research and in making methodological choices, since "analysts live in a particular spatial location and social setting within the contemporary liberal capitalist order." As such, "the relationship between researcher and interpretation underscores the discursive rather than material conception of power that underpins the analysis of meaning."[30] This inspiration causes Vincent Pouliot to argue for "sobjectivism" as constructivist methodology—looking to "recover subjective meanings to their objectification thanks to contextualization and historicization."[31] Discussing constructivists' distinct "style of reasoning," Pouliot argues that social reality, being "constructed instead of exogenously given," requires reflexive methodological approaches, including induction, interpretation, and dialectical understandings.[32]

Across work on self-described post-positivist methodology, it is largely either explicitly stated[33] or implied[34] that induction, interpretation, dialectical understandings, and perspectival knowledge are obtainable through and only through the use of methods generally understood by social scientists to be qualitative. While some dissenting voices exist,[35] texts on methodologies for reflective, post-postivist, or interpretive inquiry seem to match *post-positivist epistemology* with *interpretive methodology* and *qualitative methods.* While post-positivist epistemology and interpretive methodology *do* go together, we argue that they do not necessarily take the assumed mapping step to *qualitative methods.*

This book, then, has two goals. Its first goal is to cover the same terrain as KKV—the relationship among method, methodology, and research design—but to locate that terrain in a much broader epistemological and ontological setting. Whereas KKV provide the rules to make various methods conform to a specific narrow epistemology of social science, we suggest ways in which specific methods can conform with the methodological demands of a broader array of epistemologies. This book's second goal is to cover the same terrain as many of KKV's non-positivist competitors and critics—broad thinking about the ways in which intersubjective, interpretive, perspectival knowledge can be produced, shared, and brought to bear on the problems in contemporary global politics—but to locate that terrain *across*, rather than tied to, particular research methods. Whereas KKV provide suggestions on how to supplement the traditional methodological arsenal of IR scholars with tools that are better suited to the particular ontological predispositions of post-positivist research, we suggest ways in which that orientation overlooks some of the traditional tools of IR that might be fruitfully leveraged toward those same ends. We choose quantitative and formal methods and critical and constructivist theory, and we opt not to claim that these methods or theoretical approaches should predominate in the study of IR or that they have particular affinities for each other greater than their affinities with other methods and approaches. Rather, we choose them as sets of approaches and methods that are not often combined elsewhere and that therefore serve well to illustrate our broader claim that methodological possibilities in the study of IR are broader than what is often taught in the field.

The Disunity of Science (or the Problem with the Quantitative/Qualitative Divide)

KKV argue that "the logic of good qualitative and good quantitative research designs do not fundamentally differ,"[36] which suggests the application of "a unified logic of inference to both,"[37] because "the differences between the quantitative and qualitative traditions are only stylistic and methodologically and substantively unimportant."[38] This interpretation is shared by some of KKV's sharpest critics. For example, Henry Brady and David Collier (with Jason Seawright) make clear that their criticisms "do not amount to a rejection of the basic enterprise of striving for a shared vocabulary and framework for both quantitative and qualitative research."[39] Indeed, they "share KKV's (4–5) view that quantitative and qualitative methods are focused on similar epistemologies."[40] Brady and Collier's major contribution to the conversation is to make the argument that while KKV's view is based on the "quantitative template," there is value in looking at a "qualitative template" for both quantitative and qualitative methodology.

Both of these approaches make the mistake of conflating methods and epistemologies, understanding "quantitative" and "qualitative" templates where no such thing exists. They assume that IR's epistemological templates are defined by whether scholars use quantitative or qualitative methods to seek knowledge, rather than by understandings of what knowledge is and how it maps onto the properties of global politics. With Patrick Thaddeus Jackson, we see the qualitative/quantitative divide as "a distinction without difference," which is, if anything, orthogonal to any real distinctions across camps of IR research. As stated elsewhere, we believe that "the reification of qualitative methods as a category not only helps to cement existing in-group/out-group dynamics within the discipline" but "also creates tension within the out-group . . . by defining the boundaries of the out-group."[41] Therefore, we see the use of the categories *"quantitative"* and *"qualitative"* to describe *types of research* in IR as politically fraught and pedagogically counterproductive.[42]

Whereas KKV and Brady and Collier argue for a fundamental *unity* of political science inquiry, we argue for its *disunity*. On this axis, we contend, the discipline has been looking at the relationships among epistemology, methodology, and method in a fundamentally problematic way. We suggest that correcting this problem both leads to new insights for the application of the philosophy of science in IR and improves the field's substantive research.

The same could be said for the categories *"positivist"* and *"post-positivist."* While we use the term *neopositivist* here, following Jackson's specific definition rooted in a discussion of the philosophy of science,[43] references to positivism and post-positivism in IR often serve more as sociological and disciplinary markers than as epistemological stances. They serve different claims about how social science should be done and what counts as legitimate social science. They serve, in other words, as claims for the unity of inquiry. Eschewing the loaded categories of "positivist" and "post-positivist" as broader epistemological commitments allows us to focus on methodology as the connection between research question and method.

Methods, Methodology, and Theory

In this vein, a key part of our argument is that constructivist and critical research, whether understood by the particular practitioner as positivist or post-positivist, are compatible with quantitative methods, broadly defined. Both the substance and the importance of this argument rely on an exploration of the broader context of the relationships between research, theory, and methods. As noted earlier, the field often pairs particular methods with particular questions intuitively, limiting both the methods available to research questions and the potential of those methods. Examples include statistical modeling with neopositivist hypothesis-testing, formal modeling with rational choice theory, and individual narratives with critical theories. Obviously, we argue against such strict associations. It would be tempting to make the counterclaim, in support of a project like this one, that method is theory-neutral, that one can mix and match theories at will to suit the needs of individual research questions. But this is not quite right either.

In arguing for the disunity of science, we look to undermine the assumption that particular methods and particular epistemologies and/or research approaches neatly map one-to-one. With that assumption, we are also looking to undermine what Patrick Thaddeus Jackson describes as the disciplinary function of science, where a traditional notion of what science is plays a gatekeeping role in the discipline.[44] Recognizing what he describes as a demarcation problem, "the quest for a set of criteria that can adequately demarcate science from non-science," Jackson argues that the discipline maps particular methods to particular perspectives sociologically rather than on merits.[45]

Certain methods do bring with them particular methodological uses that are relevant to the form of theorizing. Statistical methods look for general patterns, often at the expense of the individual exception. They tell us what tends to happen, rather than what can happen or what happens at the extremes. Agent-driven models, whether rational choice models or agent-based ones, simplify to suggest general relationships given sets of prior conditions, rather than focusing on the complexity of particular events or circumstances. Again, this tells us what tends to happen rather than what is happening in a particular situation.

Still, even these traditional leanings of the methods can be capitalized on for different purposes. Statistics, for example, can play a useful role in generating the empirical basis for theoretical arguments, whether those arguments themselves are neopositivist or not. Statistical analysis can also be used to address usefulness in a Weberian sense, by helping to constitute the relationship (rather than the identity) between theory and observation. Similarly, agent-driven models can be a useful technique for exploring the internal logic of theoretical arguments. In some circumstances, quantifying a model can be a useful way of looking at its internal logic, to find out if its assumptions lead to its conclusions in a certain kind of tightly controlled setting. In these terms, within the category of generalized theory, the utility of quantitative modeling should be neither assumed nor rejected out of hand; the utility depends on the specific theory in question.

For this reason, we think, like Michael Westerman and Stephen Yanchar, who pioneered a similar project in psychology, that "the relationships between quantitative and qualitative methods, on the one hand, and the two warring camps, on the other, are quite complex. The two types of methods do not line up neatly with the two sides of the schism."[46] Noting that "the distinction between qualitative and quantitative methods is far less fundamental than most researchers think," Westerman argues "for a thoroughgoing reconceptualization of quantitative methods based on the view that it is possible, and desirable, to employ these methods in interpretive research that treats psychological phenomena as irreducibly meaningful."[47] We agree, and we therefore look to clarify the relationship among ontologies, epistemologies, methodologies, and methods.

Traditionally, the discipline of IR has (consciously or unconsciously) treated these relationships as something like this:

Ontology → Epistemology → Methodology → Method

The most popular combination in political science is an ontology of mind-world dualism, which inspires and is co-constitutive with epistemological phenomenalism, producing neopositivist methodologies, which then use both quantitative and qualitative methods to produce (positivist, objective, inferential) knowledge. A less popular, but still assumed, relationship is between an ontology of mind-world monism, which inspires and is co-constituted with epistemological transfactualism, producing reflexivist methodologies, which then use qualitative, interpretive methods to produce (intersubjective, relational) knowledge.[48]

Jackson suggests that the prioritization of ontology in this organization is at best problematic and at worse insincere.[49] Citing Colin Wight's claim that "methodologies are always, or at least should be, ontologically specific,"[50] Jackson argues that there is an internal contradiction between the idea that ontology comes first and the idea that ontological claims need warrants. For that reason, he does "not think that putting ontology first is the panacea that many seem to think it is."[51] We argue that putting ontology first contains both the mistake of *ordering* that Jackson identifies and a further mistake that he would identify as one of demarcation. That is why we argue that both of the ideal types outlined above are fundamentally limited and that those limits come from the assumption of certain specific and necessary relationships among ontology, epistemology, methodology, and method.

We suggest that methods are useful for multiple methodologies and therefore for multiple epistemologies and even multiple ontologies, as well as multiple IR (as opposed to research) paradigms. We suggest that while certain distinctions—between dualism and monism; phenomenalism and transfactualism; neopositivism, critical realism, analyticism, and reflexivity;

positivism and post-positivism; and quantitative and qualitative methods—are useful as descriptive categorizations, they are, as Jackson recognizes, ideal types rather than bounded classifications. Breaking down each of those assumed dichotomies individually or all of them together opens up the possibility for creatively pairing methods, methodologies, epistemologies, and ontologies and for the creative application of these pairings to IR paradigms. This suggestion is not so radical when we think about "qualitative" methodologies (structural realists like a good case study almost as much as critical theorists, though they are looking for different things in that study), but it seems radical when we talk about quantitative methodologies being paired with post-positivist epistemologies and constructivist or critical theorizing. We suggest that a regression, a mathematical model, or a computational model, like a good case study, can be wielded across theoretical approaches, across epistemologies, and even across ontologies.

We argue that, rather than the progression above, it is possible to see the spectrum of the production of knowledge in the discipline as follows:

Ontology ↔ Epistemology ↔ Methodology ↔ Method

Several important properties distinguish this understanding of these relationships from traditional ways of thinking about knowledge in the discipline: (1) the co-constitution of ontology and method, (2) the compatibility of not only multiple methods but multiple method-epistemology-ontology pairings, (3) the possibility of multi-epistemological research, and (4) (most importantly for this work) the freedom of methods from the constraints of particular methodologies, epistemologies, and ontologies. In the words of Jill Steans, this pushes "existing boundaries of both what we claim to be relevant in international politics and what we assume to be legitimate ways of constructing knowledge about the world," even for critical theorists who think they are already pushing those boundaries.[52] From that perspective, we suggest that quantitative/formal/computational methods are not only compatible with but situationally valuable for constructivist and critical research in IR.

Though we use potential pairings of quantitative methods and critical and constructivist IR as examples in the present book, this argument has implications beyond these potential pairings. It also suggests that not only the quantitative/qualitative divide but many of the other binaries that we use to think about research design in IR—explaining/understanding,[53] inferential/explanatory, positivist/critical, hypothesis-testing/analysis—are ultimately unsupportable oversimplifications that we deploy as signifiers of positionality along the spectrum from ontology to method, rather than defensible categories of philosophical ontology. Lost in those binaries are not only the utility of the methods presumptively matched with one side or the other but the possible payoffs of revising traditional paths *from ontology to method* into multidimensional journeys. We revisit these potential payoffs in the conclusion to this book. In the next sections of this introduction, we introduce the ideas of quantitative methods and critical and constructivist IR as we use them in this book, as well as the ways in which the contributors to this volume see these methods as potentially useful to these approaches.

Quantitative Methods

For the purposes of this project, we loosely define the term *quantitative methods* as referring to methods for IR (and the social sciences more broadly) that involve numbers and/or mathematical notation, following a common social practice in the use of that term in our discipline and others. Throughout the book, we use that term not to denote a narrow reference to statistical modeling but to describe statistical, mathematical, and computational tools that use numerical or mathematical notation. The two methods most frequently used in IR that fit into this category are statistical models and formal rational choice models, but the category also includes a variety of other methods, from agent-based modeling to network analysis. These methods have in common that they are formal, using numbers or other mathematical notation to represent the political world, rather than (or, potentially, as) narratives ("formal" being defined here as any method using a clearly specified and exact syntax). In principle, at a methodological level, formal modeling—whether in statistical, game-theoretic, or other forms—gives analyses a certain precision, in that the stages of analyses involving calculation can be shown to be mathematically correct or incorrect.

What else do these methods have in common, in a methodological and epistemological sense? We argue that while they are often assumed to share a positivist epistemological approach and a methodology that forefronts scientific precision, these methods actually share very little, if anything, methodologically or epistemologically; that is, "quantitative" methods are *not inherently* positivist or "scientific" and need not be deployed only in service of producing neopositivist hypothesis-testing. Uses that contravene these traditional assumptions are, normatively and practically, compatible with such methods.

In fact, defined broadly, as we have done here, quantitative methods fall at different points along a variety of methodological and epistemological spectra. Methodologically, they are designed to do quite different things. While statistical modeling as a method can be used for testing existing theory (among other uses), it does not (or at least should not) play any direct role in theory creation. While it can serve both causal and constitutive ends, statistical work must be deployed with particular theoretical assumptions in mind; the theory, not the method, suggests which variables should be compared, as well as the utility of particular forms of regression, time lags, variable operationalizations, and other tools.

We contend that statistical techniques can be used to analyze any data that come in numerical form, whatever purpose that analysis serves. The purpose may be simple description, or it may be theory testing, but its utility in engagement with theory is determined by data availability and statistical technique, not by the source of the theory. Game-theoretic rational choice modeling, in comparison, is primarily a mechanism for theory generation. Models are built to generate potential outcomes and to help scholars understand how outcomes might be produced. Statistical and formal models can work in tandem, as is encouraged by the NSF-funded program Empirical Implications of Theoretical Models (EITM), but there is no epistemological or methodological reason to privilege statistical models in the testing of formal ones or to use formal ones to generate theory for statistical ones. That practice is a social convention of disciplinary practice in IR (and many other social sciences), which we argue limits the application of both statistical and formal models compared to their potential uses in IR research.

Statistical analyses of formal models can provide information about which models generate more accurate predictions (within a particular epistemological framework, at least), but they cannot tell us why, because all formal choice models begin with the same basic sets of assumption. Conversely, a finding that predictions are not accurate cannot tell us whether the problem is with the basic assumption of rationality or with its application. This line of cleavage, which undermines the methodological assumption that the pairing between statistical analysis and formal models is natural for social science research, mirrors that between what Patrick Thaddeus Jackson calls neopositivism and analyticism.[54] In this understanding, formal modeling that pretends to be neopositivist is simply epistemologically confused. This does not mean that statistical techniques should never be applied to formal models. But it does mean two things. The first is that such applications should be better informed epistemologically than is currently the case, to specify what the application is intended to accomplish. The second is the original point of this section, that there is no particularly privileged relationship between the two.

Agent-based models are a form of experimental technique and therefore do not fit into quite the same categories as either statistical or rational choice models. They can be used either to generate or to test theory. While they are similar to rational choice models in being thought experiments, they are a different form of thought experiment. Rational choice models begin with a single assumption about human behavior, applied systematically (and then softened in some applications but not in others) to see where that assumption leads. Agent-based models play with assumptions about how humans think, to see what happens when they are adjusted. Both of these kinds of analyticist modeling can be usefully applied to constructivist and critical theory, for different uses, as the remainder of this project demonstrates.

Critical theorists and constructivists might respond to this discussion by observing that we must be careful with quantitative models, because both quantified data and modeling norms are socially constructed and because those constructions are themselves political. But this is no truer of quantitative or numerical claims than it is of narrative or ethnographic claims. We must read numbers with the same intellectual skepticism that we read narrative empirical claims—reflecting on their sources, their authors, and the political work that they do. There are some good examples of how to do this for quantitative or numerical claims in the existing literature,[55] but the examples are too few. We look to expand the number of these sorts of contributions and explicitly to theorize a potential pairing between quantitative work and reflexivity.

Critical and Constructivist IR

The final definitional task of this introduction is to address constructivist and critical theory. Self-identified IR constructivists have provided a number of definitions of what it means to be a "constructivist." Most of these definitions share a focus on the idea that international politics is socially constructed: "Social relations *make* or *construct* people—ourselves—into the kind of beings that we are. Conversely, we *make* the world what it is, by doing what we do with each other and saying what we say to each other."[56] Intersubjectivity and co-constitution are key components of this understanding.[57]

We see constructivism as an empirical approach to *how the world works* rather than a political theory of *how the world ought to work*. In Hayward Alker's words, constructivist research "'sociologizes' IR's disciplinary self-understanding."[58] Seeing the processes of power politics, institutions, and law as fundamentally *social*, constructivists place social structures and processes at the epistemological center of their inquiries. Studying social structure does, by definition, mean that constructivist theorists ask different questions about global politics than others, with different subjects and objects.

The employment of the term *critical theory* in IR, meanwhile, seems to date back to Robert Cox's distinction between problem solving and critical theory, where problem solvers, assuming that the system will not or is unlikely to change, try to make it function more smoothly, while critical theorists search for ways to stop the current power structures from reproducing indefinitely.[59] Cox and many others who have described and defined critical theorizing have based their arguments on Habermas's three knowledge interests: technical (understanding how to control nature and society), practical (how to make and keep order), and emancipatory (in identifying and ending oppressive social structures).[60] "Problem-solving theory" often incorporates the first two without the third. Recently, critical theorists, such as Duvall and Varadarajan, have argued, further, that "problem-solving knowledge" is itself a false premise, because it assumes a fixity that does not exist in the social and political order.[61] This assumption is an ideological bias, Duvall and Varadarajan argue, preferring (false) tidiness to (reflective) messiness in studying the social world.

When used in IR, the term *critical theory* is meant in two distinct senses that are often seen to be in tension with each other. The first sense is the use of Marxian-inspired critical social theory, which is tightly interwoven with an emancipatory project in IR; the second is a post-structuralist strand of critical theory deeply skeptical of the emancipatory project of the first. Both are compatible with the quantitative methods discussed in this volume. Similarly, although constructivists agree that international politics is socially constructed, there are theoretical divides between constructivists identified as "thick" or "postmodern" and those identified as "thin" or "neoclassical."[62] The former express concern that objective knowledge of social construction and intersubjectivity is impossible, while the latter argue that the world has a social reality that can be observed and potentially studied with objectivity. As with the distinction between Marxian-inspired and post-structural critical theories, we do not privilege one constructivist view over the other in this volume but, rather, look at ways in which quantitative methods might inform each.

For neither constructivism nor critical theory do we offer exclusive definitions that specify the boundaries of what counts as critical or constructivist and what does not: we see both constructivism and critical theory as general approaches to the study of IR and as self-defined research communities. Nor do we engage in the debate about the relationship between these approaches.[63] But since there are different approaches to constructivist and critical research in IR and since there are arguments that these approaches themselves are fundamentally at odds, can a book be about methodology in the different branches of both different approaches? Whatever degree of incommensurability exists both within and across these two research communities, we argue that they both can benefit from a discussion of the capabilities of quantitative methods.

The similar lessons for these approaches stem partly from some potential commonalities in their research, where they "reject the hegemony of a single scientific method" and "challenge rationalist conceptions of human nature and action,"[64] with a focus on "interpretive strategies" and "social construction."[65] We argue that constructivist and critical approaches to IR research have generally paired a rejection of quantitative, formal, and computational methods with a rejection of the hegemony of traditional, singular notions of science that those who use quantitative methods usually espouse. Therefore, these approaches share an underexploration and potential underutilization of quantitative/formal/computational methods, in service of their epistemological/theoretical/political ends. The employment and deployment of these methods are useful to different epistemological/theoretical/political perspectives in different ways and for different reasons. This book explores those differences as well as the potential similarities outlined above.

Quantitative Methods for Critical/Constructivist IR

We conduct this exploration largely through example. The rest of this volume consists of chapters that present uses of quantitative methods in constructivist or critical work, followed by concluding chapters that reflect on and contextualize this range of specific methods and uses. The methods represented are intended to be exemplary, rather than to constitute a comprehensive overview of quantitative methods for critical and constructivist IR; other examples of quantitative methods might include experimental designs or computer-aided content analysis. The chapters on methods are divided into two parts, with each chapter using a different method and embedded in a different version of constructivist or critical theory. The first part draws on statistical methods. The second focuses on rational choice and computational methods.

In part 1, Brooke Ackerly and her coauthors use composite indices to account for the critical concept of rights enjoyment and to cross the agent-structure divide without sacrificing countability. Suggesting that a critical theory of human rights would measure the rights enjoyment of people, the existence of institutions (social, political, and economic) to secure them, and the progress of those institutions to provide them, Ackerly and her co-authors argue that traditional, data-driven projects on human rights miss the element of individual enjoyment. This approach is hybridized, theoretically and epistemologically, and capitalizes on both critique and calculation.

In a similar vein, Cameron Thies uses constructivist theorizing to develop testable hypotheses about what to expect in war and conflict, and he employs interpretive methods to operationalize variables that he uses to test those hypotheses. He utilizes the traditional, positivist tools of statistical analysis to analyze intersubjective, co-constitutive states and their interactions, in ways that defy the traditional boundaries of the applications of those methods but that tell us something about the utility of constructivist theorizing for accounting for and predicting war and conflict.

Putting statistical methods to a different sort of use, Matthew Hoffmann uses network analysis—mapping connections, nodes, and segmentations—to explore constitution and social construction in global politics. Hoffmann shows how social network analysis can be used to explore the constitutive effects of an institution (in this case, multilateral treaty making) and of idea diffusion (in this case, about climate change). Through social network analysis, Hoffmann demonstrates that it is possible to explore the emergence and influence of a community of practice at the center of socially constructed ideas and institutions. Hoffmann's examples, drawn from very different issue areas, demonstrate that social network analysis, as a quantitative method, can provide insight into the core constructivist dynamics of constitution and social construction.

Bringing together statistical methods, a constructivist worldview, and theories of political psychology, Paul Kowert develops a methodology for studying perceptions of state identity. He argues that the existing literature on state identity either normatively applies established analytical categories to states or focuses on the details of individual cases. He uses survey data about perceptions of countries to develop a typology of perceptions of state identity. This general typology identifies the discursive palate from which such perceptions are drawn, and it thereby provides constructivist analysis of state identity with a basis on which to develop a comparative study of state identity.

Part 2, focusing on formal and computational modeling, begins with David Sylvan's chapter, which analyzes constitutive relationships in global politics through formal discourse analysis. Sylvan models sequences, narratives, and conversations to illuminate the complexities of policy agreements and the power relations therein, using examples of two conversations between British prime ministers and US presidents to make constitutive observations and temporal comparisons. He concludes with analysis that suggests that this method would be beneficial to constructivist research in global politics by enhancing the possibilities for analyzing social facts.

Ian Lustick argues that agent-based modeling used to create counterfactual scenarios, as a bottom-up method, has potential for similar purposes. Using computer simulation to explore the often nonlinear relationship between inputs at the unit level, interaction networks, and outputs at the collective level, he contends that agent-based modeling has a big payoff for complex argumentation. In many respects, the bottom-up approach built into agent-based modeling is ideal for the study of constructivist processes. Both are fundamentally oriented toward the emergent properties associated with uncoordinated but massive numbers of interactions. Lustick applies this method to an analysis of politics in Bangladesh. He seeks to identify best practices for the construction and conduct of counterfactual scenario construction in global politics.

J. Samuel Barkin's chapter argues that that there is utility to using formal modeling heuristically in service of constructivist theorizing. Barkin develops a simple rational choice model of international cooperation on issues of environmental politics. Applying this model to patterns of cooperation in international fisheries politics, he demonstrates that the model can usefully inform constructivist analysis of these politics. More broadly, he argues that formal rational choice modeling used heuristically or counterfactually can identify patterns of strategic behavior that we might expect of actors in specified social settings. Relating these expectations to observed behavior can shed light on the social structures within which strategic behavior is located and through which it is being mediated.

Laura Sjoberg and Kevin Knudson's chapter deploys the tools of geometric and computational topology to do concept mapping for critical theorizing in IR. Using the many definitions, datasets, and debates about the concept of democracy in global politics, Sjoberg and Knudson suggest that multidimensional models can both capture complexity and demonstrate malleability. They argue that "quantitative" tools that are *not* generally used in IR (particularly those of theoretical geometry) can be those best suited to the research questions of critical IR and even IR more generally.

Each of the substantive chapters in parts 1 and 2 follows a similar format. Each first discusses both the traditional assumptions about the utility of a method in the social sciences and the author's perspective on how it might be employed to serve the ends of constructivist and/or critical research in the discipline. Second, each chapter poses a research question that the method could plausibly be used to productively address in a research agenda broadly understood as constructivist or critical theorizing in IR, providing some substantive background on the research question, its situation in the field, and the appeal of inquiring into it. Each chapter therefore works through an empirical issue in global politics, although some chapters focus on more narrowly defined problems while others look at broader patterns. Third, each chapter uses its method to address the research question posed, providing an empirical example of the use of that particular method for critical/constructivist ends. Finally, each chapter discusses the lessons learned from the application of the method to the research program in the chapter, considering practical and/or policy implications, in addition to epistemological and theoretical applications.

Part 3 of this book is a reflection on the work of interpretive quantification in this study and on the future of this interpretive quantification as a scholarly enterprise. Chapter 10, by Patrick Thaddeus Jackson, reflects on the relationship among theory, methodology, and method across the chapters in this book, in the enterprise of interpretive quantification, and in the social sciences more broadly. Jackson probes not only the purposes of the deployment of particular methods but also the ways in which particular work can be interpreted, read, and used by a discipline in which there remains a hegemonic assumption about the benefit of neopositivist social science. Chapter 11, our conclusion, engages both the chapter authors and Jackson in a discussion of the role of theory and the role of method, looking to break down the disciplinary tetherings of method that make books like this rare. It engages questions of how to think about IR inquiry going forward, given the potential of interpretive quantification in its own right and as an example of the possibilities of rethinking inherited notions of how methods are chosen.

Notes

1. This paragraph is a play on the introductory paragraph in Gary King, Robert Keohane, and Sidney Verba's *Designing Social Inquiry: Scientific Inference in Qualitative Research* (Princeton, NJ: Princeton University Press, 1994), about which much more will be said over the course of this chapter.

2. For the positivist/quantitative side, see, e.g., Janet Buttolph Johnson and

H. T. Reynolds, *Political Science Research Methods* (Washington, DC: CQ Press, 2011); Craig Leonard Brians, Lars Willnat, Jarol B. Manheim, and Richard C. Rich, *Empirical Political Analysis,* 8th ed. (New York: Pearson, 2010); Paul Pennings, Hans Keman, and Jan Kleinnijenhus, *Doing Research in Political Science: An Introduction to Comparative Methods and Statistics* (London: Sage, 2006); Andrew Gelman and Jennifer Hill, *Data Analysis Using Regression and Multilevel/Hierarchical Models* (Cambridge: Cambridge University Press, 2006). For the qualitative/post-positivist side, see Audie Klotz and Deepa Prakash, *Qualitative Methods in International Relations: A Pluralist Guide* (London: Palgrave MacMillan, 2008); Audie Klotz and Cecilia Lynch, eds., *Strategies for Research in Constructivist International Relations* (London: M. E. Sharpe, 2007); Jennifer Milliken, "The Study of Discourse in International Relations: A Critique of Research and Methods," *European Journal of International Relations* 5, no. 2 (1999): 225–54; Thomas J. Biersteker, "Critical Reflections on Post-Positivism in International Relations," *International Studies Quarterly* 33, no. 3 (1989): 263–67.

3. Some will say that we are being uncharitable to those whom the discipline might identify as "qualitative methodologists" (see, e.g., James Mahoney and Gary Goertz, "A Tale of Two Cultures: Contrasting Quantitative and Qualitative Research," *Political Analysis* 14, no. 3: 227–49; Charles Ragin, *Redesigning Social Inquiry: Fuzzy Sets and Beyond* [Chicago: University of Chicago Press, 2009]). There is an extent to which that is true—we draw from some of their work in the following pages, but less from them than from either constructivist/critical theorists or what might be called "quantitative methodologists", for two reasons. First, we think that a significant amount of what might be considered the work of "qualitative methodologists" falls loosely into the scientism of the qualitative/quantitative divide. Second, as discussed in detail below, we do not see the quantitative/qualitative divide as such as marking a meaningful research difference. In our view, there are no "qualitative methodologists" or "quantitative methodologists." There may, indeed, be survey researchers, ethnographers, historians, historiographers, statisticians, game theorists, and mathematicians, but their methodologism should be read outside of the quantitative/qualitative divide.

4. Patrick Thaddeus Jackson, *The Conduct of Inquiry in International Relations* (New York: Routledge, 2010).

5. See, e.g., Stefan Titscher, Michael Meyer, Ruth Wodak, and Eva Vetter, *Methods of Text and Discourse Analysis (*London: Sage, 2000).

6. See, e.g., Janet M. Box-Steffensmeier and Christopher J. W. Zorn, "Duration Models and Proportional Hazards in Political Science," *American Political Science Review* 45, no. 4 (2001): 972–88.

7. For this argument, see J. Samuel Barkin, "Qualitative Methods?," in *Qualitative Methods in International Relations,* ed. Audie Klotz and Deepa Prakash (New York: Palgrave Macmillan, 2008).

8. Brooke Ackerly, Maria Stern, and Jacqui True, eds., *Feminist Methodologies for International Relations* (Cambridge: Cambridge University Press, 2006), 10.

9. E.g., J. Ann Tickner, *Gender in International Relations: Feminist Approaches to Global Security* (New York: Columbia University Press, 1992).

10. E.g., J. Ann Tickner, "So What Is Your Research Program? Some Feminist Answers to International Relations Methodological Questions?" *International Studies*

Quarterly 49, no. 1 (2005): 1–22; Ackerly, Stern, and True, *Feminist Methodologies for International Relations.*

11. E.g., Barbara Koremenos, Charles Lipson, and Duncan Snidal. "The Rational Design of International Institutions," *International Organization* 55, no. 4 (2001): 761–99.

12. Edward D. Mansfield and Jon C. Pevehouse, "Quantitative Approaches," in Duncan Snidal and Christian Reus-Smit, eds., *Oxford Handbook of International Relations* (Oxford: Oxford University Press, 2008), 481–98.

13. E.g., King, Keohane, and Verba, *Designing Social Inquiry.*

14. See, e.g. James D. Fearon, "Counterfactuals and Hypothesis Testing in Political Science," *World Politics* 43, no. 2 (1991): 169–95; Erik Gartzke and Yonatan Lupu, "Trading on Preconceptions: Why World War I Was Not a Failure of Economic Interdependence," *International Security* 36, no. 4 (2012): 115–50.

15. See Dvora Yanow, *Constructing "Race" and "Ethnicity" in America: Category-Making in Public Policy and Administration* (Armonk, NY: M. E. Sharpe, 2003).

16. See Mark Bevir and Asaf Kedar, "Concept Formation in Political Science: An Anti-Naturalist Critique of Qualitative Methodology," *Perspectives on Politics* 6, no. 3 (2008): 503–17; Pushkala Prasad, *Crafting Qualitative Research: Working in the Post-Positivist Tradition* (Armonk, NY: ME Sharpe, 2005).

17. See, e.g., King, Keohane, and Verba, *Designing Social Inquiry*; Johnson and Reynolds, *Political Science Research Methods*; Brians, Willnat, Manheim, and Rich, *Empirical Political Analysis*; Pennings, Keman, and Kleinnijenhus, *Doing Research in Political Science*; Henry Brady and David Collier, *Rethinking Social Inquiry: Diverse Tools, Shared Standards*, 2nd ed. (New York: Rowman and Littlefield, 2010).

18. See n. 1.

19. King, Keohane, and Verba, *Designing Social Inquiry* 7.

20. Ibid., 2.

21. Jackson, *Conduct of Inquiry*, 35.

22. For an example of scholarship that does take issue with their efforts, see James Mahoney, "After KKV: The New Methodology of Qualitative Research." *World Politics* 62, no. 1 (2010): 120–47.

23. Thomas S. Kuhn, *The Structure of Scientific Revolutions* (Chicago: University of Chicago Press, 1962).

24. Jackson, *Conduct of Inquiry.*

25. Ibid., 184.

26. Lene Hansen, "A Case for Seduction? Evaluating the Poststructuralist Conceptualization of Security," *Cooperation and Conflict* 32, no. 4 (1997): 372.

27. Ibid., 372.

28. Ackerly, Stern, and True, *Feminist Methodologies for International Relations,* 4.

29. Ibid.

30. Klotz and Lynch, *Strategies for Constructivist Research*, 10.

31. Vincent Pouliot, "'Sobjectivism': Toward a Constructivist Methodology," *International Studies Quarterly* 51, no. 2 (2007): 359.

32. Ibid., 363–64.

33. See, e.g., Tickner, "What Is Your Research Program?"; Amir Lupovici, "Con-

structivist Methods: A Plea and Manifesto for Pluralism," *Review of International Studies* 35, no. 1 (2009): 195–218.

34. See David Sylvan and Stephen Majeski, "A Methodology for the Study of Historical Counterfactuals," *International Studies Quarterly* 42, no. 1 (1998): 49–108; Alexander Wendt, *Social Theory of International Politics* (Cambridge: Cambridge University Press, 1999).

35. See Hayward Alker, *Rediscoveries and Reformulations: Humanistic Methodologies for International Studies* (Cambridge: Cambridge University Press, 1996); Brooke Ackerly, "Why a Feminist Theorist Studies Methods," *Politics and Gender* 5, no. 3 (2009): 431–36; Laura Sjoberg and Jeffrey Horowitz, "Quantitative Methods in Critical Security Studies," *Critical Approaches to Security: An Introduction to Theories and Methods, ed. Laura J. Shepherd* (London: Routledge, 2013), 103–17.

36. King, Keohane, and Verba, *Designing Social Inquiry,* vii.

37. Ibid., 3.

38. Ibid., 4.

39. Brady and Collier, *Rethinking Social Inquiry,* 19.

40. Ibid., 19.

41. Barkin, "Qualitative Methods?," 218.

42. Ibid., 211.

43. Jackson, *Conduct of Inquiry*, 37.

44. Ibid.

45. Ibid., 10.

46. Michael Westerman and Stephen C. Yanchar, "Changing the Terms of the Debate: Quantitative Methods in Explicitly Interpretive Research," *Theory and Psychology* 21, no. 2 (2011): 141.

47. Michael Westerman, "Conversation Analysis and Interpretive Quantitative Research on Psychotherapy Process and Problematic Interpersonal Behavior," *Theory and Psychology* 21, no. 2 (2011): 158, 155.

48. Our use of the terms *mind-world dualism, mind-world monism, phenomenalism,* and *transfactualism* follows that of Jackson in *Conduct of Inquiry.*

49. Jackson, *Conduct of Inquiry.*

50. Colin Wight, *Agents, Structures, and International Relations: Politics as Ontology* (Cambridge: Cambridge University Press, 2006), 259.

51. Jackson, *Conduct of Inquiry*, 27.

52. Jill Steans, "Engaging from the Margins: Feminist Encounters with the 'Mainstream' of International Relations," *British Journal of Politics and International Relations* 5, no. 3 (2003): 445.

53. Martin Hollis and Steve Smith titled their book on IR theory *Explaining and Understanding International Relations* (Oxford: Clarendon, 1991).

54. Jackson, *Conduct of Inquiry.*

55. See, e.g., Lars-Erik Cederman, *Emergent Actors in World Politics: How States and Nations Develop and Dissolve* (Princeton, NJ: Princeton University Press, 1997); Matthew J. Hoffmann, *Ozone Depletion and Climate Change: Constructing a Global Response* (Albany: State University of New York Press, 2005); Georgios Karyotis and Stratos Patrikios, "Religion, Securitization, and Anti-immigration Attitudes: The Case

of Greece." *Journal of Peace Research* 47, no. 1 (2010): 43–57; Stéphane J. Baele and Olivier C. Sterck, "Diagnosing the Securitisation of Immigration at the EU Level: A New Method for Stronger Empirical Claims," *Political Studies* 63, no. 5 (2014): 1120–39.

56. Nicholas Greenwood Onuf, "Constructivism: A User's Manual," in *International Relations in a Constructed World, ed.* V. Kubalkova, Nicholas Greenwood Onuf, and Paul Kowert (London: M. E. Sharpe, 1998), 59 (emphasis in the original).

57. See Friedrich V. Kratochwil, "Theory and Political Practice: Reflections on Theory Building in International Relations," in *Principled World Politics: The Challenge of Normative International Relations, ed.* Paul Kevin Wapner, Lester Edwin J. Ruiz, and Richard A. Falk (Lanham, MD: Rowman and Littlefield, 2000), 50.

58. Hayward R. Alker, "On Learning from Wendt." *Review of International Studies* 26, no. 1 (2000): 141.

59. Robert Cox, "Social Forces, States, and World Orders: Beyond International Relations Theory," *Millennium: Journal of International Studies* 10, no. 2 (1981): 126–55.

60. Jurgen Habermas, *Knowledge and Human Interests* (Boston: Beacon, 1972).

61. Raymond Duvall and Latha Varadarajan, "On the Practical Significance of Critical International Relations Theory," *Asian Journal of Political Science* 11 (2003): 76–88.

62. The labels "thick" and "thin" come from Wendt, *Social Theory of International Politics*; "postmodern" and "neoclassical" from John G. Ruggie, "What Makes the World Hang Together? Neo-utilitarianism and the Social Constructivist Challenge," *International Organization* 52, no. 4 (1998): 855–85.

63. See, e.g., Duvall and Varadarajan, "Practical Significance of Critical International Relations Theory"; Alexander D. Barder and Daniel J. Levine, "'The World Is Too Much with Us': Reification and the Depoliticising of *Via Media* Constructivist IR," *Millennium: Journal of International Studies* 40, no. 3 (2012): 585–604; Richard Wyn-Jones, ed., *Critical Theory and World Politics* (Boulder, CO: Lynne Rienner, 2001), particularly Alexander Wendt, "What Is International Relations For? Notes Toward a Postcritical View"; Richard Price, ed., *Moral Limit and Possibility in World Politics* (Cambridge: Cambridge University Press, 2008); Ted Hopf, "The Promise of Constructivism in International Relations Theory," *International Security* 23, no. 1 (1998): 171–200.

64. Richard Price and Christian Reus-Smit, "Dangerous Liaisons? Critical International Theory and Constructivism," *European Journal of International Relations* 4, no. 3 (1998): 259–94.

65. Duvall and Varadarajan, "Practical Significance of Critical International Relations Theory," 82.

PART I

Statistical Methods

CHAPTER 2

Measuring Critical Theories of Human Rights

BROOKE ACKERLY, WITH JOSÉ MIGUEL CRUZ, ANNA CARELLA, AND BISHAWJIT MALLICK

> [I]t is the great error of reformers and philanthropists . . . to nibble at the consequences of unjust power, instead of redressing the injustice itself.
>
> —J. S. Mill, *Principles of Political Economy* (1848), book 5, chapter 11, section 9

Numbers matter. If someone tells you there are ants in your kitchen, you will want to know whether the ants number twenty or two million. Although it seems as if numbers tell us what kind of problem we have, it is our *interpretation of them* that actually does that work. Numbers alone cannot tell us if the ants came from the garden or if they are nesting in the wall. Numbers *help* us know what kind of problem we are facing and what kind of concepts we will need to study the problem and know how to address it, but the work of asking a research question and interpreting data is *ours*.

In fact, we do not want to know *how many* ants we have in our kitchen as much as we want to know *why* we have ants in our kitchen. Numbers do not speak for themselves. Ants in the kitchen could be evidence of a small problem in the kitchen but a *big* problem in the garden, a big problem in the kitchen, or no problem at all. To interpret numerical data, we need theories *and the right research questions.* The wrong theories make us ask the wrong research questions, count the wrong things, or interpret the numbers incorrectly. Political science and international relations (IR) are disciplines that can answer the whys of politics and power relations if we ask the right questions.

Most quantitative studies of universal human rights treat rights as privileges secured for individuals by states; critical theories of rights criticize that conceptualization of human rights. What good can quantitative methods be to critical human rights theory? In this chapter, I (Brooke Ackerly), argue, with José Miguel Cruz, Anna Carella, and Bishawjit Mallick (with whom I have worked on various the parts of this chapter), that quantitative methods can be useful to critical human rights inquiry. The theoretical concept of human rights deployed by many quantitative analyses is one of rights as privileges (not of *universal* human rights) and of states as duty bearers (not of universal responsibility for human rights). By contrast, a critical theory of human rights challenges the normative assumptions of rights as privileges and of the state as uniquely capable of bearing responsibility for human rights.[1] A critical theory of human rights requires that we study human rights dynamics within states and can utilize both qualitative and quantitative methods for doing so.

In keeping with the theme of this book and the structure of the chapters proposed by its editors, I here first set out the challenges of a noncritical constructivist quantitative approach to the study of human rights. Next, I stipulate the key features of a quantitative empirical study of human rights that is guided by feminist critical theory. The subsequent two sections describe two key features of a research agenda for the critical quantitative study of human rights and demonstrate their use in contemporary research. The first is a single-method quantitative approach. José Miguel Cruz and I used existing data to operationalize "rights enjoyment" as a measure of whether people feel that people have rights.[2] The findings of our study provide some empirical evidence for the conditions under which rights are enjoyed. Most important among these is the need to study rights enjoyment with consideration of community-level factors and paying attention to differences in rights enjoyment across subgroups. In that light, these findings suggest additional methodological innovations necessary to further explore the empirical hypotheses of a critical human rights theory. The second research design explores these questions. It uses the same measure of rights enjoyment but changes the method of data collection to a geolocated survey, with sample sizes large enough to detect variations among communities. This chapter concludes with the methodological (and epistemological) implications of these interpretations.

Challenges of Constructivism without Critical Theory (in the Quantitative Study of Human Rights)

When political science is confronted with a puzzle such as *how the transformations of formal political institutions and informal practices of social life that are the goals of human rights conventions lead to increased rights enjoyment,* we are asking *both* what it means to enjoy human rights and which political institutions and practices contribute to that enjoyment. This two-part question calls out for the conceptualization of human rights as enjoyment and for an empirical search for broad patterns that bring about rights enjoyment. The first is a question for normative human rights theory: for what do those struggling for human rights *struggle*?[3] The second is a question for quantitative empirical methods: what are the patterns of rights enjoyment?

From a critical perspective, every time a political scientist studies a question, the scholar engages two questions: *(1) what is the political meaning of what I am studying* and *(2) how shall I study it?* Much criticism of quantitative research has been aimed at revealing the unexamined epistemological biases of research concealed within a study's framing.[4] Without first reflecting on the normative underpinnings of a study's core conceptual apparatus, *quantitative approaches cannot describe the world; tautologically, they describe only what they measure.*

By focusing on state-level measures of rights enjoyment for cross-national comparison, most quantitative studies of human rights (perhaps inadvertently) import two normative claims into their empirical studies. First, they compare the privileges of rights enjoyment across states (not the *impediments* to rights enjoyment for some groups within each state). In this way, rights are individual privileges or entitlements, not the fabric of a shared political life.[5] Second, again by focusing on state-level measures of rights enjoyment for cross-national comparison, these studies treat the state as the appropriate unit for recognizing the right holder and the right and for bearing the duty of securing the right.[6] Responsibility for human rights is a shared political responsibility of actors within and outside of any given state.

Constructivist theorists who have used quantitative cross-national regression models have employed state-level aggregate data of both de jure (formal)[7] and de facto (in practice)[8] rights achievements. With state-level measures, human rights scholars have used quantitative methods to study the effects of foreign aid on human rights,[9] but, of course, the dynamics that affect effectiveness of aid may be local-level politics or the forces of global political economies. These studies show that democratic institutions support human rights,[10] but, of course, a country with formal democratic institutions can have democratic rights curtailed in significant ways for subpopulations (as in the United States). Quantitative studies at the state level can show that economic growth supports human rights modestly;[11] clearly, if we understood the ways in which the benefits of growth are distributed throughout a society, we might realize that household livelihood improvement, not GDP per capita growth, increases rights enjoyment. Aggregate studies may find that social norms affect women's rights[12] or that neither democracy nor human rights ensure women's security.[13] Many of these findings—for example, that electoral political participation and accountability are important for aggregate realization of rights[14]—make more pressing the need to study the dynamics of the ways in which formal and informal institutions affect political engagement and democratic accountability within states.

Ostensibly, all human rights theory and practice is about changing the world. Which theory of human rights should guide political inquiry into the patterns of human rights enjoyment if the goal is to change the world? Some theorists do not even think that human rights can change the world; in their interpretation, the concept itself essentially relies on a particular (conservative) notion of human.[15] To put their objection as a philosophical problem, a human rights claim is at minimum two claims: (1) the claim to be the kind of person who gets to make a rights claim and (2) the claim that something is a right.[16] People who are suspicious of human rights' critical potential worry that the lack of the political standing to make a claim is a political obstacle to the usefulness of the concept of human rights for political emancipation.[17] I argue, rather, that for all human rights claims, most of the work is on that first political claim. Once recognized, making the claim is not easy, but without that recognition, it is impossible.[18] This approach of arguing *simultaneously* for the political standing to make a claim and for the particulars of the claim has been part of feminist human rights scholarship and activism.[19] In critical feminist interpretation, this is what human rights are and how they function as a conceptual institution.[20]

Viewed in this way, constructivist and critical human rights theories are not *competing* theories; they are alternative theories that imply different epistemologies and normative expectations about the role of empirical inquiry in injustice. Both have been used to generate empirically testable hypotheses, but not the same hypotheses and not the same data. Alternative theories call us not to put away numbers, but rather, to look more closely at how we use them. For example, both constructivist and critical studies might use Freedom House data, but constructivist quantitative studies might use the Freedom House scores of civil liberties in a country-level analysis,[21] whereas a critical theory approach might look at the rights violations within a country, noticing, for instance, that oppression of labor within the garment industry and insecure land tenure rights have been chronic sites of violations of civil liberties in Bangladesh under a range of regimes (see figure 2.1).[22]

The next section sets out the key features of a quantitative empirical study of human rights that is guided by an explicitly feminist critical theory. These considerations should not be unique to feminist approaches, but they have been developed and popularized through feminist scholarship and its influence on critical theory (and constructivist) approaches to international relations scholarship.

A Feminist Critical Theory of Human Rights

Rights claims vary widely, from things that need to be secured (about which theorists often use the language of negative freedom) to those that need to be cultivated (about which theorists use the language of positive freedoms or capabilities). A feminist critical theory of human rights is a normative theory of human rights that grounds its analytical purchase in both kinds of claims. A rich empirical understanding of these claims is the foundation of the normative implications of a feminist critical theory for the quantitative study of human rights.

I have elsewhere argued that a feminist critical theory of rights enjoyment holds that (1) rights are interdependent (my enjoyment is related to that of those around me and, indeed, of all humanity; no one can enjoy a right to health if there is an epidemic in their community or is not a safe supply of drinking water), (2) rights are indivisible (no one can enjoy their right to health if they do not have a reliable source of livelihood, water, and nutrition), and (3) rights are enjoyed or threatened structurally in groups and subgroups (social norms and political institutions have strong effects on whether rights are enjoyed).[23] A feminist critical theory of human rights follows in the tradition of Marx, Gramsci, Cox, or Linklater but is more firmly grounded in the struggles of the most marginalized, including, but not limited to, women and girls.[24] With Jacqui True[25] and Katy Attanasi,[26] I have argued that a *feminist critical theory* guides both theoretical and empirical research, using "critical inquiry and reflection on social injustice by way of gender analysis, to *transform*, and not simply explain, the social order."[27] In this way, a feminist critical theory studies not only the research subject but also the power of a researcher's conceptual framework to shape the research subject and the study thereof. Feminists treat the critical project as a *grounded* project, whose concepts and empirics are informed by the people who are contesting the concepts. Rights grounded in struggle[28] and rights claims based on recognition of claimants[29] are key to this approach. This approach differs from that (discussed in the introduction and first section of this chapter) in which rights claims are treated as entitlements that may or may not be universally distributed. In a feminist critical approach, rights are not distributed at all but are enjoyed politically together.

A broad range of critical theories question the ways in which material conditions *constrain* our imaginations about the nature of work and human interaction. In this vein, feminist critical theories question the ways in which gender norms *constrain* our imaginations about the range of behavior, roles, and treatment that is "normal" in our society (whichever social reference we use to define "our" society). In this way, feminist critical human rights theory tells us that universal human rights are not enjoyed by the political collective if they are not enjoyed by each and every individual within the collective. Conventional human rights IR measures actually measure not *enjoyment* but, rather, legal standards and average social, political, or economic achievement.[30] These measures may focus on the public sphere (like rule of law) or on state enforcement or practice (like torture) and thereby omit or overlook the patterns of abuse that women experience.[31] Conceptually, in a critical theory of human rights, we enjoy our rights not "against some individual or group" or the state but, rather, *with* others. In a critical theory of human rights, if rights are not enjoyed by all, they are not *enjoyed* by any, because the human rights of each depend on the enjoyment of the rights of all. Where rights are privileges, they are insecure in practice even for those who have them affirmed in treaties or constitutions. In sum, to study critical human rights with quantitative methods, scholars need to measure rights enjoyment at the individual level and also to aggregate individual-level measures to construct a community or national measure suitable for cross-community or cross-national comparison.

Feminist critical theory has a second methodological implication for the empirical study of human rights, which is to focus on processes of injustice, not merely on their harmful consequences. A detailed discussion of the processes of injustice is not possible here. Feminist analyses highlight three: (1) overt and covert oppression, (2) power inequalities, and (3) normalization. These three processes make rights violations sometimes invisible, often because they inhibit the recognition of the rights *claimants,* less often because those with privilege do not recognize the claim. Recognizing injustice of either form is only half of confronting injustice, however. The other half is being overtly committed to cultivating a just world.[32] *Both* the recognition of injustice and the commitment to reject it, in critical terms, are situated in a context where the epistemology of the society, the theorist, and the empiricist can separately, together, or partly *contribute* to the injustice itself. Confronting injustice reflexively entails a commitment to notice and redress invisibility, diversity, and disagreement.[33]

For both defining rights enjoyment and identifying processes of injustice, the metamethodological implication of a critical approach to empirical studies is to use grounded methodologies that reveal the content of the struggles to be recognized as rights claimants and to have one's claims recognized. The methodological challenge posed to international relations scholars by the notion of enjoying rights *with others* is that while it would be easiest to study rights violations at the level of the state (because of the availability of national datasets), subgroups within states often enjoy rights differently. An approach that looked within the state may seem *a priori* to limit the potential generalizability of findings.[34]

This limitation is problematic for two reasons. First, much experience and qualitative research shows that when rights violations occur within a country, these violations usually disproportionately affect certain identifiable subgroups of the population: women[35] or particular ethic groups.[36] Sometimes this empirical problem can be solved with national-level disaggregated data—for example, on the basis of gender, race, ethnicity, geography, and socioeconomic status.

The second reason is more challenging for quantitative empiricists. Subgroup rights are also violated in subgroups of those groups. For example, the rights of women are based on *gender,* and gender differences vary by the ways in which social values, practices, and norms group people into economic, political, or social subgroups. For instance, in a natural disaster, women are four times as likely as men to die, and *poor women* are eight times as likely as men to die.[37] Even at the aggregate level, we can sometimes see that disaggregated data on those impacted can help us better understand the obstacles to rights enjoyment as it relates not only to a specific violation of that enjoyment (in this case, natural disaster) but also to other rights violations. For example, though the specifics vary across sites, where social norms constrain women's mobility, they are less likely to be able to survive a natural disaster. To think of their oppression as "more so" is too simplistic.[38] It is qualitatively different. In this way, social constraints on women's mobility inhibit their rights enjoyment, but these constraints function differently across subgroups of women and by community.

To be engaged with that struggle and not constrained by previously asserted meanings, the quantitative study of human rights needs to develop methods that reflect our competing theoretical understandings of processes, as well as ways of testing those methods. These studies may use existing data, but they should not do so unreflectively. The availability of existing data can be a resource, but we must question why those data are collected, and we must consider *what we would collect from scratch if no data were available.*[39]

In sum, in a feminist critical theory approach, we look not just to have hypotheses confirmed or rejected by our model but also to study anomalies, outliers, and puzzles raised by patterns in the data or by outliers to those patterns. We look for evidence that oppression, normalization, or power inequalities in political life *or in our studies of political life* are rendering the injustices experienced by some invisible. As we will see in the next section, inquiries about epistemology, research questions, conceptualization, operationalization, and measurement lead us to innovate methodologically in order to study the injustice of human rights in a way that illuminates struggles for rights and their obstacles. As we will see in the following section, *community-level factors, not just intersecting factors* like gender and poverty, affect rights enjoyment.

Critical Theory of Human Rights in Quantitative Practice: Measuring Enjoyment

In IR, the primary challenge for an empirical quantitative study of human rights is the operationalization of the concept of rights enjoyment with a theoretically appropriate measure that allows the study of differences and change both across *and* within states.[40] In a study that I will refer to here as the Ackerly-Cruz study, José Miguel Cruz and I began to explore operationalizing rights enjoyment using a dataset of cross-national public opinion data that included the following question:

> To what extent do you think that citizens' basic rights are well protected by the political system of [your country]?[41]

This is a conceptually good measure of rights enjoyment, because it reflects the theorization of rights as indivisible, interrelated, and enjoyed through formal structures and practices. A respondent may reflect on his or her own experience of human rights or on that which he or she observes. It is an empirically good measure, because it measures rights enjoyment at the individual level, can be aggregated by community or any other subgroup of a population (including the nation-state), and shows significant variation. It also enables cross-national quantitative study, because each national survey within the Ackerly-Cruz study is intended to provide a nationally representative sample.

With this measure, Cruz and I embarked on a new research agenda: the quantitative study of human rights as a *concept* in struggle for *people* in struggle. For the purposes of my argument here, I will not review the independent variables, the controls, and their sources or even summarize the findings of the study; rather, I will highlight a couple of findings that illustrate the potential insights from studying critical questions with empirical methods. These insights chart a course for a research agenda guided by a critical feminist theory of human rights that, at the moment, is part of qualitative, but not quantitative, constructivist approaches to human rights.

Cruz and I found that governance variables measured at the individual level and experienced locally (e.g., participation, functioning of government, and rule of law) are correlated with rights enjoyment. By contrast, governance variables measured at the state level (e.g., freedom of expression) do not correlate with rights enjoyment.[42] In fact, of the aggregate state-level measures, only GDP per capita is correlated with rights enjoyment. People in a country feel their rights protected to the extent that *they experience* their government performing well. By contrast, the commonly used measures of torture and curtailment of individual rights that are calculated by experts at Amnesty International and the US State Department are not associated with the typical person's perceptions of rights enjoyment.[43] Additionally, the commonly used state-level measures cannot assess how rights are experienced differently across the geography and subpopulations of a state.[44]

The findings of the Ackerly-Cruz study shed light on the oppression, normalization, and power dynamics of injustice, illustrating that different parts of a population who experience the rule of law and effectiveness of government differently also express differences in rights enjoyment. However, by studying subgroups within the population, Cruz and I found patterns that were the opposite of what we might have expected. For example, given that education is available to those of relative privilege and generally brings about more relative privilege, we would expect those with more education to have a relatively higher expectation that rights are enjoyed in their country, but their expectation was lower. This suggests that those with greater education are *more attuned to* the human rights deprivations of themselves and others. Recall how the question is phrased: "To what extent do you think that citizens' basic rights are well protected by the political system of [your country]?"

Similarly, given the documented problems of violence against women, health disparities by gender, and gendered income disparities, we might have expected women to report less rights enjoyment than men, but we found instead that they had higher average levels of rights enjoyment than men. This suggests that women are either less attuned to the rights violations of others or more accepting of injustices experienced through social, economic, and political norms. This finding is inconsistent with qualitative studies of women's discourse[45] and women's activism[46] and thus requires further inquiry.

These puzzles suggest more empirical questions for a critical theory of human rights. What are people's sources of security and insecurity? When do they understand their social and economic rights politically? What experiences develop a sense of entitlement to claim human rights? These questions can be pursued through a combination of, on the one hand, qualitative data that allows us to explore the plausible mechanisms of causality and power relations and, on the other hand, quantitative data that enables us to reveal patterns in the qualitative data. However, these puzzles also affirm the appropriateness of a critical theory of human rights, one that treats human rights as a dynamic concept, changing with reference to people's reconception of themselves as rights claimants and as having the right to make claims. As Fariss notes, the constructivist approach also has to face the dynamics of conceptualization, because it relies on datasets constructed by experts from Amnesty International and the US State Department, who utilize "increasingly stringent assessments of state behaviors."[47] The theory and the findings of the Ackerly-Cruz study suggest that quantitative research can be an important tool for critical human rights theory.

Critical Theory of Human Rights in Quantitative Practice: Disaggregation

As we saw above, studying rights enjoyment through nationally representative polling data reveals interesting findings about the import of the local experience of governance and about the differences among groups within a population. Methodologically, these findings raise puzzles for quantitative studies of rights across contexts and confirm the critical theorist's suspicions about aggregate measures of human rights, whether de jure or de facto. A feminist critical theory can support an empirical research program, if findings from one study can be used to inform other studies and if *puzzles* from one study can generate hypotheses that can be explored through similar or other methods. As a *critical* theory, however, such a research program has to be particularly attentive to the epistemologies and power relations revealed in the study.

The Ackerly-Cruz study found that people enjoy their rights locally, that is, in *community* or in association with others similarly located. The study found that local governance is an aspect of community that affects rights enjoyment. However, without knowing what other community-level factors affect oppression, normalization of injustices, and power inequalities, it is difficult to generate hypotheses about *which* community-level factors are relevant to rights enjoyment.

Since 2012, I have been exploring these questions with qualitative and quantitative data from communities in southwestern Bangladesh, which is a context of environmental strain, economic strain, and moderate political stability (see fig. 2.1).[48] After preliminary research, qualitative research conducted in 2012 and 2013 indicated that within a narrow geography, there were significant differences among communities in terms of their threat from environmental forces and their ability to respond to it. The Polder 32 study was sited in an embanked island, or polder, of southwestern Bangladesh for which satellite imagery had revealed significant destruction due to Cyclone Aila in 2009 (see fig. 2.2).[49] That imagery also revealed that one part of the polder recovered sooner than the rest (see fig. 2.3).

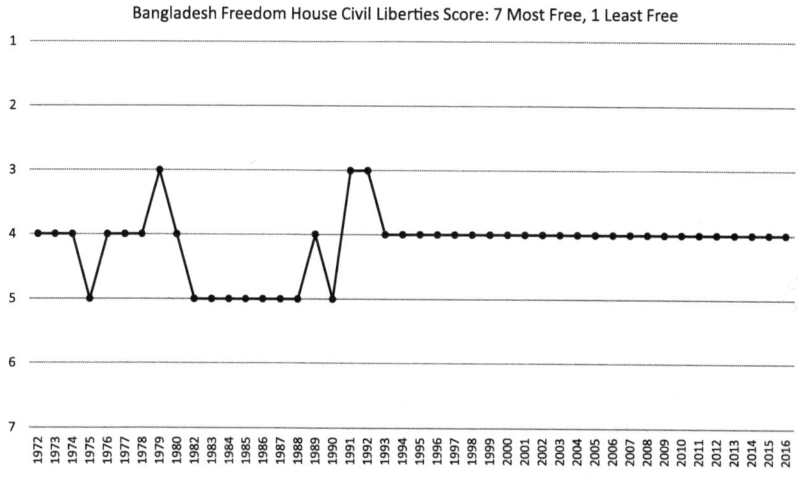

Fig. 2.1. Freedom House civil liberties score, Bangladesh. (From Freedom House, Freedom in the World.)

Through ethnographic observation and qualitative interviews, the Polder 32 study revealed that the concept of "community" was defined by the people narrowly, as a community of fate, and that people worked together within their communities to solve local environmental challenges. People within the communities agreed on who was in them (and on who was marginal within them). For example, the community in the northeast of the polder recovered sooner and more permanently than the communities

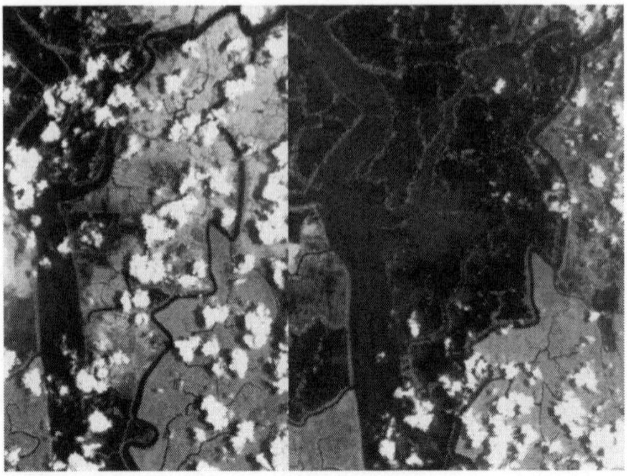

Fig. 2.2. Landsat imagery enhanced to reveal wet and dry terrain in Polder 32, Dacope, and Khulna, Bangladesh, seven days before Aila (left) and nine days after Aila (right). White is cloud, lighter gray is dry, darker gray is mangrove forest, and darkest gray or black is wet. The dark lines are rivers and canals, often with a built embankment, the other areas being flooded due to breaches in embankments.

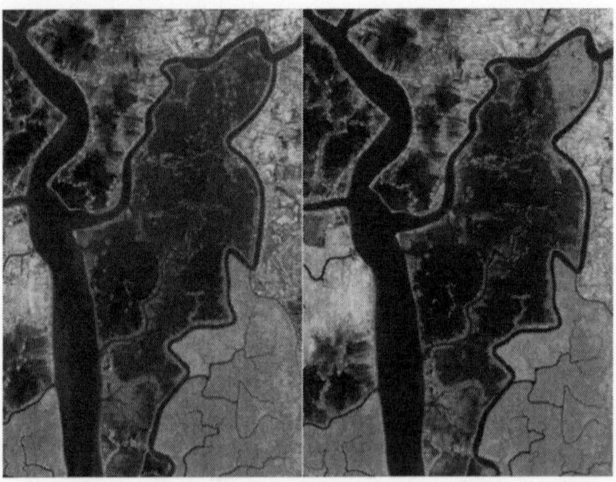

Fig. 2.3. Landsat imagery enhanced to reveal wet and dry terrain in Polder 32, Dacope, and Khulna, Bangladesh, six months after Aila, November 11, 2009 (left), and sixteen days later, November 27, 2009 (right). The light gray area in the upper right (surrounded by dark water) is the community of Uttar Kamarkhola.

further south and west because they worked together to restore an interior barrier that protected their land from being flooded by tidal waters from the west.

In 2014, following the Polder 32 study and reflecting on its finding of the scale at which to define community, Bishawjit Mallick, Anna Carella, and I studied twenty-three communities. Geographically distributed across the southwest of Bangladesh, these communities experienced differing degrees of a range of environmental concerns: vulnerability to cyclones, a dynamic natural environment in which land use and river use are slowly changing, and reliance on rainwater for drinking water because the aquifer is saline. We call this the MAR study, because the twenty-three sites were selected on the basis that they were about to receive a water project that used an engineering technology called managed aquifer recharge (MAR), in which fresh rainwater is stored in the aquifer in order to deal with the last of these three common environmental concerns. Using qualitative methods, as with the Polder 32 study, we defined the boundaries of the community according to the community's self-understanding.

The population of each community was enumerated with our own geolocated photo census of all households (defined as those who shared a kitchen) in each community (community size ranged from 68 to 298 households).[50] Survey researchers were assigned randomly selected households and given a map, photo, and name for each house. Geolocation of interviews conducted and photos of houses confirmed that sampled houses were surveyed. Given dense population and the preference for interviewing outdoors due to the heat, these methods were necessary to yield a random sample and not a quasi-convenient sample. All interviews were audio recorded for quality assurance. The study used the same measure of rights enjoyment used in the Ackerly-Cruz study. The question on that measure was incorporated into a ninety-minute interview that spanned environmental, economic, and political issues.

Figure 2.4 shows that rights enjoyment across communities varies significantly in magnitude and direction. In site 34, over 80 percent of respondents do not feel that rights are enjoyed in Bangladesh, with eleven (nearly half) of the communities surveyed having 50 percent or more respondents with a negative opinion about rights enjoyment in Bangladesh. Only three communities have 50 percent or more of respondents having a positive view of rights in Bangladesh. To understand puzzles such as *why* there is such variety across communities within the same region, we generally turn to qualitative data. The right quantitative data can also shed light on these

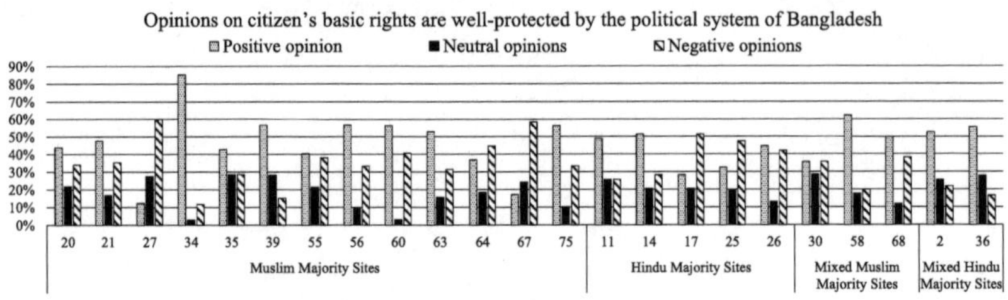

Fig. 2.4. Community variation in rights enjoyment

problems. I here pose some of the puzzles and describe the methodologies we are using to explore them.

By analyzing the qualitative data of outliers and comparative cases, we can see the sources for the range of experience of governance that we saw in the Ackerly-Cruz study. Qualitative data from ethnographic data gathered at the same time as the survey tells us that sites 67 and 56 are resettlement sites where landless people were offered government land (see fig. 2.5). However, site 67 has a very high percentage of people enjoying their rights, whereas site 56 does not. This difference reflects the political economy. In site 56, the people are exposed to pirates and have to travel outside of their village for work, even for day labor. In site 67, the recently resettled people experience the government as functioning well, partly due to the resettlement and partly due to the supplementary services they receive through nongovernment organizations (NGOs). In site 56—resettled in 1995, exposed to pirates, and receiving infrequent resources through NGOs—the people do not enjoy their rights as much.

There is significant variation across communities as to their sources of insecurity (see fig. 2.6). However, the reporting in this case has reliability issues and requires interpretation. For example, since the pirates do not live among the villagers of site 56, the villagers felt free to speak about the threat the pirates pose. Other issues, particularly those experienced due to gender norms or localized power dynamics, cannot be discussed openly and require more sophisticated qualitative research techniques to be revealed. A feminist critical theory of human rights needs to use these sophisticated methods to reveal those aspects of oppression, normalization, and power relations that cannot be revealed in patterns or by exploring the details of the outliers.

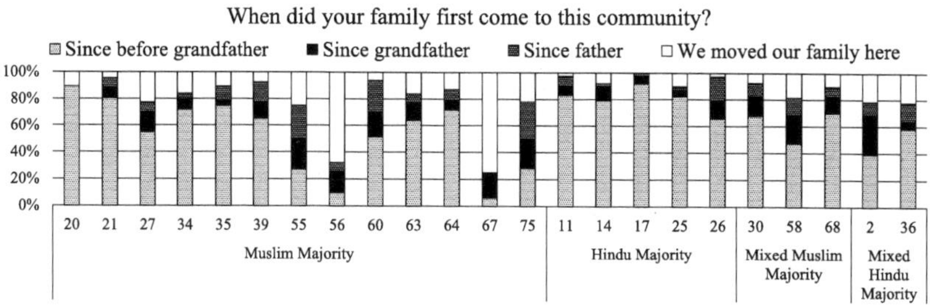

Fig. 2.5. History of family migration by generation, site, and religion

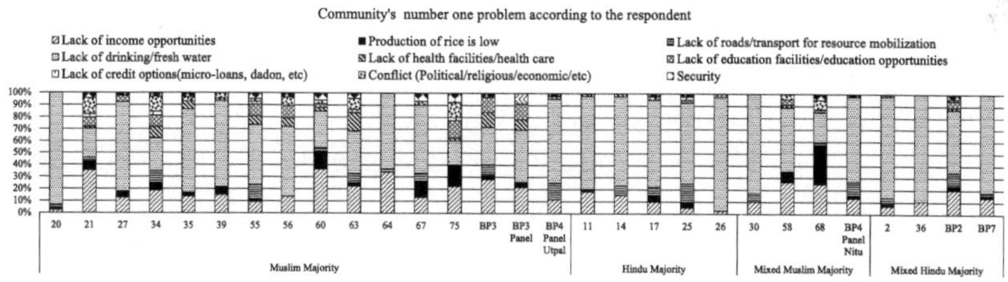

Fig. 2.6. Community's number one problem

Quantitative analysis can give us some insight into the relationship between income, relative income, income inequality in a community, and perceptions of rights. We would expect more negative attitudes toward rights in communities with significant income inequality as compared with communities with relative income equality (see fig. 2.7). For example, site 34, with low views of human rights, has high income inequality. Site 67, with high views of human rights, has low income inequality, including few in the lowest income category. Does that pattern bear out across the sites? We can further refine our understanding with hierarchical linear modeling, the hypothesis being that individuals in a community with greater income equality would be more likely to enjoy their rights than otherwise similar individuals situated in communities with less income equality. We can refine our understanding still further with an internal experiment in which a treatment group is primed to notice income inequality prior to answering questions about rights, the hypothesis being that those primed to perceive that there is income inequality that disadvantages them would be less inclined to enjoy their rights.

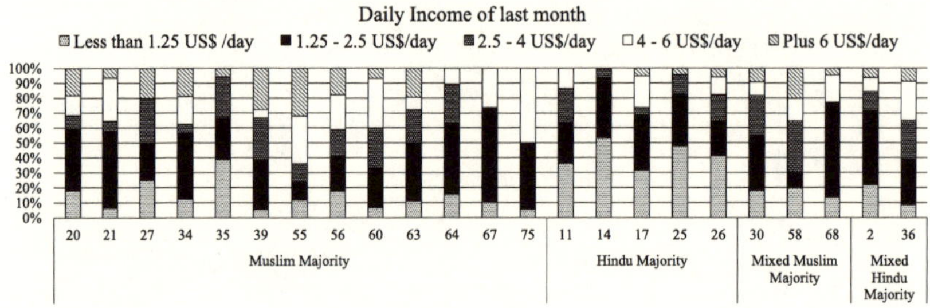

Fig. 2.7. Income diversity

In sum, qualitative and quantitative tools can explore the paradoxes of rights enjoyment. Different household experiences affect people's sense of rights enjoyment differently. Some of these experiences are *shared* within a community; for example, a resettled community has a common experience of resettlement. Some of these are experienced in a *context* of a community, such as income equality, sufficient local employment and therefore not much migration, or certain powerful elite. Households within these communities experience these conditions differently, depending on other features. Further, quantitative data and qualitative data at the community level suggest that macro-level trends in rights enjoyment are not experienced in the aggregate but can vary significantly by and within communities. Understanding those differences is essential to human rights praxis.

Conclusion: Complexity, Ethics, and Money

A critical theory of human rights has to address oppression, normalization, and power dynamics not only as a subject of research but also in the research process. Substantively, critical theories guide us to study human rights violations at the relevant scale. The quantitative research shared here shows us that rights enjoyment varies by and within communities and subgroups. The multimethod study of individual, household, community, and national quantitative data combined with qualitative and experimental data in some of these sites may enable us to unravel some of the puzzles related to the complexity of local, national, and global forces in a particular context. Our generalizations from these quantitative findings are not so general as to be practically meaningless even though statistically significant.[51] Yet we cannot rely on them to resolve the contractions created by the dynamics of rights enjoyment.

Just as we may use quantitative skills to explore a range of critical approaches to human rights, we can, in light of critical theories, develop new ways of analyzing qualitative data so that we can compare and study at the appropriate scale, being attentive to differences, emerging patterns, and outliers. While it is too early to share findings from these more recent studies, it is not too early to recognize that their findings are guided by critical theory *and rely partly* on quantitative data and analyses. Guided by the appropriate research question, model, and operationalization of variables, quantitative methods can be an essential part of a critical theory of human rights. Quantitative methods for the study of human rights enable us to study a critical theory of human rights *and* to contribute to a better understanding of the challenges to human rights enjoyment, by enabling the study of these processes at the scale at which they are experienced. Properly conceived, they are an important part of the empirical projects of critical theory.

These are not, however, the only concerns of a critical empiricist, who also reflects on the ways in which power dynamics affect research. Consider the power dynamics related to the funding sources and the international research team of this project. First, the quantitative studies shared here were made possible by federally funded grants. Where publicity does not pose a political problem for respondents and their communities, these data are or will be publicly available in some format. In the first instance, the data were not collected with a particularly critical theory in mind. Cruz and I used data from the Latin American Public Opinion Project for a critical quantitative research design. The cost of doing this critical quantitative project was incremental and minimal. The Polder 32 and MAR studies, by contrast, were initiated *because* of a grant. The research design was informed by earlier work, but due to the exploratory nature of the grant, the funding allowed and encouraged methodological innovation. By contrast, some forms of funding are constrained by disciplinary norms. This funding was made possible *because* it promised to be methodologically innovative and interdisciplinary. A critical theory approach expects that we will be responsible custodians of our resources regardless of their sources. Moreover, we consider the resources of the project not merely to be financial but also to include the time of the respondents.

Second, in a critical theory approach to empirical research, we think about all aspects of power relations, including those between project leader and research team members, particularly those who are developing new research skills. In international work, there are extra layers of power inequalities, including those having to do with the relative ease with which people of certain nationalities can move between countries, obtain advanced degrees, and design the research projects of our choosing. In addition to the substantive findings of the research, with a feminist critical theory lens, the researcher bears ethical responsibility not merely for those ethics questions of interest to human subjects review committees but also for those ethics questions raised by the norms and power dynamics of research itself.

Notes

1. See Brooke Ackerly, *Universal Human Rights in a World of Difference* (Cambridge: Cambridge University Press, 2008); Ackerly, "Human Rights Enjoyment in Theory and Activism," *Human Rights Review* 12, no. 2 (2011).

2. Brooke Ackerly and José Miguel Cruz, "Hearing the Voice of the People: Human Rights as if People Mattered," *New Political Science* 33, no. 1 (2011).

3. For a richer account of the theory used in this chapter, see Ackerly, *Universal Human Rights*. The question of what those in struggle *are struggling for* could also be empirical but could not be answered without normative work on the meaning of the concepts in question.

4. See Dvora Yanow, "Conversations across Epistemological Divides: Critical Methodologies for International Relations," in *Bridging Multiple Divides* (San Francisco: International Studies Association, 2008); Dvora Yanow and Peregrine Schwartz-Shea, eds., *Interpretation and Method: Empirical Research Methods and the Interpretive Turn*, 2nd ed. (Armonk, NY: M. E. Sharpe, 2013, 2006); J. Ann Tickner, "You Just Don't Understand: Troubled Engagements between Feminists and IR Theorists," *International Studies Quarterly* 41, no. 4 (1997); Tickner, "What Is Your Research Program? Some Feminist Answers to International Relations Methodological Questions," *International Studies Quarterly* 49, no. 1 (2005).

5. This is not even true in those states where a strong centralized authority is uniquely responsible for rights violations. See Michael E. Goodhart, *Democracy as Human Rights: Freedom and Equality in the Age of Globalization* (New York: Routledge, 2005).

6. See Emilie M. Hafner-Burton, "A Social Science of Human Rights," *Journal of Peace Research* 51, no. 2 (2014).

7. See Wade M. Cole, "Hard and Soft Commitments to Human Rights Treaties, 1966–2001," *Sociological Forum* 24, no. 3 (2009); Jay Goodliffe and Darren G. Hawkins, "Explaining Commitment: States and the Convention against Torture," *Journal of Politics* 68, no. 2 (2006); Ryan Goodman and Derek Jinks, "How to

Influence States: Socialization and International Human Rights Law," *Duke Law Journal* 54, no. 3 (2004); Oona A. Hathaway, "Why Do Countries Commit to Human Rights Treaties?," *Journal of Conflict Resolution* 51, no. 4 (2007); Ellen L. Lutz and Kathryn Sikkink, "International Human Rights Law and Practice in Latin America," *International Organization* 54, no. 3 (2000); Andrew Moravcsik, "The Origins of Human Rights Regimes: Democratic Delegation in Postwar Europe," *International Organization* 54, no. 2; Eric Neumayer, "Qualified Ratification: Explaining Reservations to International Human Rights Treaties," *Journal of Legal Studies* 36, no. 2 (2007); James Raymond Vreeland, "Political Institutions and Human Rights: Why Dictatorships Enter into the United Nations Convention against Torture," *International Organization* 62, no. 1 (2008); Christine Min Wotipka and Kiyoteru Tsutsui, "Global Human Rights and State Sovereignty: State Ratification of International Human Rights Treaties, 1965–2001," *Sociological Forum* 23, no. 4 (2008).

8. See M. Rodwan Abouharb and David L. Cingranelli, "The Human Rights Effects of World Bank Structural Adjustment, 1981–2000," *International Studies Quarterly* 50, no. 2 (2006); Rodwan Abouharb and David L. Cingranelli, *Human Rights and Structural Adjustment* (Cambridge: Cambridge University Press, 2007); Bruce Bueno De Mesquita et al., "Thinking Inside the Box: A Closer Look at Democracy and Human Rights," *International Studies Quarterly* 49, no. 3 (2005); David Cingranelli and Mikhail Filippov, "Electoral Rules and Incentives to Protect Human Rights," *Journal of Politics* 72, no. 1 (2010); Christian Davenport, "Multi-Dimensional Threat Perception and State Repression: An Inquiry into Why States Apply Negative Sanctions," *American Journal of Political Science* 39, no. 3 (1995); Davenport, "State Repression and the Tyrannical Peace," *Journal of Peace Research* 44, no. 4 (2007); Axel Dreher, Martin Gassebner, and Lars H. R. Siemers, "Globalization, Economic Freedom, and Human Rights," *Journal of Conflict Resolution* 56, no. 3 (2012); Neil A. Englehart, "State Capacity, State Failure, and Human Rights," *Journal of Peace Research* 46, no. 2 (2009); Emilie M. Hafner-Burton, "Sticks and Stones: Naming and Shaming the Human Rights Enforcement Problem," *International Organization* 62, no. 4 (2008); Oona A. Hathaway, "Do Human Rights Treaties Make a Difference?," *Yale Law Journal* 111, no. 8 (2002); Linda Camp Keith, C. Neal Tate, and Steven C. Poe, "Is the Law a Mere Parchment Barrier to Human Rights Abuse?," *Journal of Politics* 71, no. 2 (2009); Eric Neumayer, "Do International Human Rights Treaties Improve Respect for Human Rights?," *Journal of Conflict Resolution* 49, no. 6 (2005); Steven C. Poe, C. Neal Tate, and Linda Camp Keith, "Repression of the Human Right to Personal Integrity Revisited: A Global Cross-National Study Covering the Years 1976–1993," *International Studies Quarterly* 43, no. 2 (1999); Emilia Justyna Powell and Jeffrey K. Staton, "Domestic Judicial Institutions and Human Rights Treaty Violation," *International Studies Quarterly* 53 (2009); David L. Richards and Ronald D. Gelleny, "Good Things to Those Who Wait? National Elections and Government Respect for Human Rights," *Journal of Peace Research* 44, no. 4 (2007); Joseph K. Young, "State Capacity, Democracy, and the Violation of Personal Integrity Rights," *Journal of Human Rights* 8, no. 4 (2009).

9. Steven C. Poe, "Human Rights and US Foreign Aid: A Review of Quantita-

tive Studies and Suggestions for Future Research," *Human Rights Quarterly* 12, no. 4 (1990); Poe, "Human Rights and Economic Aid Allocation under Ronald Reagan and Jimmy Carter," *American Journal of Political Science* 36, no. 1 (1992).

10. See Steven C. Poe and C. Neal Tate, "Repression of Human Rights to Personal Integrity in the 1980s: A Global Analysis," *American Political Science Review* 88, no. 4 (1994); Bueno De Mesquita et al., "Thinking Inside the Box."

11. See Steven C. Poe, C. Neal Tate, and Linda Camp Keith, "Repression of the Human Right to Personal Integrity Revisited."

12. See Steven C. Poe, Dierdre Wendel-Blunt, and Karl Ho, "Global Patterns in the Achievement of Women's Human Rights to Equality," *Human Rights Quarterly* 19, no. 4 (1997).

13. See Mary Caprioli, "Democracy and Human Rights versus Women's Security: A Contradiction?," *Security Dialogue* 35, no. 4 (2004).

14. See Bueno De Mesquita et al., "Thinking Inside the Box." See also Srilatha Batliwala, *Engaging with Empowerment: An Intellectual and Experiential Journey* (New Delhi: Women Unlimited, 2013).

15. Generally, these critics think of human rights as a cultural concept connected to a particular liberal, modern, Western, and economic notion of the person. In what follows, I take a more theoretical understanding of the obstacle. See, for comparison, V. Spike Peterson, "Whose Rights? A Critique of the 'Givens' in Human Rights Discourse," *Alternatives* 15 (1990).

16. See Ackerly, *Universal Human Rights*; Jacques Rancière, "Who Is the Subject of the Rights of Man?," *South Atlantic Quarterly* 103, no. 2 (2004); Hannah Arendt, *The Origins of Totalitarianism*, 1st ed. (New York: Harcourt, 1951); Karen Zivi, *Making Rights Claims: A Practice of Democratic Citizenship* (New York: Oxford University Press, 2012). In my research, I enrich this two-part understanding of rights. Here I focus on just these two, as this is a familiar and yet underutilized disaggregation of the concept "rights claim."

17. See Peterson, "Whose Rights?"; Wendy Brown, "Suffering Rights as Paradoxes," *Constellations* 7, no. 2 (2000). Cf. Goodhart, *Democracy as Human Rights*.

18. See my development of the concept "terrain of difficulty" in *Universal Human Rights*, chaps. 7 and 8.

19. See Charlotte Bunch, "Women's Rights as Human Rights: Toward a Re-Vision of Human Rights," *Human Rights Quarterly* 12, no. 4 (1990). Other theorists emphasizing this distinction include Bina D'Costa, "The Humanitarian Frontline: Rohingya Refugees and the 'Right to Have Rights'" *Forum Monthly, the Daily Star* (2012); Natalie Oman, "Hannah Arendt's 'Right to Have Rights': A Philosophical Context for Human Security," *Journal of Human Rights* 9, no. 3 (2010); James Ingram, "What Is a 'Right to Have Rights'? Three Images of the Politics of Human Rights," *American Political Science Review* 102, no. 4 (2008); Rancière, "Who Is the Subject of the Rights of Man?"

20. See Ackerly, *Universal Human Rights*; Ariel Kohen, *In Defense of Human Rights: A Non-Religious Grounding in a Pluralistic World*, Routledge Innovations in Political Theory (London: Routledge, 2007); Zivi, *Making Rights Claims*.

21. See Beth A. Simmons, *Mobilizing for Human Rights: International Law in Domestic Politics* (Cambridge: Cambridge University Press, 2009).

22. See Freedom House, "Bangladesh," in *Freedom in the World*, 1998–2014.
23. Ackerly, *Universal Human Rights*.
24. For my critical assessments of critical theory in IR, see "Uncritical Theory," in *Critical Theory in International Relations and Security Studies: Interviews and Reflections*, ed. Shannon Brincat, Laura Lima, and João Nunes (New York: Routledge, 2012).
25. For an account of what a research ethic guided by feminist critical theory entails, see Brooke Ackerly and Jacqui True, "Studying the Struggles and Wishes of the Age: Feminist Theoretical Methodology and Feminist Theoretical Methods," in *Feminist Methodologies for International Relations*, ed. Brooke Ackerly, Maria Stern, and Jacqui True (Cambridge: Cambridge University Press, 2006).
26. For an account of global feminism as not only a theory but also a pedagogy and ethics, see Brooke Ackerly and Katy Attanasi, "Global Feminisms: Theory and Ethics for Studying Gendered Injustice," *New Political Science* 31, no. 4 (2009).
27. Brooke Ackerly and Jacqui True, *Doing Feminist Research in Political and Social Science* (Basingstoke, UK: Palgrave Macmillan, 2010), 2.
28. See Ackerly, *Universal Human Rights*.
29. See ibid.; Zivi, *Making Rights Claims*; Rancière, "Who Is the Subject of the Rights of Man?"
30. See Poe, Tate, and Keith, "Repression of the Human Right to Personal Integrity Revisited."
31. See Caprioli, "Democracy and Human Rights versus Women's Security."
32. For more on responsibilities of rights-based theoretical and empirical inquiry, as well as rights-based activism, see Ackerly, *Universal Human Rights*.
33. See ibid., chap. 7; Brooke Ackerly, "The Hardest Cases of Global Injustice: The Responsibility to Inquire," in *Justice, Sustainability, and Security: Global Ethics for the 21st Century*, ed. Eric Heinze (New York: Palgrave Macmillan 2013).
34. See Robert O. Keohane, "International Relations Theory: Contributions of a Feminist Standpoint," *Millennium: Journal of International Studies* 18, no. 2 (1989).
35. See, e.g., V. Spike Peterson and Laura Parisi, "Are Women Human? It's Not an Academic Question," in *Human Rights Fifty Years On: A Reappraisal*, ed. Tony Evans (Manchester, UK: Manchester University Press, 1998); Bunch, "Women's Rights as Human Rights."
36. See Keith J. Bybee, "Essentially Contested Membership: Racial Minorities and the Politics of Inclusion," *Legal Studies Forum* 21, no. 4 (1997).
37. See Eric Neumayer and Thomas Plümper, "The Gendered Nature of Natural Disasters: The Impact of Catastrophic Events on the Gender Gap in Life Expectancy, 1981–2002," *Annals of the Association of American Geographers* 97, no. 3 (2007).
38. See Susan Moller Okin, "Gender Inequality and Cultural Differences," *Political Theory* 22, no. 1 (1994).
39. See Ackerly and Cruz, "Hearing the Voice of the People."
40. For a review of how others have operationalized human rights see ibid.; Hafner-Burton, "A Social Science of Human Rights"; Maria Green, "What We Talk About When We Talk About Indicators: Current Approaches to Human Rights Measurement," *Human Rights Quarterly* 23, no. 4 (2001).
41. Ackerly and Cruz, "Hearing the Voice of the People." We thank the Latin American Public Opinion Project, or LAPOP (www.vanderbilt.edu/lapop/), and its

major supporters (the US Agency for International Development, the United Nations Development Programme, the Inter-American Development Bank, and Vanderbilt University) for making the data available.

42. This paragraph restates and cites Ackerly and Cruz, "Hearing the Voice of the People," 20.

43. In cases of extreme political repression or civil war, we might expect these to be more closely correlated if the violations are widespread and not concentrated in particular communities.

44. See, e.g. Simmons, *Mobilizing for Human Rights.*

45. See Maria Stern, *Naming Security—Constructing Identity: "Mayan Women" in Guatemala on the Eve of "Peace"* (Manchester, UK: Manchester University Press, 2005).

46. See Ackerly, *Universal Human Rights.*

47. Christopher J. Fariss, "Respect for Human Rights Has Improved over Time: Modeling the Changing Standard of Accountability," *American Political Science Review* 108, no. 2 (2014): 297.

48. This research is part of ISEE Bangladesh (http://www.vanderbilt.edu/ISEEBangladesh/about.php), a multidisciplinary, multiuniversity (Vanderbilt, Columbia, Dhaka, Khulna, and Jahangirnagar) project studying community and regional resilience to environmental change in coastal Bangladesh. The partnership is funded by the US Office of Naval Research (Vanderbilt IRB approval 120454). The data and analysis from this research that are referenced in this chapter were collected from 2012 to 2013 using qualitative comparative analysis of twelve communities in and around Polder 32 in southwest Bangladesh and of twenty-three sites more geographically disbursed across the region, selected on the basis of variability in their vulnerability to sea-level rise, cyclones, and inadequate freshwater throughout the year. The research includes the study of sedimentology, hydrology, sociology, economics, and politics in a historical perspective. Additional data collection and analysis is ongoing. Persons whose efforts significantly contributed to the data in this chapter include Steve Goodbred (physical), Leslie Wallace (physical), John Ayers (physical), Jonathan Gilligan (physical and technical), "Labib" Mujibul Anam (social), Sayed Muhammad Saikh Imtiaz (social), Bishawjit Mallick (social), and Anna Carella (social). Significant partnership with Kazi Matin Uddin Ahmed (geology, Dhaka University) informed site selection regarding salinity.

49. Figures 2.2 and 2.3 include Landsat imagery distributed by the Land Processes Distributed Active Archive Center, located at the United States Geological Survey's Earth Resources Observation and Science Center in Sioux Falls, South Dakota (http://lpdaac.usgs.gov).

50. The authors are happy to provide technical details and software for those interested in the technological specifics.

51. This is the criticism in Bueno De Mesquita et al., "Thinking Inside the Box."

CHAPTER 3

Quantitative Methods and Constructivist Theorizing for Conflict Studies

CAMERON G. THIES

Statistical Methods for Constructivist International Relations

The academic discipline of International Relations (IR) has been the subject of a number of so-called Great Debates in its history, including at least one over methodology. The Second Great Debate, between behavioralism and what Hedley Bull called the "classical approach," set the stage for much of the subsequent, methodological debate between those who prefer the use of quantitative methods of one type or another and those who prefer more qualitative forms of analysis.[1] Different subfields later emerged with particular configurations of theory and methodology. For example, the subfield of security studies is primarily characterized by a realist theoretical orientation and qualitative methodology, whereas the subfield of conflict studies contains elements of both realist and liberal IR theory while maintaining a focus on quantitative methodology. In this chapter, I focus on how statistics has been used within the context of conflict studies and how it could be used to inform a constructivist approach to conflict studies. Since constructivism is a metatheory rather than a specific theory applicable to a specific domain of IR, I use conflict studies as the context in which I demonstrate that statistics can be useful to constructivism.

Statistical analysis has been used in political science since the onset of the behavioral revolution, most often to test hypotheses derived from verbal or mathematical theories. Within our discipline, a hypothesis is usually stated in causal terms, such that an independent variable (the purported cause) is producing a change in the dependent variable (the purported effect), subject to the effects generated by any number of relevant control variables (known correlates of the dependent variable that are not the primary focus of the investigation). The results of the statistical analysis will reveal the direction of the effect (positive or negative), as well as the magnitude (size) of the effect and its significance (the likelihood that the result occurred as a result of chance). While purely inductive work is possible using statistics, the preference of the discipline is to follow some version of a deductive approach that generates testable hypotheses.

The use of statistics is a central feature of the subfield of conflict studies, which focuses on actors involved in interstate or intrastate conflict. Statistical approaches depend on quantified data, and conflict studies as a subfield has often looked to established datasets about potential correlates of large-scale conflict as the source of its data. The best known of these is the Correlates of War (COW) Project, which, like many data collection efforts that sprang up as a result of the behavioral revolution, focuses on collecting data on the attributes of actors, behavior, and events. In the case of COW, most of those attributes are material variables rooted in traditional realism—population size, gross domestic product (GDP), territory, contiguity, material capabilities, alliance membership, and so on. Other data gathering projects have produced data on regime type, trade, membership in intergovernmental organizations (IGOs), and so on, which statistical analyses increasingly incorporate alongside traditional realist variables in order to demonstrate that liberals also have something to say about world politics.[2] "Realist" variables could coexist easily alongside "liberal" variables in a statistical analysis and fit well into the traditional theoretical divide in the discipline between realism and idealism/liberalism.

Partly because of the dominance of the COW approach, conflict studies has largely grounded its theory in versions of realism and liberalism and ignored constructivism's entry into the discipline in the 1990s. One way to begin to incorporate a statistical approach and constructivism into conflict studies is to simply identify "constructivist" variables to test alongside realist and liberal variables. As Choi and Caporaso suggest, we could take "variables central to constructivism, such as norms and institutions," and engage in a typical exercise of comparative hypothesis-testing.[3] We could then see if constructivist variables actually have "value added" compared to realist and liberal explanations of phenomena. But which variables would conflict studies associate with constructivism? Would this include all identity variables, such as measures of ethnicity, religion, or language group? Many of these variables are routinely used in studies with a primarily rationalist and materialist theoretical perspective. Democracy is a "type" identity according to Wendt, but it is also commonly considered a liberal explanatory variable. IGOs are sometimes ceded to constructivists, since they provide the opportunity for member states to be socialized and learn, yet they are also claimed by liberals.[4] Labeling variables as "constructivist" once and for all is probably misguided, because variables may represent concepts associated with multiple theoretical perspectives.

A more promising way to bring a statistical approach to constructivism in the context of conflict studies is to match constructivist theorizing about concepts to data. For example, Atkinson argues that we can observe US hegemonic socialization (a potential "constructivist" concept) through US officer training and military exchanges.[5] Her statistical evidence suggests that the US is able to socialize authoritarian states through these types of exchanges, resulting in the increased likelihood of transition to greater levels of democracy. Yet, compare this perspective to a traditional conflict studies article by Ruby and Gibler, whose empirical findings suggest that US professional military education reduces the likelihood of a coup attempt.[6] While the former argument is rooted in a constructivist theoretical framework, the latter is grounded loosely in the literature on civil-military relations and democratization. The empirical results are largely the same. A skeptic from the conflict studies community would probably suggest that we did not need the constructivist theorizing, since existing theoretical perspectives explain the outcome.

I will try to move the conversation along further by drawing on my own work on rivalry, a concept in IR that emerged squarely within the conflict studies community. Its original proponents were Paul Diehl, who has long been associated with the COW project, and Gary Goertz. The operational development of rivalry outpaced the conceptual development at first, as militarized interstate disputes (MIDs) were used to observe rivalries.[7] William Thompson criticized this approach and developed a conceptual approach to rivalry that relied on mutual perception.[8] Both approaches have been widely used in the conflict studies literature, and I suggest that the latter offers an empirically observable bridge to constructivist theorizing.

I begin by making the case for rivalry as a concept that can bridge conflict studies and constructivist research. I then discuss two research projects in which constructivist theorizing is paired to statistical analysis through the rivalry concept. Both projects are heavily influenced by Wendt's work and heed his advice to combine constructivist insights with other theoretical perspectives, to develop testable hypotheses about militarized conflict, on the one hand, and regional orders, on the other.[9] After discussing these projects, I then discuss the benefits of using statistical analyses with constructivism and sketch out an agenda for constructivist research in conflict studies.

Rivalry: A Bridge Concept between Constructivism and Conflict Studies

The rivalry concept is an ideal bridge between materialist and more ideational approaches to world politics. The concept has been developed by those located squarely in the COW tradition who use the frequency of MIDs or crises to identify rivals.[10] In this materialist approach, a rivalry is typically constituted by competition over some (in)tangible good between a pair of states over an extended period of time. Operationally, this usually amounts to identifying how many observed conflicts or crises occur in a dyad within a defined period of time. For example, Goertz and Diehl's original operational definition of an enduring rivalry required "conflicts between the same two states that involve at least five militarized disputes in a period lasting at least ten years."[11] Goertz and Diehl originally identified rivalries via empirical observation and then created categories of enduring rivalry and proto-rivalry, as a way to categorize relationships between states with varying amounts of MIDs over varying periods of time. Over time, their approach developed more conceptual and theoretical language to catch up with the early empirical observations. The primary finding from this approach was that most conflict and wars in the world were contained within rivalries.

Others in the tradition have attempted to bring in issues as a way to tackle ideas, but still within a primarily materialistic framework suited to traditional conflict studies.[12] The approaches that focused on issues were an attempt to better date the beginning and endings of rivalries, as well as to make sure that something held the conflicts within a rivalry together, by ensuring that the same issue or set of issues connected recurrent conflict across the life span of the rivalry. Rather than relying on the MID data to tell *ex post* which states were rivals (as in the early Diehl and Goertz approach), Bennett, as well as Mitchell and Thies, used various sources of data to identify when issues came into contention between states, to mark the beginning of a rivalry, and then when those issues were settled, to mark the end. The rivalries themselves were identified as contention over a single issue or sets of issues. Even later iterations of the Diehl and Goertz approach began to incorporate issues as the source of competition between states.[13] Even so, issues in these approaches are often tied to material attributes of states, such as territory, border disputes, maritime zones, and riparian disputes.

Thompson actually grounds his approach to rivals in perceptions, which is unusual for conflict studies.[14] He was critical of the early dispute density approaches favored by Diehl and Goertz, since it produced some rather unlikely pairings (e.g., U.S.-Haiti, Russia-Sweden) due to massive imbalances in capabilities, and it also missed some of the historic great power rivalries of the nineteenth century, such as that between Great Britain and France. Instead, Thompson argues that we could identify rivals only by looking at the "key decision makers' own observations about who they thought their principal enemies and opponents were."[15] Only "principal" opponents could really be considered rivals, which is a perceptual approach that is independent of the measurement of disputes over set periods of time. Thompson's principal rivalries approach morphed into his strategic rivalry approach.[16] Conceptually, strategic rivals must view each other as "(a) competitors, (b) the source of actual or latent threats that pose some possibility of becoming militarized, and (c) enemies."[17] Thompson's approach, while still rooted in material sources of conflict, pushes the envelope for typical conflict research by incorporating decision makers' perceptions of self and other identities. It is doubtful that Thompson intended to open the door to identity with his approach, since he was really looking for a better way to categorize pairs of states for traditional conflict analysis. However, the unintended by-product of his work is a conceptual and operational approach to rivalry that is consistent with constructivist theoretical understandings of the rival role.

Wendt identifies three role identities—friend, rival, and enemy—that are claimed to constitute particular cultures of anarchy.[18] He argues that role identities are learned and reinforced in response to how states are treated by significant others, through a process of cultural selection or socialization.[19] For example, if the state is treated as an enemy by others, the state will internalize that belief in its own role identity. As more states treat each other as enemies, a tipping point is reached whereby all members are assumed to be enemies. This process results in the Hobbesian culture of anarchy, while the dominance of the rival role identity produces a Lockean culture, and the friend role identity produces a Kantian culture of anarchy. Anarchy is therefore "what states make of it" as a result of treating each other as friends, rivals, or enemies, rather than always an enemy-dominated environment as assumed by realism. Wendt's judgment is that the modern interstate system is actually dominated by a Lockean culture of anarchy. According to him, the Lockean culture based on the rival role identity generates four tendencies in the international system.[20] First, interstate conflict is accepted but constrained, since rivals recognize each other's sovereignty and do not attempt to destroy or conquer each other as enemies might. Second, the constrained nature of conflict produces low rates of state death. Third, the mutual recognition of sovereignty produces the balancing of power among states, rather than as a result of anarchy. Finally, neutrality is a recognized status, because states need not compete militarily in such a "live and let live" system.

If Wendt's theoretical account of rivalry is compatible with Thompson's more empirically oriented measures of rivalry, we have established a unique theoretical bridge between constructivism and traditional conflict studies, allowing for statistical tests of constructivist hypotheses generated about rivalry. I have elsewhere suggested that Wendt's and Thompson's approaches are compatible, in several articles that will be referenced below to illustrate the potential of such a combination. There are some obvious metatheoretical differences between the two approaches: Wendt's approach to constructivism is methodologically holist and ideational, while Thompson's work is rooted in methodological individualism and materialism. Yet they share common ground in perceptions that lead to mutual identification of rivals. In Wendt's world, if the self perceives the other as a rival and treats the other as a rival, the other is likely to form a rival relationship with the self. In Thompson's world, we must mutually perceive each other as our principal opponent to be considered a rival. This common ground allows us to use a variety of forms of constructivist theorizing to generate hypotheses about rivals and their behavior that can be tested using Thompson's operational measure. I will focus on several studies that illustrate how this has been done, before speculating, in this chapter's conclusion, on other potential fruitful areas for cross-fertilization between constructivism and conflict studies, via the use of statistical methods.

Examples of Statistical Analyses of Rivalry Grounded in Constructivist Theorizing

Rivalrous Paths to Conflict

Kowert and Thies set out to theoretically unpack the concept of rivalry and to identify different images of rivalry that may be associated in different ways with militarized conflict.[21] As noted above, rivalry is typically conceptualized as being constituted by militarized conflict in the traditional conflict studies literature, or as one of three generic role identities in Wendt's theoretical analyses of cultures of anarchy. Yet it is possible that rivalry may mean different things in different contexts. Kowert and Thies make this argument by focusing on how images of conflict associated with rivalry are responses to violations of particular forms of order that rest on one of the three characteristic types of linguistic rules.[22]

The argument is motivated by three images of threat, each associated with a particular type of rival. The first image, of threat based on institutional legitimacy, is motivated by Iraq following the invasion of Kuwait and the 1991 Persian Gulf War. Hussein's failure to conform to international norms represents the threat of recklessness and aggressiveness with which a rogue dictator could use power, as well as a deficiency in institutional character and leadership in Iraq. Hussein borrowed the image of the lion from Nebuchadnezzar and the ancient Babylonians to represent himself, and we use the lion as the symbol of institutional rivalry. The second image, of threat based on competition, is represented by the Asian Tigers in the 1980s, such as Japan, Singapore, Hong Kong, Taiwan, and South Korea. This threat represents unfair or unrestrained competition to those who perceive it, such as the United States and Europe during that time period. The third image, of strategic threat, is motivated by the Russian/Soviet bear during the Cold War. This image rests on violations of international security norms, which, in that case, meant evolving norms of cooperative security. The Iraqi lion, Asian tiger, and Russian bear are meant to be stylized images of threat associated with types of interstate rivalry (institutional, economic, and strategic, respectively).

Each of these types of rivalry is a result of violations of particular forms of order. We are indebted to Wendt for labeling these forms of order Hobbesian, Lockean, and Kantian,[23] though they rest on different theoretical foundations. A Kantian order rests on the ability of states to commit themselves to the transformation of anarchy into community. Expectations of peace in this order are connected with the institutional form of the state. Threats to a Kantian order rest on divergence from democratic institutional forms. A Hobbesian order rests on trust in a general system of expectations, such that by announcing policies of deterrence and collective security, states signal norms of international behavior. The main threat to this type of order is that the basic directives associated with international society will not be obeyed. This kind of threat is most associated with strategic rivals who have a history of violating each other's sovereignty through conflict. The Lockean order rests on cooperation in service of the public good. In such a system, states are encouraged to behave responsibly by allowing access to domestic markets in accordance with liberal principles. Any behavior that challenges fair play and fair competition yields the economic rival as an unfair competitor.

The Kantian order thus rests on the qualities of the agents themselves, the Hobbesian order rests on enforcement of norms, and the Lockean order rests on acceptance of norms in service of the public good. Onuf links acceptance to a specific category of speech act; namely, assertion, while enforcement is linked to directives, and trust (of the agents themselves) is linked to commissive speech acts.[24] While Wendt and Onuf provide structural accounts of these three forms of order, Onuf and Kowert and Thies, consider the underpinning linguistic. Each image of threat is therefore rooted in violations of a particular normative order that rests on a foundation of linguistic rules. The type of rivalry produced in each account (institutional, strategic, or economic) is a result of threats to Kantian, Hobbesian, and Lockean normative orders.

Kowert and Thies suggest that each of these types of rivalry should be positively related to conflict, which they measure in the form of MIDs.[25] The three forms of rivalry representing three images of threats to underlying normative orders should generate conflict. Kowert and Thies draw on Thompson's measure of rivalry to capture what they mean by strategic rivalry.[26] Yet considerable attention is spent on generating measures of the other forms of rivalry from existing data. Economic rivalry is measured as the interaction of mutual dependence and asymmetric dependence. Mutual dependence is measured as the arithmetic mean of each state's trade dependence in a dyad. Asymmetric dependence is measured as the absolute value of the difference between the trade dependence of each state in a dyad. Interacting the two suggests that as the average trade dependence increases along with the difference in trade dependence, we should be more likely to observe competitive threats to fair play and fair competition. In an economic rivalry so measured, the importance of trade between the two states is increasing as one state is benefiting more than the other. Institutional or regime rivalry is created as the interaction of the average regime measure and the regime difference measure. The average regime measure is the arithmetic mean of the polity score for a dyad, while the regime difference measure is the absolute value of the difference between the polity scores for both states in the dyad. The logic of the regime rivalry variable is that as the average regime score for the dyad increases alongside the widening of the regime score difference, we are likely to see increased threats to institutional order. Kowert and Thies suggest that this is also implicitly a perceptual measure, much like the strategic rivalry variable.[27]

Kowert and Thies conducted a logit analysis of MID incidence using a typical array of control variables from conflict studies: contiguity, distance, alliance, capabilities, joint IGOs, peace years, and three cubic splines.[28] The control variables performed as expected in large-*n* statistical analyses (ca. five hundred thousand observations), and each of the types of rivalry was found to have a positive, statistically significant effect on MID incidence. These results suggest that there are different kinds of rivalries and that they do exhibit the expected positive effect on conflict, where previous analyses only focused on strategic rivalry. Conceptually, these different types of rivalry could inform constructivist theorizing, such as the small but growing literature on constructivist approaches to international political economy, constructivist accounts of the democratic peace, or regional security complexes. The results also suggest that conceptual and operational definitions of rivalry that are independent of measures of conflict like MIDs are useful in that they give an independent conceptual status to rivalry. Future work could examine how these types of rivalry require different types of foreign policy to manage interstate conflict. Strategic rivalry is underpinned by different conceptions of the normative order and more foundational linguistic rules than economic or regime rivalries, yet each is a path to conflict. How can policy-makers armed with such knowledge develop norms or other institutional forms that arrest conflict?

Zones of Peace / Cultures of Anarchy / Regional Orders

I merged Kacowicz's approach to zones of negative peace with Wendt's Lockean culture of anarchy to generate some theoretical expectations for the rival role in creating regional interstate cultures, and I conducted related statistical analyses based on Thompson's measure of strategic rivalry.[29] This approach could be generalized beyond Kacowicz's work, since a number of approaches in the literature attempt to explain regional peace and security. Most approaches categorize peace and security on a continuum with reference to Deutsch's early work on pluralistic security communities.[30] Kacowicz describes regions in terms of zones of negative peace, zones of stable peace, and pluralistic security communities.[31] Adler and Barnett focus mainly on pluralistic security communities, though they acknowledge nascent, ascendant, and mature phases of security community.[32] Miller labels his "ideal types" of regions as experiencing a cold peace, normal peace, or warm peace.[33] Buzan and Waever's regional security complexes include conflict formations, security regimes, and security communities, based on underlying patterns of amity and enmity, which they compare directly to Wendt's Hobbesian, Lockean, and Kantian cultures of anarchy, respectively.[34] It does not appear that any of these conceptual schemes would be hostile to a constructivist account that might flesh out parts of their arguments or to an empirical approach rooted in statistical analysis, even though all of these are qualitative accounts.

Kacowicz's work proposes a number of hypotheses responsible for the maintenance of the negative peace of a region, which he groups into realist, liberal, and neo-Grotian categories.[35] I match these to Wendt's three degrees of the institutionalization of sovereignty norms: coercion, self-interest, and legitimacy.[36] The first degree is the realist path to a Lockean culture of anarchy based on coercion, which suggests that states are forced to respect sovereignty norms by others who are more powerful. Kacowicz includes the presence of a hegemon (regional or extraregional), a regional balance of power, an external threat to the states in the region, and geographical isolation, irrelevance, and impotence to wage wars as potential realist explanations of the zone of negative peace.

The second degree is the liberal path to a Lockean culture of anarchy based on self-interest, which suggests that states respect sovereignty norms because of their self-interest in achieving other goals, such as increased trade. The presence of liberal democratic regimes, high levels of economic development and prosperity, economic interdependence, and integration and transnational links are expected by Kacowicz to support the negative peace. But Ripsman's analysis suggests that these liberal factors would move regions away from a zone of negative peace and toward a zone of stable peace, if sufficiently present.[37]

The third degree is what Wendt refers to as the constructivist path to a Lockean culture of anarchy based on legitimacy. This path suggests that states respect sovereignty norms because they are seen as legitimate, unquestioned parts of the interstate order. The related neo-Grotian explanation offered by Kacowicz is that a common cultural framework and normative consensus about conflict management and resolution helps to keep the negative peace.[38]

Kacowicz then analyzes Latin America and West Africa using traditional qualitative techniques, including in-depth historical analyses and some small-*n* types of comparisons in his conclusion considering other regions not analyzed in detail in the book.[39] The main difficulty that one encounters when examining a small number of cases is that it is difficult (or perhaps impossible) to rule out competing explanations, of which Kacowicz has nine. I have reasoned elsewhere that a combination of Wendt's and Kacowicz's theoretical work, Thompson's measure of strategic rivalry, and plenty of existing data to measure the other realist, liberal, and neo-Grotian (or constructivist) hypotheses would enable us to sort out the findings with large-*n* statistical tests.[40]

The rival role identity becomes the linchpin of these analyses, since Wendt argues that the dominance of the rival role identity should produce the Lockean culture of anarchy. If a Lockean culture of anarchy is functionally equivalent to a zone of negative peace, we should be able to devise a statistical analysis that incorporates Kacowicz's nine factors to explain its maintenance. The statistical analysis uses simultaneous equation modeling where the Lockean culture of anarchy is operationalized as the number of rival role relationships present in the region, using Thompson's measure of strategic rivalry. This is not a variable that varies across dyads in a year but from year to year in the region. The second equation models the existence of a rival role relationship within a state dyad, again using the Thompson measure. This variable varies from year to year within each dyad. Thus we have two equations, one predicting the Lockean culture of anarchy and one predicting rivalry, even as they both predict each other. This simultaneous equations analysis uses the method developed by Keshk to analyze two endogenous covariates, one continuous (size of Lockean culture of anarchy) and the other dichotomous (presence of rivalry).[41]

This statistical technique is particular helpful in that it allows us to capture, however imperfectly, some aspect of the simultaneous "constitution" of agents and structures. What two-stage least-squares offers as a statistical technique is that rather than presuming that the direction of effect is one-way, as in traditional regression models, it allows for two-way effects. The regional culture should result from previous regional and dyadic interactions, just as the dyadic role relationship is a result of previous dyadic and regional characteristics. Admittedly, this work is somewhat imprecise about the relationship between constitution, causation, and correlation. Statistical analysis can only tell us whether a relationship between the occurrences of two things is not due to chance. Correlational analysis is one tool to help us identify both causation and correlation, even though it alone does not identify either.[42] The use of multiple methods in the attempt to triangulate either constitution or causation would make for a more convincing case, and narrative analysis is used for this purpose in both the West African and Latin American cases.

The Lockean culture of anarchy is predicted in this model by variables representing the nine realist, liberal, and neo-Grotian hypotheses, as well as the presence of a rival role relationship in the dyad. The rival role relationship is predicted by typical measures associated with rivalry, as well as the size of the Lockean culture of analysis. As I have noted elsewhere, we must be careful when interpreting the signs on the coefficients in the statistical analyses.[43] A positive sign indicates that the variable increases the size of the

Lockean culture of anarchy. A negative sign means that the variable diminishes the Lockean culture of anarchy, but it could also suggest that the variable is moving the regional culture toward a Hobbesian culture of anarchy and or a Kantian culture of anarchy. The statistical evidence cannot be used to adjudicate between the two alternative scenarios, since the variable representing the Lockean culture of anarchy is constructed based on the rival role identity and not the enemy or friend role identities.

Table 3.1 presents the part of the model that captures the size of the zone of negative peace or Lockean culture of anarchy in West Africa and Latin America. In both regions, the formation of a rival role relationship increases the size of the Lockean culture of anarchy. Increases in the size of the Lockean culture of anarchy also increase the likelihood of rival role relationships in the dyad (this result is not shown in the table; refer to the two articles discussed for the full models). This is some evidence that agents and structures are mutually constituted and that the rival role identity works empirically in the way that Wendt describes in his purely theoretical account (see table 3.1).

In both regions, the realist path to a Lockean culture of anarchy based on coercion is fairly well supported in the statistical accounts. For example, hegemonic presence and activity by the French in West Africa and by the United States in Latin America support the zone of negative peace, though cumulative intervention and the perception of overwhelming US capabilities has the opposite effect. The interpretation in the literature is that this is the result of the United States acting as an overly intrusive caudillo, which would suggest movement toward a zone of conflict. The remaining realist variables have varying effects in the regions, and each analysis contains variables pertinent to the region, so they are not directly comparable across regions. The liberal path based on self-interest receives mixed support in the regions (but may be interpreted as leading to a stable peace). For example, higher levels of democracy move the region away from a negative peace, while regional trade agreements support a negative peace, and regional economic development has mixed effects. Finally, the constructivist path based on legitimacy demonstrates that higher levels of regional satisfaction move the region away from negative peace (and possibly toward stable peace), the presence of unresolved territorial issues supports the negative peace in West Africa as expected, and negotiations to settle territorial issues in Latin America moves the region away from negative peace (and possibly toward stable peace).

Overall, the results largely conform to Kacowicz's qualitative analysis, but we have much more precise information about effect of realist, liberal, and constructivist paths to a zone of negative peace or Lockean culture of anarchy. We can say with much more confidence which path supports the regional order and which paths seem to move the order away from negative peace. The variables on the realist path mostly support the zone of negative peace, though some aspects of global and regional hegemonic activity seem to undermine this order (most likely in the direction of a zone of conflict). Variables on the liberal and constructivist paths exhibit more mixed effects

Table 3.1. Zones of Negative Peace / Lockean Cultures of Anarchy

	West Africa		Latin America	
Variables	Coefficient	Standard error	Coefficient	Standard error
Rival role relationship	.0059*	.0028	.2531***	.0382
Realist path				
French hegemonic role	1.0359***	.1263		
US hegemonic role			.8294***	.0345
French intervention	.1469***	.0371		
US intervention			.1611***	.0220
French cumulative intervention	.2034***	.0233		
US cumulative intervention			-.1584***	.0070
French economic dependence	-1.4054	1.2068		
US economic dependence			-.0093	.0199
US capabilities			-.3874***	.0109
Nigerian hegemonic role	-14.1890***	.4023		
Regional balance of power	-.0911	.0621	-1.3228***	.0293
System shock	.9168***	.0380	-.6009***	.0246
Domestic shock			.0686***	.0116
Distance			.0237**	.0075
Liberal path				
Regional polity average	-.0673***	.0106	-.0925***	.0063
Regional economic development	-.0006**	.0002	.0004***	.0000
ECOWAS		1.2797***	.0473	
Regional trade agreement			.1660***	.0197
Constructivist path				
Regional satisfaction	-1.8921***	.1051	-5.8602***	.5237
Regional territorial issues	.4071***	.0188		
Negotiated territorial issues			-.1784***	.0379
N	3807		5791	
R^2	.80		.64	

Note: All significance tests are two-tailed. This table is adapted from those found in Thies (see n. 29, "Construction of a Latin American Interstate"; "Explaining Zones"). The simultaneous equations predicting the rival role relationship in these analyses are not shown.

$^{*}p < .05$; $^{**}p < .01$; $^{***}p < .001$

but are suggestive of moves away from a zone of negative peace or Lockean culture of anarchy toward a zone of stable peace or Kantian culture of anarchy. Unfortunately, as previously mentioned, the statistical results cannot adjudicate the direction of the movement; they just do not support the zone of negative peace. Further, a snapshot coefficient on a regression analysis cannot truly indicate movement over time. We do not know if the negative signs are a result more of recent activity or of past activity averaged over the dyad-years that are the unit of analysis.

The Benefits of Combining Constructivist Theorizing with Statistical Methods for Conflict Studies

What are the net benefits of using statistical methods for the aforementioned examples, compared to the typical qualitative approach that constructivists take in international relations studies? First, constructivists have tended to avoid empirically explaining interstate conflict. As Farrell notes, constructivism has made inroads into the subfield of security studies by offering theoretical explanations of phenomena like strategic and organizational culture, balance of power, the security dilemma, the democratic peace, and isomorphism in military development.[44] Yet none of these approaches connect abstract theorizing about underlying conceptual issues to the explanation of classes of events such as MIDs or interstate wars. The tendency in the constructivist literature is to stick to theorizing and provide selective confirmatory evidence from a few cases, much like realist security studies. By combining constructivist theoretical insights with statistical analysis, we can begin to explain larger classes of events. For example, Kowert and Thies connected constructivist theorizing about images of conflict associated with certain forms of rivalry to actually observed MIDs.[45]

Second, relatedly, constructivist concepts often remain in rather imprecise form even when operationalized. For example, Wendt's discussion of the rival role highlights some general behavioral features of rivals,[46] but moving to Thompson's operational definition completes the specification of when states perceive and treat each other as rivals. This specification allowed Kowert and Thies to incorporate that measure, along with several other constructivist-inspired measures of rivalry, into our explanation for MIDs.[47] It also allowed me to offer the first statistical tests of the zones of peace argument.[48]

Third, statistical analyses offer a way of analytically leveraging the coaction of agents and structure that was central to the original constructivist critique of IR theory. Thies used two-stage least-squares models with a quantitative measure of rivalry at the agent level as one endogenous covariate and a count of the number of rivalries at the regional/cultural level as the other endogenous covariate, such that both were used to simultaneously predict the other.[49] One could also imagine the use of multilevel modeling to capture both agent and structural/cultural variables, as another possibility to leverage constructivist theory. A multimethod approach combining statistical analyses with case studies might allow for a more in-depth analysis of the underlying mechanisms of co-constitution of agents and structures as well.

Finally, if constructivism can allow for variable correlations to represent constitution (as they are often argued to represent causation in mainstream conflict studies), then constructivism might prompt renewed theorizing about potential variables like rivalry. There may be other similar concepts that could be similarly used as a bridge between conflict studies and constructivism. Wendt's role identities of enemy and friend might be developed further. Thompson's coding of strategic rivalry seemed to conflate it with the enemy role, but (as mentioned above) this was largely to ensure nonanonymity in a dyad coded as a rival.[50] Rivals may seem to be enemies, but the vast majority of the time that actors spend in a rivalry does not involve war to eliminate the other. Instead, there are period between militarized conflicts where feelings are cooler. The enemy role identity, where two actors want to eliminate each other, is a rare occurrence. Perhaps enemy role identities are only salient during periods of outright warfare or for short periods before, during, and after warfare. The enemy role identity could proceed with theorizing from Wendt and coding along similar lines to Thompson's approach to rivalry. Similarly, we might explore the concept of "friend." Are there countries that adopt friend role identities and enact friend role relationships? Does the Anglo-American special relationship count as a friendship? Would members of supranational organizations like the European Union be counted as friends, or would a European identity be more of a corporate (rather than role) identity in Wendt's account? Further conceptual and operational analysis would be necessary to flesh out both the enemy and friend role identities. Such a development would allow for a cross-regional analysis over time for Wendt's cultures of anarchy argument. We could examine the networks of rivals, enemies, and friends that emerge, thrive, and collapse over time. Network analysis would be ideal to examine the cultures of anarchy that result.

The resurgence of role theory in foreign policy analysis might help to generalize the notion that role identities are significant features of international relations.[51] Role theory is arguably compatible with constructivism, especially since it preceded constructivism as a whole and within the field of foreign policy and international relations.[52] Holsti's pioneering piece introducing the field to role theory identified a number of familiar roles that could be subject to quantitative analysis, including regional leader, regional protector, defender of the faith, faithful ally, active independent, bastion of revolution–liberator, liberation supporter, bridge, isolate, and so on.[53] Wendt draws on identity theory, which is itself a merger of role theory and symbolic interactionism, to generate his role identities (i.e., rival, friend, enemy).[54] Wendt's description of the social act in which actors socialize others into their appropriate roles is a partial account of how role theorists suggest that role identities are adopted. Contemporary role theory research focuses a great deal on the domestic contestation associated with the adoption of a role identity and on the role location process that a state follows as it tries to convince others that its role identity is appropriate and to form role relationships with it (since all role identities require a counterrole identity). The role location process is essentially the foreign policy process, and depending on the cues and demands received from others, the state may abandon a role identity, attempt to force enactment of that role identity on others, or modify the role identity so that it is more palatable to others.[55] There is no reason that aspects of the role location process cannot be quantified.[56]

Wendt's typology of identity includes corporate, type, role, and collective identity.[57] The illustrations in the present chapter focus on the rival role, but hints abound as to other forms of identity that could be explored more carefully through constructivist theorizing and statistical analysis in conflict studies. Corporate identity consists of the basic self-organizing features of identity that make something a state. Studies related to nationalism could usefully be theorized from this perspective. For example, in my own work, I statistically tested African interventions to make more of a nation-state, derived from Herbst.[58] These included the use of a national currency versus adopting a foreign currency, *jus soli* vs. *jus sanguinis* citizenship rules, and interventions in patterns of land tenure (chiefs vs. state).[59] These interventions were also paired to types of political geographies inherited by states (i.e., difficult, hinterland, neutral, favorable). The point of this work is to figure out how to make more of a corporate identity given the type of state inherited from the colonizers. A conceptual and operational approach to "stateness" derived from constructivism could be a useful addition to the conflict studies literature, as the issue of state capacity is frequently invoked as a determinant of interstate conflict, civil conflict, state failure, human rights violations, and the like.

Beyond corporate identities, type identities such as democracy have already found their way into conflict studies research. Elsewhere, Mitchell and Powell look at how the type of domestic legal system (civil, common, or Islamic law) affects acceptance of the jurisdiction of international courts, as well as the durability and design of those commitments.[60] Other work on these state types has looked at interstate conflict and human rights practices. "Rogue" states have also drawn attention in the literature as comprising a type of state thought to be violating international norms. I have discussed role identities above; what makes this form of identity most compatible with conflict studies is that it is relational. Roles always require counterroles to form role relationships. The relational aspect of roles also fits well with the preeminent position of dyadic analysis in the conflict studies literature. Thus rival role relationships (or rivalries in conflict studies), allied role relationships (or simply alliances in conflict studies), role relationships between hegemon followers and challengers, and so on have long been part of conflict studies, even if they are viewed primarily in material terms. Collective identities offer up some interesting ways to move the conflict studies literature forward. Continued interest in the possibilities of a systemic democratic peace, as opposed to the dominant dyadic approaches, matches well with the notion of an emerging collective identity underlying a Kantian Peace.[61] As we found in the above illustration of zones of peace, constructivist theorizing at the systemic level can be combined with quantitative measures not only at that level but also at the dyadic and monadic level. More systematic systemic theorizing would be a breath of fresh air in the conflict studies literature that has adopted dyadic theorizing almost exclusively, despite the knowledge that not all processes are purely dyadic.

Conclusion

In this chapter, I have argued that the combination of constructivist theorizing and statistical analysis is a fruitful approach to conflict studies. If constructivism could open itself up to statistical analyses, then its appeal might spread within conflict studies and to many other areas currently dominated by quantitative methods in the field. Not all forms of constructivism are amenable to quantitative analysis, even though constructivist theorizing might have something to say about most forms of conflict that we study. Conflict studies is unlikely to give up its material foundations (grounded in realism) any time soon. Various forms of identity have found their way into conflict studies analyses, but they are incorporated in ways that do not disturb the underlying form of statistical analysis. This may provide space for other forms of mathematical modeling or agent-based modeling to pick up where statistical models leave off. Constructivism can be theorized in terms of linguistic rules or other types of rule-based behavior that may find compatibility with other types of modeling already present in conflict studies.

Given that conflict studies has already begun to incorporate some of what it terms "constructivist" variables, this is a natural area for focus by constructivist scholars willing to use statistical methods. Of course, the real goal would be to generate constructivist theories of interstate and intrastate conflict, testable hypotheses, and measurable concepts that could be analyzed through some quantitative method. Such an effort will likely require a change in how constructivists and students in conflict studies are trained. A broader view of what counts as science is critical to this endeavor on the part of both constructivists and scholars in conflict studies. Constructivism can gain from statistical analyses, and conflict studies can gain from constructivism. The more studies that are published that go beyond just incorporating "constructivist" variables, the more likely we are to see the combination of constructivist theorizing and statistical methods become a standard way of contributing to the field.

Notes

1. See Hedley Bull, "International Theory: The Case for the Classical Approach," *World Politics* 18, no. 3 (1966): 361–77; Morton A. Kaplan, "The New Great Debate: Traditionalism vs. Science in International Relations," *World Politics* 19, no. 1 (1966): 1–20.

2. See, e.g., John R. Oneal and Bruce Russet, "The Kantian Peace: The Pacific Benefits of Democracy, Interdependence, and International Organizations, 1885–1992," *World Politics* 52, no. 1 (1999): 1–37.

3. Young Jong Choi and James A. Caporaso, "Comparative Regional Integration," in *Handbook of International Relations, ed.* Walter Carlsnaes, Thomas Risse, and Beth A. Simmons (London: Sage, 2002).

4. For constructivists, see Michael N. Barnett and Martha Finnemore, "The Politics, Power, and Pathologies of International Organizations," *International Organization* 53, no. 4 (1999): 699–732. For liberals, see Oneal and Russett, "Kantian Peace."

5. Carol Atkinson, "Constructivist Implications of Material Power: Military Engagement and the Socialization of States, 1972–2000," *International Studies Quarterly* 50, no. 3 (2006): 509–37.

6. T. Z. Ruby and D. M. Gibler, "US Professional Military Education and Democratization Abroad," *European Journal of International Relations* 16, no. 3 (2010): 339–64.

7. For an example, see Gary Goertz and Paul F. Diehl, "The Empirical Importance of Enduring Rivalries," *International Interactions* 18, no. 2 (1992): 151–63.

8. William R. Thompson, "Principal Rivalries," *Journal of Conflict Resolution* 39, no. 2 (1996): 195–223; Thompson, "Identifying Rivals and Rivalries in World Politics," *International Studies Quarterly* 45, no. 4 (2001): 557–86.

9. See, e.g., James Fearon and Alexander Wendt, "Rationalism v. Constructivism: A Skeptical View," in *Handbook of International Relations*, ed. Walter Carlsnaes, Thomas Risse, and Beth Simmons (Thousand Oaks, CA: Sage, 1998).

10. For frequency of MIDs, see Goertz and Diehl, "Empirical Importance"; Gary Goertz and Paul F. Diehl, "Enduring Rivalries: Theoretical Constructs and Empirical Patterns," *International Studies Quarterly* 37, no. 2 (1993): 147–71. For crises, see J. Joseph Hewitt, "A Crisis-Density Formulation for Identifying Rivalries," *Journal of Peace Research* 42 (2005): 183–200.

11. Goertz and Diehl, "Empirical Importance," 155.

12. See D. Scott Bennett, "Security, Bargaining, and the End of Interstate Rivalry," *International Studies Quarterly* 40, no. 2 (1996): 157–84; Bennett, "Measuring Rivalry Termination, 1816–1992," *Journal of Conflict Resolution* 41, no. 2 (1997): 227–54; Bennett, "Integrating and Testing Models of Rivalry Duration," *American Journal of Political Science* 42, no. 4 (1998): 1200–1232; Sara McLaughlin Mitchell and Cameron G. Thies, "Issue Rivalries," *Conflict Management and Peace Science* 28, no. 3 (2011): 230–60.

13. See James P. Klein, Gary Goertz, and Paul F. Diehl, "The New Rivalry Dataset: Procedures and Patterns," *Journal of Peace Research* 43, no. 3 (2006): 331–48.

14. See Thompson, "Principal Rivalries"; Thompson, "Identifying Rivals."

15. Thompson, "Principal Rivalries," 201.

16. Ibid.

17. Thompson, "Identifying Rivals," 560. The "enemy" condition is designed to ensure nonanonymity in the identification of rivals, rather than to indicate a separate enemy role (Thies 2001: 697–98; Mitchell and Thies, "Issue Rivalries," 235). Thies (2001) develops a social psychological account of the formation of enduring rivalries through competition and socialization mechanisms, which is also compatible with constructivism. Cameron G. Thies, 2001, "Social Psychological Approach to Enduring Rivalries," *Political Psychology* 22, no. 4: 693–725.

18. Alexander Wendt, *Social Theory of International Politics* (Cambridge: Cambridge University Press, 1999).

19. Ibid., 327.

20. Wendt, *Social Theory*, 283–85.

21. Paul A. Kowert and Cameron G. Thies, "(Babylonian) Lions, (Asian) Tigers, and (Russian) Bears: A Statistical Test of Three Rivalrous Paths to Conflict," *Journal of International Relations and Development* 16, no. 3 (2013): 406–33.

22. See Nicholas G. Onuf, *World of Our Making: Rules and Rule in Social Theory and International Relations* (Columbia: University of South Carolina Press, 1989).

23. Wendt, *Social Theory*.

24. Onuf, *World of Our Making*.

25. Kowert and Thies, "(Babylonian) Lions," 420.

26. Ibid., 421.

27. Ibid., 423.

28. Ibid., 423–26.

29. Cameron G. Thies, "The Construction of a Latin American Interstate Culture of Rivalry," *International Interactions* 34, no. 3 (2008): 231–57; Thies, "Explaining Zones of Negative Peace in Interstate Relations: West Africa's Regional Culture of Interstate Rivalry," *European Journal of International Relations* 16, no. 2 (2010): 391–415. For negative peace, see Arie M. Kacowicz, *Zones of Peace in the Third World: South America and West Africa in Comparative Perspective* (Albany: State University of New York Press, 1998); for the Lockean culture of anarchy, Wendt, *Social Theory*.

30. Karl Deutsch, *Political Community and the North Atlantic Area: International Organization in the Light of Historical Experience* (Princeton, NJ: Princeton University Press, 1957).

31. Kacowicz, *Zones of Peace*, 9–10.

32. Emmanuel Adler and Michael Barnett, eds., *Security Communities* (Cambridge: Cambridge University Press, 1998), 49–57.

33. Benny Miller, "When and How Regions Become Peaceful: Potential Theoretical Pathways to Peace," *International Studies Review* 7, no. 2 (2005): 229–67.

34. Barry Buzan and Ole Waever, *Regions and Powers: The Structure of International Security* (Cambridge: Cambridge University Press, 2003), 53–54.

35. Kocawicz, *Zones of Peace*.

36. Wendt, *Social Theory*, 285–90.

37. N. M. Ripsman, "Two Stages of Transition from a Region of War to a Region of Peace: Realist Transition and Liberal Endurance," *International Studies Quarterly* 49, no. 4 (2005): 669–93. Ripsman considers some of these "liberal" factors to be "constructivist," such as democratic regimes and IGOs.

38. Kacowicz, *Zones of Peace*, 39.

39. Ibid.

40. Thies, "Construction of a Latin American Interstate Culture of Rivalry"; Thies, "Explaining Zones."

41. Omar Keshk, "CDSIMEQ: A Program to Implement Two-Stage Probit Least Squares," *Stata Journal* 3, no. 2 (2003): 157–67.

42. For a thoughtful discussion of the relationship between causal and correlational analyses of the COW project, see David Dessler, "Toward a Causal Theory of War," *International Studies Quarterly* 35, no. 3 (1991): 337–55.

43. Thies, "Explaining Zones," 19.

44. Theo Farrell, "Constructivist Security Studies: Portrait of a Research Program," *International Studies Review* 4, no. 1 (2002): 49–72.

45. Kowert and Thies, "(Babylonian) Lions."

46. Wendt, *Social Theory*.

47. Kowert and Thies, "(Babylonian) Lions."

48. Thies, "Construction of a Latin American Interstate Culture of Rivalry"; Thies, "Explaining Zones."

49. Ibid.

50. Thompson, "Identifying Rivals."

51. See, e.g., Cameron G. Thies, "Role Theory and Foreign Policy," in *The Inter-*

national Studies Encyclopedia, ed. Robert Denemark (Malden, MA: Wiley-Blackwell, 2010); Cameron G. Thies and Marijke Breuning, "Integrating Foreign Policy Analysis and International Relations through Role Theory," *Foreign Policy Analysis* 8, no. 1 (2012): 1–4; Sebastian Hanisch, Cornelia Frank, and Hanns Maull, eds., *Role Theory in International Relations: Approaches and Analyses* (Abingdon: Routledge, 2011).

52. See Marijke Breuning, "Role Theory Research in IR: State of the Art and Blind Spots," in Hanisch, Frank, and Maull, *Role Theory in International Relations*; Thies, "Role Theory and Foreign Policy."

53. K. J. Holsti, "National Role Conceptions in the Study of Foreign Policy," *International Studies Quarterly* 14, no. 3 (1970): 233–309.

54. Wendt, *Social Theory*.

55. For the role location process as a foreign policy process, see Stephen G. Walker, ed., *Role Theory and Foreign Policy Analysis* (Durham: Duke University Press, 1987). For an expansion of role location, see Cameron G. Thies, "International Socialization Processes vs. Israeli National Role Conceptions: Can Role Theory Integrate IR Theory and Foreign Policy Analysis?," *Foreign Policy Analysis* 8, no. 1 (2012): 25–46; Thies, *The United States, Israel, and the Search for International Order: Socializing States* (New York: Routledge, 2013).

56. See many of the contributions in Walker, *Role Theory and Foreign Policy Analysis*.

57. Wendt, *Social Theory*, 75–79.

58. For reference, see Jeffrey Herbst, *States and Power in Africa: Comparative Lessons in Authority and Control* (Princeton, NJ: Princeton University Press, 2000).

59. Cameron G. Thies, "National Design and State Building in Sub-Saharan Africa," *World Politics* 61, no. 4 (2009): 623–69.

60. Sara McLaughlin Mitchell and Emilia Justyna Powell, *Domestic Law Goes Global: Legal Traditions and International Courts* (Cambridge: Cambridge University Press, 2011).

61. See, e.g., Nils Petr Gleditsch and Håvard Hegre, "Peace and Democracy: Three Levels of Analysis," *Journal of Peace Research* 41, no. 2 (1997): 283–310; Ewan Harrison, "The Democratic Peace Research Program and System-Level Analysis," *Journal of Peace Research* 47, no. 2 (2010): 155–65.

CHAPTER 4

Exploring Constitution and Social Construction through Network Analysis

MATTHEW HOFFMANN

Social constructivism, in its many variants, is fundamentally concerned with constitutive dynamics—how social facts, intersubjective knowledge, and communities of practice emerge, change, and shape political dynamics.[1] Constructivists generally pursue these questions through interpretive and qualitative methods, tracing nuanced processes of social construction in particular empirical contexts. But answering these questions favored by constructivists is not logically or philosophically tied to particular methods. As the editors of the present volume discuss in the introductory chapter, *methods* are appropriately tied to questions, and diverse tools can be deployed within and across multiple epistemological or ontological systems of thought. In this chapter, I explore the use of social network analysis (SNA) for analyzing constitutive dynamics. SNA, a quantitative tool developed by sociologists, has not had wide uptake among constructivists, even though it shares similar ontological roots with constructivism (especially concerning the primacy of relational dynamics)[2] and offers a range of visualization and statistical tools suited for exploring some constructivist questions. A different means for approaching constructivist analysis, SNA may produce new insights and empirical fodder for advancing constructivist theorizing.

This chapter develops and substantiates this argument in three sections. First, I briefly introduce the practicalities of SNA and its potential utility for constructivist analysis. I then turn to two empirical examples and demonstrate how SNA can be used to generate insight from a constructivist perspective. One example illustrates how SNA can be used to explore the constitutive effects of an institutional form—multilateral treaty making. Arguably, treaty-making is more than a tool that states use instrumentally to reach their goals; it is a practice that constitutes states as states. SNA can be used to partially substantiate this argument empirically. The other example illustrates how SNA can illuminate the diffusion of ideas that constitute communities of practice and through which those communities influence social construction—in this case, the social construction of carbon markets. SNA reveals the contours and evolution of communities of practice that have worked to develop and deploy this approach to climate governance that is shaping the global response to climate change. These examples, drawn from very different issue areas, demonstrate that SNA can provide insight into core constructivist dynamics—constitution and diffusion—in a way that catalyzes further theoretical development. I conclude with a discussion of the utility and limitations of SNA for constructivist research in light of the overarching themes of this volume. SNA can be a useful tool for uncovering and generating insights about constructivist dynamics and is worth exploring, even if it does not ultimately end up in every constructivist's methods toolbox.

Social Network Analysis and Social Constructivism

SNA is a tool that utilizes graph theory and visualization software to map and statistically analyze the structure of relationships between distinct actors or nodes in a system. This method was developed mainly by mathematical sociologists, and there is now a robust field and community of social network analysts, research, and literature. This section outlines how SNA works and how it has been applied thus far in the field of International Relations (IR). It concludes with a discussion of how a constructivist deployment of SNA, different than what is so far in evidence in the IR literature, is reasonable given the conceptual foundation of relational sociology from which SNA emerges.

The SNA Method

SNA includes mapping networks and analyzing network statistics to obtain information about the nodes (agents) in the network and the network characteristics as a whole.[3] Both the visualization of network relationships and the statistical analysis provide insight useful for exploring constructivist research questions.

The first step in SNA is defining the network. Put simply, a network is made up of nodes and edges. Nodes are the agents of interest in the study, and edges are the links or relations between the nodes. This is not a very limiting definition. Nodes can range from individuals to groups, organizations, or more abstract "agents," such as treaties. Edges can be defined as directly observable linkages between agents, like common membership in a nongovernmental organization, or as more subjective relations, like affinity or friendship. Information used directly in network analysis is simply an array of nodes and edges. Generally, one begins with a two-dimensional array (see table 4.1), where both the nodes (states) and edges (memberships in intergovernmental organizations) are represented, and transposes that into a one-dimensional array (see table 4.2), where the number of connecting edges comprises the data.

This is all the information that is required to create a network map , a visual representation of nodes and how they are linked (see figures 4.1–4.3 below). Mapping is essentially a descriptive, though quantitative, enterprise. It is a picture of the agents' relationships/linkages specified by the researcher.[4] Mapping can be simple or more elaborate. The representation of the nodes and edges can be linked to other data and/or network statistics (discussed below). For instance, the thickness of the line connecting two nodes could be drawn so as to represent the strength of the tie (in the example above,

Table 4.1. Two-Dimensional Array of IGO Memberships

	United Nations	Organization of American States	European Union	Group of 77
United States	X	X		
China	X			X
France	X		X	
Brazil	X	X		X
Germany	X		X	

Note: Rows = agents (nodes); columns = relationships (edges).

Table 4.2. One-Dimensional Array of IGO Memberships, with States as Nodes

	United States	China	France	Brazil	Germany
United States	X	1	1	2	1
China	1	X	1	2	1
France	1	1	X	1	2
Brazil	2	2	1	X	1
Germany	1	1	2	1	X

Note: Headings = agents (nodes); data = relationships (edges).

the link between the US and Brazil would be thicker than that between the US and China, because the US and Brazil share in common more memberships in intergovernmental organizations). Alternatively, the edges can be nondirected or directional, with arrows representing affinity (or enmity) or a specific direction in the relationship between the nodes (flow of information from one node to another). Nodes in the network map can themselves be differentiated. For instance, a researcher may use color to indicate different categories of nodes (level of development or region, for instance, if nodes are states) or may alter the size of nodes based on network statistics (e.g., using the centrality measures discussed below).

While mapping is a descriptive enterprise, it can have significant analytic value. Nonobvious patterns and relationships can emerge in the network mapping, and mapping provides snapshots of social relations that are especially interesting for social constructivist approaches, because the way that agents are connected has potentially significant implications for many constructivist mechanisms (e.g., socialization, diffusion, learning, persuasion). Creating network maps from time series data on relationships provides a way to see, through multiple snapshots, how relationships change over time.

In addition to its use for descriptive mapping, SNA has a direct analytic component. Through the use of graph theory in mathematics, SNA statisticians have developed a number of sophisticated measures for characterizing both nodes and networks as a whole. Nodal analysis tools calculate attributes for individual nodes in relation to the population of nodes and structure of the network. These measures tell us about how each node is situated in the network and its position vis-à-vis all the other nodes in the network. These statistical measures are data that can tell us about the behavior and potential of nodes. Crucially, for constructivist thinking, the expectations of behavior and potential of nodes is derived from their network/structural positions rather than from independent, individual attributes.

Some of the most popular and widely used nodal statistics focus on various measures of centrality. Centrality statistics are diverse ways to represent each node's connectedness and relative position. For example, *degree centrality* measures how many other nodes a node is connected to (in the above example, all the nodes have a degree centrality of 1 or 2). *Betweenness centrality* measures the structural significance of a node, by capturing how important a node is to the connectivity of the network. Nodes with high betweenness centrality can be thought of as key junctures in the network; if you removed them, the network would fragment. For instance, in a friendship network, there may be one person connecting two groups of friends (i.e., he or she is the only one that is a member of both groups); that person would have high betweenness centrality. This measure provides a way to think about how different nodes affect the structure of the network and condition the possibilities for flow through it. *Closeness centrality* measures the length of the path from one node to all other nodes. These measures can help us to understand how flows (of information or material) move through the network and which agents may be more influential. For instance, high levels of betweenness are often associated with agents' abilities to act as brokers in a network, because they exist at key junctures in the network.

Beyond centrality, social network analysts are also interested in nodal measures of structural equivalence—discerning which nodes in a network are alike in the sense of having similar structural positions. The idea here is that nodes in similar structural situations will behave similarly. Instead of comparing states with similar gross domestic products or populations, structural equivalence measures provide a way to categorize states based on the way that they fit into the network of states (defined by whichever relationships the analyst is investigating).

Nodal analysis, in terms of both centrality and structural equivalence, can provide useful insights on its own for constructivist analyses. Knowing which agents are strategically placed in a network to best effect socialization, for instance, can enhance our understanding of how constitutive dynamics play out in a specific situation. The key is that the data generated from SNA statistics about individual actors is derived from the actors' relationships and structural positions. The statistics are thus measures of socially determined position and a characterization of social position, rather than reflecting individual attributes that actors possess outside of social relations.

SNA statistics can also be used to characterize entire networks. There are quantitative metrics that characterize and explain the structural qualities of the networks. This kind of analysis can be done qualitatively. For instance, Wendy Wong used qualitative network analysis in a study of nongovernment organizations concerned with human rights and found that variation in their internal network structure shaped their effectiveness in influencing the dynamics of the human rights regime.[5] However, quantitative SNA statistics can be calculated for a number of structural features that can be deployed in constructivist research.

In undertaking network-level analyses, the statistics can be used to compare empirical networks (as a whole), an empirical network against a hypothetical ideal, or an empirical network against a theoretically derived set of expectations. This can be done in multiple ways. Statistics of density and connectedness measure the concentration of links in a network (relative to other networks). Core-periphery statistical measures indicate the level of stratification in a network. This kind of analysis can be used to illuminate the emergence of network structure, to compare the trajectories of different systems, and to explain how outcomes differ in different systems because of the structure of the network. For constructivists, network-level analyses potentially offer a way to "see" the emergence of social structure—the distribution of ideas and interactions—in a way that is not available qualitatively. Further, it allows for a visualization of social structure that is more analogous to how material structure is visualized (i.e., distribution of capabilities), while retaining the crucial element of sociality that constructivists require.

Positioning SNA in International Relations

The appearance of SNA in the tool kits of researchers in international relations and political science is a relatively recent phenomenon and has been accompanied by a number of works that lay out what SNA can do for political scientists.[6] Lazer highlights the multiple strands of SNA applications, differentiated by whether they focus on the effects of networks (flows through networks, regulation of individual behavior, and the relationship between network position and control/power) or on the origins/structure of networks.[7] Essentially, he is categorizing SNA studies by whether network structure is an independent or dependent variable. Hafner-Burton and her coauthors specifically lay out a number of ways that SNA can be used to enhance research in international relations.[8] First, they claim that it can be a fruitful source of hypotheses for behavior in IR studies where network structure becomes an independent variable in attempts to explain political behavior and outcomes. Second, SNA can be used as a means of testing alternative IR theories. Network and nodal attributes and even network maps can be used to adjudicate between empirical expectations generated by IR theories.

This latter approach has become the most common means of integrating SNA into IR research. Networks are graphed, and nodal analysis statistics are generated to produce data that is associated with each node (e.g., degree centrality would be calculated for each node). The data generated through nodal analysis is then used in other (mainly statistical) analyses, in conjunction with other data, to test hypotheses. Cao, for instance, has examined how measures of network position can help to explain economic policy convergence.[9] Similarly, Hafner-Burton and Montgomery examine the relationship between structural positions in international organizations and trade networks and conflict.[10] These kinds of research designs tend to be used to answer causal questions that come from (relatively) rationalist research programs. The data that SNA generates is used to test hypotheses about patterns of behavior and outcomes. SNA provides data on the network relationships and structural positions of the actors, variables that can potentially explain the dependent variable of interest. It becomes another source of data for econometric analysis, and nodal attributes derived from network positions are treated as attributes carried by individual actors. Variation in these measures is then used to explain variation in the dependent variables, behavior or interactions of actors.

Constructivists have engaged less with SNA at this point—somewhat ironically, given the method's origins in relational sociology. Hafner-Burton and her coauthors note that SNA could help constructivists further develop and empirically explore "underspecified" dynamics, such as socialization and diffusion.[11] Yet there has been scant discussion of how constructivists could benefit from employing SNA techniques, and there has been even less exploration of what SNA research by IR constructivists would look like.

This is a curious lacuna. Beyond the method's nuts and bolts discussed above, SNA is built on a set of assumptions about the nature of causation and social ontology that conceptually fits well with certain variants of social constructivism in IR.[12] The core idea is that the structural position of agents and network characteristics shape nodal (or agent) behavior and characteristics. The foundational assumption of this kind of relational analysis is that the "regular network patterns beneath the often complex surface of social systems" are important for understanding and explaining social and political dynamics.[13] SNA seeks to "describe these patterns and use their descriptions to learn how network structures constrain social behavior and social change."[14] Relationships, interactions, and social structure shape (at least) the behavior of actors in the system, and, of course, their behavior (in terms of the relationships that they engage in) creates the social structure of the system. There is a close affinity here with mutual constitution.

The apparent similarity between constructivism and SNA goes beyond ontological resemblance, however, because, like social constructivism, "network analysis is not a formal or unitary 'theory' that specifies distinctive laws, propositions, or correlations, but rather a broad strategy for investigating social structure."[15] SNA is a perspective on social life and a theory of social process, rather than a substantive theory of IR (or any other social milieu).[16] The conceptual core of SNA is compatible with constructivist thinking about the importance of social structure and relations. Like constructivism, SNA rejects methodological individualism, because the attributes of individual actors cannot be the sole (or even significant) foundation for explanations of behavior and therefore social (and political) outcomes.[17] Rather, the structure of relationships among individual actors is of paramount importance. This approach fits well with the constructivist notion that social structure not only constrains agents but constitutes them as well. Relations, socially constructed practices, and intersubjectively held beliefs and ideas are the stuff of constructivist explanations for social and political behavior and outcomes.[18] As a relational approach, SNA also privileges social relations in explanations and focuses on the structured processes of interaction. From the SNA perspective, agents do not have ontologically prior interests and identities; their interests and identities develop through and are constituted by social relations and network structure.

The conceptual match between constructivism and SNA is close enough, then, to warrant significant attention and empirical exploration. The next step is to consider what kind of constructivist questions SNA can appropriately address and to operationalize those questions with SNA tools.[19] The following section takes up these tasks in the form of two brief examples of SNA used in empirical constructivist research. Each example begins with a research question that has some significance for constructivist research. Each then proceeds to discuss how SNA can provide (partial) answers and feedback to enhance constructivist theorizing.

SNA and the Constitutive Practice of Treaty Making

Martha Finnemore made a groundbreaking argument about how states come to understand that certain practices are indicative or constitutive of modern statehood, specifically looking at the proliferation of science bureaus across the population of states.[20] The example discussed in this section examines how states are constituted as states, in relation to a key type of institutional practice and interaction, multilateral treaty making.[21] The goal is to see if multilateralism is more than an instrumental practice that states undertake to facilitate transboundary relationships and is instead a practice that constitutes states as states.[22] The claim investigated with SNA is thus that multilateral treaty making[23] has become a constitutive practice—constructing what states are, constituting what it means to be a state, not just something that states do. States are multilateral treaty-making entities (among other things), and to be a state is to make multilateral treaties.

There are multiple ways that constructivists could go about substantiating this claim. One could examine changes in state structure over time, to see, in the spirit of Finnemore, how states have changed internally and materially to orient themselves toward making treaties.[24] One could count the number of treaties made over time and observe the expansion of issue areas in which states make multilateral treaties.[25] One could look for historical junctures when we might expect states to interact differently if treaty making was not a constitutive practice for statehood—for instance, after major wars or with the establishment of new states—and then do in-depth process-tracing case studies to see if/how the practice of treaty making shapes the pursuit or establishment of statehood.[26]

The position of this chapter is that SNA should potentially be added to this list of approaches. Toward that end, creating a network map of multilateral treaty-making relationships at particular points in time allows us to explore what treaty-making relationships look like and whether those relationships provide evidence of constitutive effects. The brief example presented here works from a network map of multilateral treaty-making relationships from 1961 to 1975—a key period for decolonization, when a range of newly independent states emerged and had to choose how to manage their transboundary relationships (see figure 4.1).

This map was developed from a comprehensive database of multilateral treaty signing, developed at the University of Delaware and the University of Toronto.[27] In this map, nodes are states, and the edges are treaties signed in common. It depicts a degree 4 network, meaning that an edge represents four or more treaties signed in common.[28] The network in this map is undirected, meaning that the ties between nodes have no direction. This network map reveals a number of interesting observations that speak to the question of whether treaty making is a constitutive practice and how. Two observations are particularly relevant.[29]

First, while figure 4.1 is only one slice in time, it covers a critical juncture—the most active period of decolonization, when an explosion of newly independent states entered the international system. If treaty-making was not taken for granted as a constitutive aspect of statehood, we might expect new states to experiment with a number of tools for managing transboundary and international issues. In fact, before multilateral treaty making became taken for granted as a tool of international coordination/cooperation in the middle to late nineteenth century, there were multiple tools in serious use, especially international conferences and unions.[30] Figure 4.1 shows, however, that immediately after decolonization, new states began making and signing multilateral treaties in significant numbers.[31] The African cluster is especially relevant here. These newly independent states followed in the footsteps of newly independent states in Latin America—whose treaty-making clusters are older but still distinct in this period (the evident Latin American treaty networks emerged in the nineteenth century

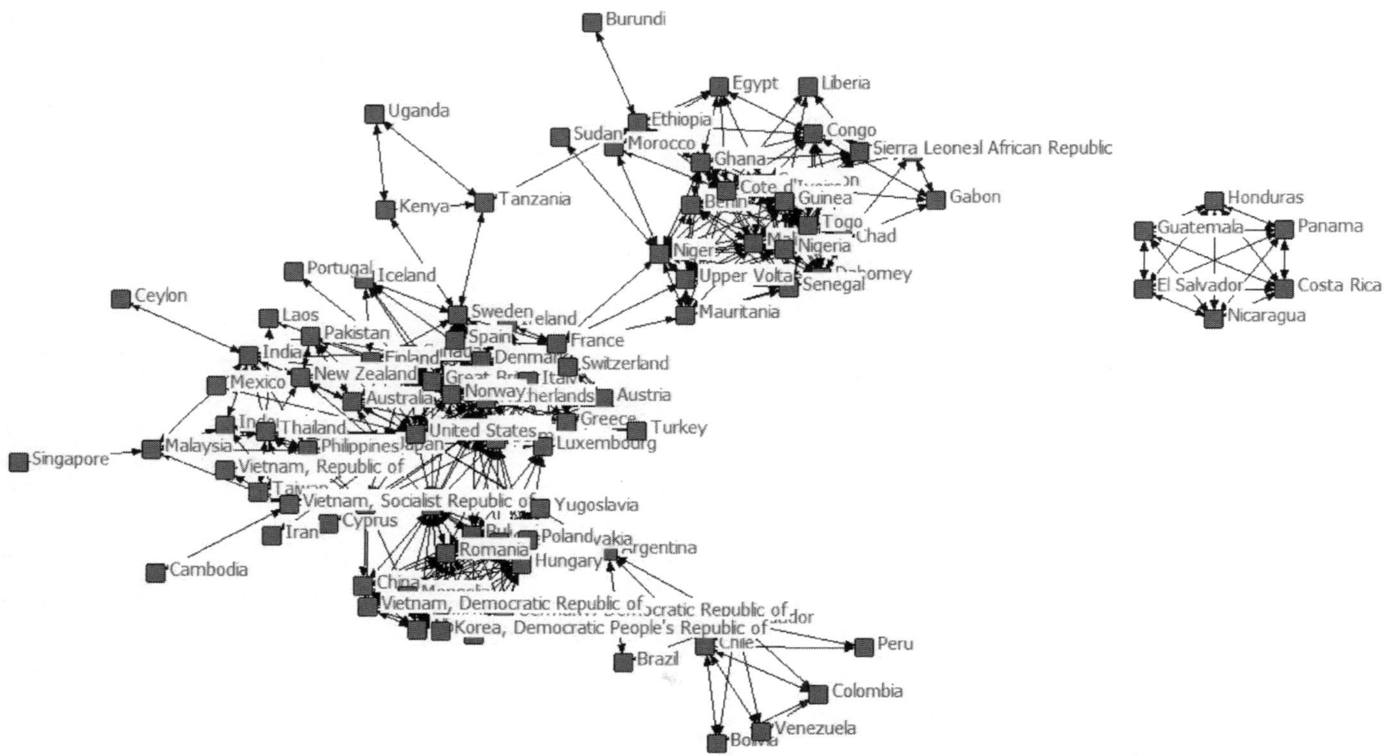

Fig. 4.1. Multilateral treaty network (degree 4), 1961–75

and are observable in earlier network maps as well)—and exercised statehood by signing multilateral treaties.

This treaty-signing network map does not, by itself, confirm constructivist expectations for a constitutive practice, but it is a piece of evidence that supports the constructivist perspective on the role of multilateralism. Looking to act like states, newly independent states take on functions that have been socially constructed to define what counts as acting like states. To act like a state, they negotiated and signed multilateral treaties. Yet SNA can take this argument further and beyond what other strands of constructivist data might allow. It can provide insights into how the constitutive practice travels and the way that it plays out in this specific instance.

Second, focusing in on the African cluster, two patterns jump out. First, there are ties back to colonial powers, most notably between France and West African states. Such ties are suggestive of a mechanism of socialization (and potentially a coercive one) whereby newly independent nations "learned" one of the necessities of statehood from colonial powers. However, the links back to the core European cluster of treaty making are quite sparse, even with the relatively low threshold of four treaties signed in common. What we see, secondly, is the emergence of a dense regional cluster (and perhaps three clusters) that exhibits less robust ties to Europe. These newly independent states are enacting statehood through treaty-making in a way not directed by former colonial powers, in a dense regional treaty-making network.[32]

Observing treaty-making relationships in the network map—who signs treaties with whom or the network structure of treaty-making from 1961 to 1975—provides evidence that constructivist expectations about treaty-making as a constitutive practice of statehood are plausible. It also provides empirical fodder for theorizing the conditions under which social construction takes place. The structure of the treaty-making network suggests that a mix of colonial/core influence and regional interaction may be at work. This indicates that it may be fruitful to consider that new states both were socialized by the European core and learned to be states by acting like states within a peer group.

Of course, SNA cannot reveal what treaty-making means to the states that sign them or if different states interpret multilateral treaty-making differently, which is why multiple tools (e.g., process tracing and content analysis) are needed for constructivist analysis. Yet mapping relations of interest can make constitutive dynamics observable in ways not necessarily possible with qualitative methods. For instance, it is unlikely that there will be textual evidence available where officials from newly independent states say that they are making treaties in order to act like states (though this is sometimes possible[33]). It also prods theorizing about the conditions under which general constitutive dynamics play out.

SNA and the Diffusion of Emissions Trading

How do ideas flow? Constructivism rose to prominence partly by demonstrating the importance of ideational factors in determining political behavior and outcomes. The literature has explored how ideas and norms shape what is possible and what outcomes we should expect. To be convincing with these explanations, constructivists have had to develop analytic frameworks for understanding how ideas emerge and move through communities. SNA can potentially provide a way to make sense of how ideas and norms diffuse and a better understanding of the contours of socialization, by uncovering the structural opportunities and obstacles to the flow of ideas in a community (and comparisons between communities). This section develops this potential with an examination of how ideas about what counts as governance of climate change diffused.[34] Specifically, the idea that the appropriate response to climate change included the use of mechanisms of emissions trading emerged in the 1980s and diffused rapidly in the international community.[35] The claim for this example is that ideas about what counts as appropriate governance of climate change significantly shape the global response to climate change. This is especially the case when we discuss the tools available to respond to climate change. Tools based in carbon markets—means of commoditizing or pricing carbon pollution as a way to use market mechanisms to reduce that pollution—and especially emissions trading have become dominant, though contested in important ways, in the global response.[36] Processes of social construction, especially socialization and diffusion, have made emissions trading a centerpiece of climate governance, with significant consequences for how humanity deals with this crucial issue.[37]

As in the treaty-making example, constructivists can and have worked to substantiate this claim. Mostly through qualitative case studies and discourse analysis, they have looked to understand the emergence of this idea and how states and other actors came to see it as an appropriate part of the global response to climate change. SNA can add to the analysis of the social construction of emissions trading as an appropriate governance tool, by giving us greater insights into *how* the idea has diffused and set the foundation for the politics of carbon markets.

The network mapping in this example is of the individuals (who carry ideas) and organizations that worked to develop emissions trading systems for climate change over time and in various places. The goal is to uncover the contours of diffusion—what pathways were possible in the spread of the idea of carbon markets and what difference those diverse pathways could make. In figure 4.2, a degree 1 network map, individuals are nodes, and edges are defined as common participation in one or more venues dedicated to advancing, planning, or developing emissions trading systems.[38] In figure 4.3, a degree 2 network map, organizations are the nodes, and the edges represent common participation in two or more of the venues.[39] The size of the nodes in both of these figures is related to the betweenness score of the node. The larger the square is, the higher the betweenness score is for that node, and thus the more central to the network that node is (in terms of structural significance and how the absence of the node would fragment the network).

Combining visualization through network mapping with nodal-level statistical analysis provides a number of insights important for investigating constructivist claims about diffusion of ideas and the importance of ideational factors in shaping outcomes. Three insights are particularly relevant for this discussion. First, the SNA informs an understanding of how contestation over or diverse instantiations of an accepted idea develop. Constructivists have often struggled with understanding how norms and other social facts can change over time—how the reifying dynamics of mutual constitution can also allow for change (ironically, given how constructivism rose to prominence on the basis of its perceived advantage at explaining change). The constructivist literature has come up with multiple ways to think about how ideas that are taken for granted can provide fodder for contestation as different groups of agents differently interpret and act on "what everyone knows."[40] SNA provides a way to demonstrate how this happens and a structural account for divergence and contestation over accepted ideas.

The original intellectual foundations of emissions trading were developed and discussed in the small venues that emerge in the lower right quadrant in figure 4.2.[41] These clusters of individuals are distinct groups of economists and early policy professionals that developed the intellectual foundation of ideas of carbon markets. The map shows that connections between these early intellectual leaders and the following clusters of individuals working on operational venues (all the rest of the clusters, representing venues where actual trading systems were developed) are both sparse and bifurcated. The top mass of individuals come from two North American venues (the Regional Greenhouse Gas Initiative and the Western Climate Initiative), and the bottom clusters are all European and international venues (Kyoto, the European Union, and the United Kingdom). Distinct flavors of thinking about emis-

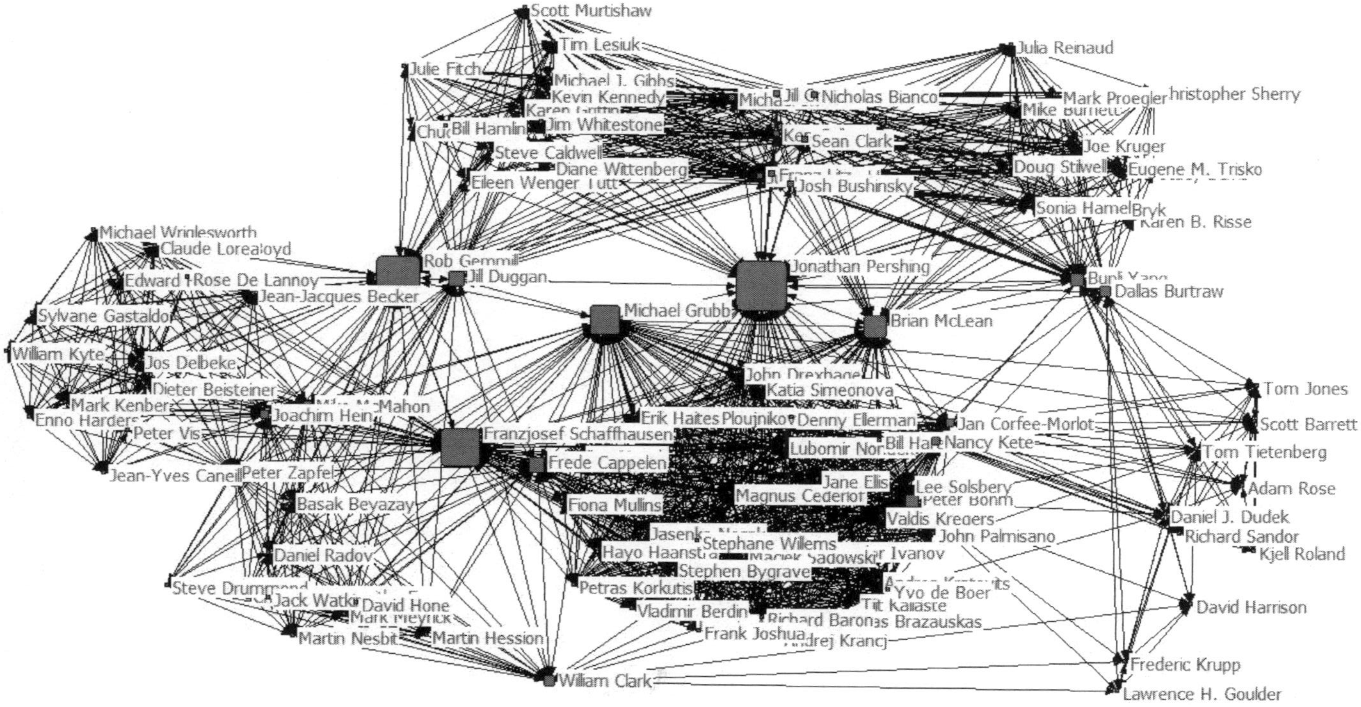

Fig. 4.2. Individual network of emissions trading

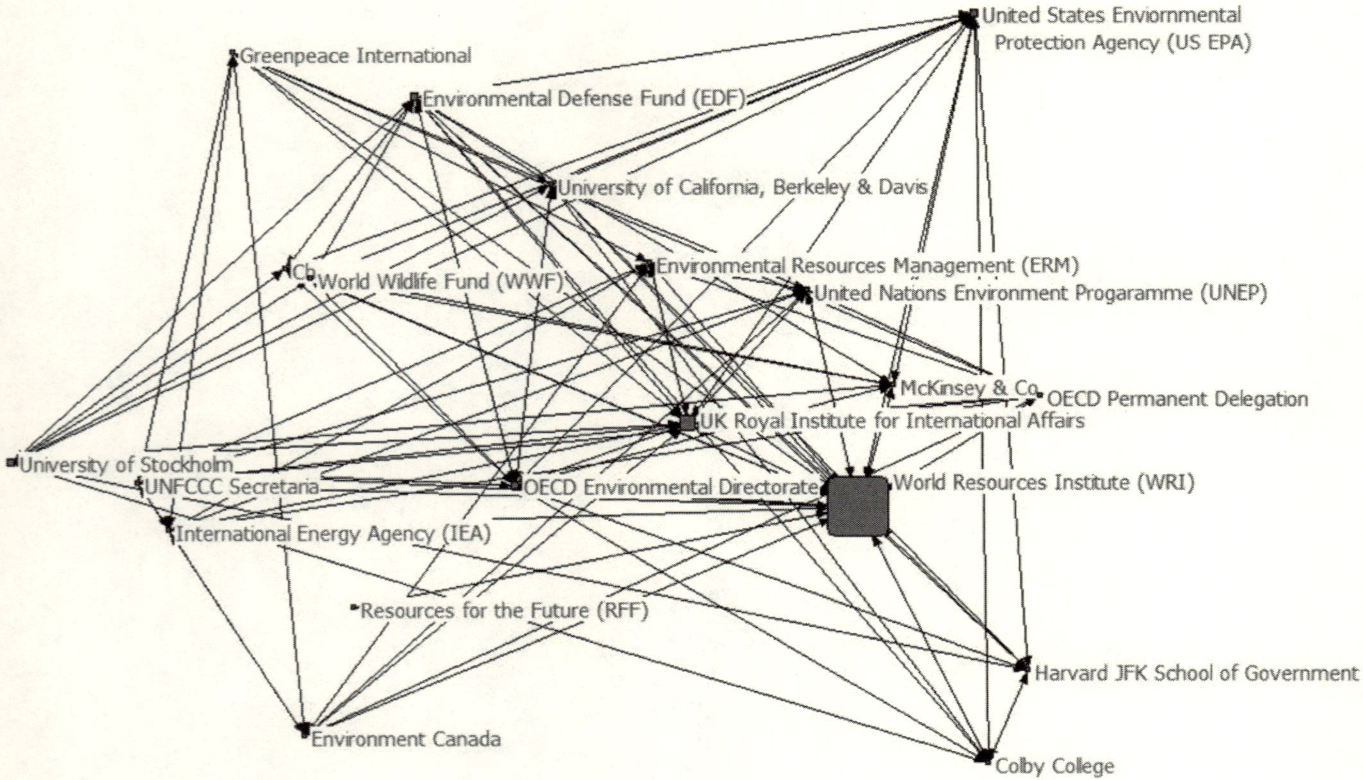

Fig. 4.3. Organizational network of emissions trading

sions trading traveled in the European and North American venues, shaping very different politics of emissions trading.[42] It is plausible that when accepted ideas diffuse through networks with specific structures, different interpretations and instantiations of those accepted ideas can emerge. This is another way to think about norm and idea contestation. Mutual constitution does tend to reify norms and foundational ideas, but the population of actors who have internalized norms are not necessarily uniform. Instead, they are distributed in networks, which alters the way in which ideas come to constitute the intersubjective playing field.

Second, in figure 4.2, intravenue relations are significantly denser than extravenue relations. This has significant implications for diffusion and the way that the foundational idea of emissions trading could influence politics.[43] Because of the contrasting density of intravenue and extravenue networks, there are opportunities for the emergence of key brokers who may be able to channel diffusion and shape the way that the ideas of emissions trading have and will travel from venue to venue. This structure also suggests that diffusion is working through two levels (at least) of politics: (1) a relatively sparse transnational network of individuals that are working across venues and (2) relatively dense venue-specific networks where the politics and details of putting emissions trading into practice are worked out.

Finally, by changing the identity of the nodes in the emissions trading network from individuals to the organizations they represent, figure 4.3 reveals additional insights about the diffusion process around emissions trading and how this foundational idea moves through the climate governance community. When the network is viewed organizationally, a very different picture emerges. The venues do not emerge in the network map as distinct clusters of relationships (as was clear in figure 4.2) suggesting that organizations are likely to work across venues, whereas individuals tend to focus more on a particular venue or two. This is not entirely surprising, but the comparison of the two networks is crucial. The map and distribution of highly central actors suggests the existence of a strata of transnational actors participating relatively widely across venues and providing the ideational glue that holds the fragmented emissions trading system together (relatively speaking) and that influences the development of individual emissions trading systems. Further, that strata is largely transnational, rather than transgovernmental, contra to the expectations that have developed in the diffusion literature about which kind of actors drives diffusion of global policy.[44]

Empirically, it is clear that emissions trading, as a key tool for climate governance, diffused and has shaped the global response to climate change.

SNA provides a means to observe the pathways through which this diffusion has taken place, which furthers our understanding both of why diverse instantiations of the idea of carbon markets have developed and of the kind of politics through which diffusion has played out.[45] For constructivists, SNA provides additional evidence in support of their ideational arguments and further allows for a refinement of constructivist theorizing on how network structure influences ways in which foundational ideas construct politics.

Conclusion

SNA is not a revolution for constructivist work. It reinforces, rather than challenges, the underlying ontology with which many constructivists work. At a fundamental level, it does not add significantly, in a conceptual sense, to a perspective that already buys into relational analysis and that has developed a number of sophisticated ways to apprehend social dynamics. It does, however, add another methodological tool for exploring and advancing constructivist claims. It adds another stream of data/analysis that constructivists can use to interrogate their claims and extend their (middle-range) theorizing. Constructivism reveals processes of social construction in ways simply not available through qualitative methods, and it expands the number of constructivist questions that can be subjected to empirical scrutiny. The use of two very different examples in this chapter was intended to demonstrate how SNA can facilitate constructivist analysis. SNA not only helps to confirm that constructivist expectations are plausible; it also shows how constructivist processes play out in specific instances, and it helps to identify sets of factors that influence how they play out. In this way, SNA can be generative of advances in constructivist theorizing, in addition to being a valuable tool of empirical analysis.

The match is not perfect, however, and two sources of conceptual caution for constructivists serve to put boundaries on the kind of constructivist questions this method can be used to explore. First, SNA is clearly a structural approach to analysis that leaves little room for agency. As Emirbayer and Goodwin argue, it is a perspective that "questions the explanatory potential of all those conceptual strategies that emphasize . . . purposive actions of individuals or collectivities."[46] Constructivists pursuing SNA should take care to remember that this method and perspective is only concerned with the structural side of the mutual constitution dynamic.[47] In addition, SNA may sit uncomfortably with constructivists who adhere to postpositivist or interpretivist epistemologies. For many applications of SNA, the observation of nodes and ties is done from the outside. Once the observer/analyst defines the nodes (which is potentially problematic from a relational perspective) and the relationships that count as links, he or she builds the network from that perspective. There is less discussion about the differential meaning that links might have from the subjective perspective of individual nodes, and the differentiation of links at all is often constrained to relatively quantitative measures—strength (conceptualized as number of relations) and direction. One could, hypothetically, develop a network whereby the nodes in the network defined the linkages themselves (there are some applications of this in terms of friendship networks), but SNA generally sits more comfortably within the kind of positivist or pseudopositivist epistemology practiced by modernist constructivists.[48]

These caveats aside, the conceptual fit of SNA with constructivism makes it plausible that SNA can provide useful insights, but perhaps it is necessary to use the method differently than the conventional uses we see in the current literature. Specifically, SNA can help constructivists empirically uncover and more directly observe constitutive mechanisms at the heart of constructivist approaches. Constructivist theory expects that through mutual constitution, social structure should shape who actors are (identity), their interests (what they want), and their behaviors (what they do). Socially situated interests and behaviors create and re-create actors and constitute their social context. SNA gives constructivists another way to observe empirical traces of these constitutive dynamics at work *and* to grasp and observe the conditions under which constitutive dynamics are likely to play out in different ways.

Three types of constructivist uses for SNA suggest themselves, and all three differ from the conventional approaches that use SNA to find actor-level attributes that are generated by network position or network effects and that use those attributes (independent variables) to try and explain political outcomes (dependent variables). First, the mapping applications of SNA can be used to visualize and provide empirical evidence of arguably otherwise unobservable processes. Constitutive practices can be unveiled and observed in the relationships that actors form in particular networks. For instance, if actors are socialized to act in a certain way, constructivism has an expectation that they will form certain kinds of relationships. Mapping of relationships through SNA can reveal the implications of constitutive practices. Further, the mapping can uncover specific conditions for how constitutive practices are playing out, which can help to improve constructivist theorizing.

Second, mapping provides a way to observe the evolution of community structures over time. Social structure is not given in constructivist theory; it emerges from the actions and interactions of actors. SNA is a way to visualize the interactions of actors in a rigorous way. If the important parts of international structure are intersubjective and relational, rather than the distribution of material capabilities, constructivists need a way to conceptualize and observe social structure—the distribution of intersubjective knowledge and the relations and interactions that produce social structure. SNA mapping and statistical analysis can provide a way to do so.

Finally, SNA can help constructivists specify pathways of socialization and diffusion. Constructivist theory provides a series of expectations about the important role of idea or norm diffusion and processes of socialization. The details of how ideas or notions of appropriate behavior move (since they do not float freely) has not been as clearly articulated. SNA provides a tool for observing and analyzing how flows of ideas work in specific contexts, because it uncovers the specific structure of relationships in a community through which ideas are flowing. Here, nodal attributes become important in understanding power over diffusion and the potential pathways and discourse communities that develop in the network. This can be helpful in both theorizing diffusion and explaining particular outcomes of diffusion empirically.

Going further with constructivism and SNA entails three avenues of research that dovetail with the kind of questions asked in the introductory chapter. First, there needs to be a full exploration and consideration of the kind of constructivist questions that can be answered through SNA tools. This suggests not method-driven research but, rather, that constructivists should engage with SNA tools to better understand its possibilities and limits and to do more on matching constructivist questions with SNA tools. This trial-and-error process will require more empirical work and more experimentation with the statistical tools of SNA.

Second, more conceptual work is needed to see if and where the underlying precepts of SNA—relational sociology and the network perspective—can be incorporated into constructivist theorizing. This chapter did not delve deeply into the ontological and epistemological implications of using SNA to address constructivist questions. Further work conceptually aligning the method of SNA with constructivist systems of thought will better delineate the boundaries of where SNA can be useful for constructivists.

Third, SNA must, in most instances, be used as a complement to other (often qualitative) methods. Without additional data on the nature of linkages and processes at play, SNA can produce spurious correlations. For instance, in the example of emissions trading discussed above, the data on common presence at the same venues that was used to construct the network map does not provide evidence or data about the nature of the interactions at the common venues (or if there even was direct interaction). Content analysis, process tracing, elite interviewing, and participant observation can be used in conjunction with SNA to gain fuller insight from the network dynamics. Further reflection on how these methods fit together is thus imperative.

The additional work I have recommended here will no doubt uncover areas where SNA can push constructivist research ahead. It is also likely to uncover areas where SNA is incompatible with the goals and perspectives of constructivists. Yet there is enough potential here to cautiously advocate that constructivists invest the time and energy necessary for fully exploring this powerful methodological tool.

Notes

1. See, e.g., Emanuel Adler, "Seizing the Middle Ground: Constructivism in World Politics, " *European Journal of International Relations* 3, no. 3 (1997): 319–63.

2. See Patrick Thaddeus Jackson and Daniel Nexon, "Relations before States," *European Journal of International Relations* 5, no. 3 (1999): 291–332.

3. For accessible introductions to SNA statistics, see J. Scott, *Social Network Analysis* (London: Sage, 1990); S. Wasserman and K. Faust, *Social Network Analysis: Methods and Applications* (New York: Cambridge University Press, 1997).

4. The number of SNA software packages that can be used to visualize networks has exploded in recent years. Netdraw, Gephi, packages in R, and others are now available. Some of these visualization tools are paired with analytic packages, such as UCINet, while others bundle visualization with statistical analysis.

5. Wendy Wong, *Internal Affairs: How the Structure of NGOs Transforms Human Rights* (Ithaca: Cornell University Press, 2012).

6. See Emilie Hafner-Burton, Miles Kahler, and Alexander Montgomery "Network Analysis for International Relations," *International Organization* 63 (2009): 559–92; David Lazer, "Networks in Political Science: Back to the Future," *PS* 44 (2011): 61–68.

7. Lazer, "Networks in Political Science."

8. Hafner-Burton, Kahler, and Montgomery, "Network Analysis for International Relations."

9. Xun Cao, "Global Networks and Domestic Policy Convergence: A Network Explanation of Policy Changes," *World Politics* 64, no. 3 (2012): 375–425; Cao, "Networks as Channels of Policy Diffusion: Explaining Worldwide Changes in Capital Taxation, 1998–2006," *International Studies Quarterly* 54, no. 3 (2010): 823–54.

10. Emilie Hafner-Burton and Alexander Montgomery, "War, Trade, and Distrust: Why Trade Agreements Don't Always Keep the Peace." *Conflict Management and Peace Science* 29, no. 3 (2012); Hafner-Burton and Montgomery, "Power Positions: International Organizations, Social Networks, and Conflict. *Journal of Conflict Resolution* 50, no. 1 (2006): 3–27.

11. Hafner-Burton, Kahler, and Montgomery, "Network Analysis for International Relations."

12. See, e.g., Barry Wellman, "Social Network Analysis: Some Basic Principles," *Sociological Theory* 1 (1983): 155–200; Mustafa Emirbayer, "Manifesto for a Relational Sociology," *American Journal of Sociology* 103, no. 2 (1997): 281–317; Mustafa Emirbayer and Jeff Goodwin, "Network Analysis, Culture, and the Problem of Agency," *American Journal of Sociology* 99, no. 6 (1994): 1411–54; Lazer, "Networks in Political Science."

13. Wellman, "Social Network Analysis," 157.

14. Ibid., 157.

15. Emirbayer and Goodwin, "Network Analysis, Culture, and the Problem of Agency," 1414.

16. See Adler, "Seizing the Middle Ground."

17. See Emirbayer and Goodwin, "Network Analysis, Culture, and the Problem of Agency," 1415; Adler, "Seizing the Middle Ground."

18. See Adler, "Seizing the Middle Ground."

19. A range of topics would seem likely targets for constructivist use of SNA, including multiple instances and types of diffusion, such as cascading revolutions, norm diffusion, and influence of transnational activist networks. For some examples of work that does use SNA, from within constructivism or at least in conversation with constructivism, see R. Charli Carpenter, "Vetting the Advocacy Agenda: Network Centrality and the Paradox of Weapons Norms," *International Organization* 65, no. 1 (2011): 69–102; Jean-Frédéric Morin, "The Two-Level Game of Transnational Networks: The Case of the Access to Medicines Campaign," *International Interactions* 36, no. 4 (2010): 309–34; Mely Caballero-Anthony, "Understanding ASEAN's Centrality: Bases and Prospects in an Evolving Regional Architecture," *Pacific Review* 27, no. 4 (2014): 563–84.

20. Martha Finnemore, *National Interests in International Society* (Ithaca: Cornell University Press, 1996).

21. This example is drawn from an ongoing research project in which I participated, with Robert Denemark, Aarie Glas, and Cliff van der Linden. Parts of the analysis and some passages draw directly on current work (Aarie Glas, Cliff van der Linden, Matthew Hoffmann, Robert Denemark, "Understanding Treaty-Making as a Constitutive Practice of Global Politics" [paper presented at the annual meeting of the International Studies Association, 2013]) and previous work (Robert Denemark and Matthew Hoffmann, "Not Just Scraps of Paper: The Dynamics of Multilateral Treaty-Making," *Cooperation and Conflict* 43, no. 2 [2008]: 185–219).

22. See John Ruggie, ed., *Multilateralism Matters* (New York: Columbia University Press, 1993).

23. This section focuses exclusively on multilateral treaty making.

24. See Finnemore, *National Interests.*

25. See Denemark and Hoffmann, "Not Just Scraps of Paper."

26. See Alan Milward, *The European Rescue of the Nation-State*, 2nd ed. (London: Routledge, 2000).

27. For more on the database, see Denemark and Hoffmann, "Not Just Scraps of Paper."

28. The choice of degree is somewhat arbitrary. For instance, the degree 1 network for this example is too dense to show any useful patterns. The degree 4 network has

enough treaty-making relations to screen out noise (relatively rare treaty relations) while capturing most of states' treaty-making activity.

29. There is not room here for a full discussion of what SNA can provide for this question, so I am focusing on just two kinds of insight.

30. Craig Murphy, *International Organization and Industrial Change: Global Governance since 1850* (New York: Oxford University Press, 1994).

31. I am not including here the before and after pictures showing that treaty relations and networks among new states emerged with decolonization and then solidified in the 1980s, but that data and those images are available. Other work in which I have collaborated examines treaty networks before and after World War II and in the aftermath of the Russian Revolution of 1917, to demonstrate the constitutive nature of treaty making. See Glas, van der Linden, Hoffmann, and Denemark, "Understanding Treaty-Making."

32. An objection to this point—discussed in much more detail in Glas, van der Linden, Hoffmann, and Denemark, "Understanding Treaty-Making")—is that the regional cluster is more dense because relatively local transboundary issues are much more prevalent than international issues involving both European and African states (ibid.). This truth is trivial here, because it misses the point that the obviousness of regional treaty networks emerging among newly independent states presupposes that multilateral treaty making is the accepted way that states appropriately and must deal with such issues. This is the very point constructivists make—that states are constituted, only known as states, by socially constructed practices. However, in this chapter, I am not fully exploring the alternative to the constructivist arguments; rather, I am illustrating how constructivist analysis can be advanced by using SNA.

33. See Milward, *European Rescue.*

34. This example is drawn from ongoing work with colleagues (Matthew Paterson, Steven Bernstein, and Michele Betsill). It draws specifically on work published in Matthew Paterson, Matthew Hoffmann, Michele Betsill, and Steven Bernstein, "The Micro Foundations of Policy Diffusion toward Complex Global Governance: An Analysis of the Transnational Carbon Emission Trading Network," *Comparative Political Studies* 47, no. 3 (2014): 420–49.

35. See Paterson et al., "Micro Foundations"; Michele Betsill and Matthew Hoffmann, "The Contours of 'Cap and Trade': The Evolution of 41 Emissions Trading Systems for Greenhouse Gases," *Review of Policy Research* 28, no. 1 (2011): 83–106.

36. See Betsill and Hoffmann, "Contours"; Peter Newell and Matthew Paterson, *Climate Capitalism: Global Warming and the Transformation of the Global Economy* (Cambridge: Cambridge University Press, 2010).

37. See Betsill and Hoffmann, "Contours"; Steven Bernstein, Michele Betsill, Matthew Hoffmann, and Matthew Paterson, "A Tale of Two Copenhagens: Carbon Markets and Climate Governance," *Millennium: Journal of International Studies* 39, no. 1 (2010): 161–73.

38. There are, of course, other ways that individuals involved in emissions trading might be linked. An obvious way is through citation networks, which would have implications for how ideas about emissions trading have diffused.

39. The venues include relatively informal gatherings where the idea of emissions trading was discussed among experts and policy makers in the abstract: in the United

States, Project 88, a bipartisan-sponsored expert-based initiative focused initially on developing the policy case for market mechanisms for US domestic clean air policy; the Organization for Economic Cooperation and Development and the United Nations Conference on Trade and Development, both of which sponsored reports on emissions trading; and the Annex I Working Group, or AIXG, the principal forum for discussing emissions trading in the negotiations of the United Nations Framework Convention on Climate Change (UNFCCC) before Kyoto in 1997. The venues also include specific instances where emissions trading was developed and designed into working systems: Kyoto/Marrakesh (UNFCCC negotiations in Marrakesh produced the 2001 Marrakesh Accords, in which parties finalized the rules of implementation for the 1997 Kyoto Protocol) and four venues that are or were operational—the United Kingdom, the European Union, the Regional Greenhouse Gas Initiative, and the Western Climate Initiative. For more on the data collection and development of the network mapping, see Paterson et al., "Micro Foundations."

40. See Matthew Hoffmann, "Norms and Social Constructivism in International Relations," in *The International Studies Encyclopedia,* ed. Robert Denemark et al. (Oxford: Wiley-Blackwell, 2010); Wayne Sandholtz, *International Norms and Cycles of Change* (New York: Oxford University Press, 2008); Antje Wiener, "Contested Compliance: Interventions on the Normative Structure of World Politics," *European Journal of International Relations* 10, no. 2 (2004): 189–234.

41. This map does not contain data on the dates when the venues were in operation (the overall data represents activities from the late 1980s through the mid-2000s). Contextual knowledge and other data is what allows us to see these clusters as venues.

42. See Paterson et al., "Micro Foundations."

43. It is of interest that "venues" are recognizable just by looking at the linkages between individuals working on emissions trading.

44. See Anne-Marie Slaughter, *A New World Order* (Princeton, NJ: Princeton University Press, 2004).

45. The diffusion of ideas is clearly an area where constructivists have done significant work: see, e.g., Peter Hall, ed., *The Political Power of Economic Ideas: Keynesianism across Nations* (Princeton, NJ: Princeton University Press); Finnemore, *National Interests*; Amitav Acharya, "How Ideas Spread: Whose Norms Matter? Norm Localization and Institutional Change in Asian Regionalism," *International Organization* 58, no. 2 (2004): 239–75. SNA is another tool for exploring these dynamics.

46. Emirbayer and Goodwin, "Network Analysis, Culture, and the Problem of Agency," 1416.

47. SNA might therefore be most compatible with the sociological institutionalist varieties of constructivism (see, e.g., Finnemore, *National Interests*).

48. On the different variants of constructivism, see Richard Price and Christian Reus-Smit, "Dangerous Liaisons? Critical International Theory and Constructivism," *European Journal of International Relations* 4, no. 3 (1998): 259–94; Adler, "Seizing."

CHAPTER 5

Dimensions of Identity Construction and the Measurement of Differences among Countries

PAUL A. KOWERT

Constructivism in International Relations (IR) is far from novel in its philosophical conceits. To the extent that it is recognizable by its emphasis on the problem of identity—the identity of things in general, and of agents in particular, that can be constructed in various ways—it is closely linked to its philosophical roots in the ontological problem of identifying or naming things. Even within the field of IR itself, constructivism builds on a persistent interest in this problem. One thing in need of identification has been the state. Consequently, multiple research traditions have grappled with the problem of describing or identifying the state in the context of IR. Are there different kinds of states, or are states essentially homogeneous units? If the former is the case, how many different kinds of states are possible? How many of their differences are relevant to an understanding of foreign policy? Such questions have informed the contemporary explosion of interest in constructivism and identity politics.

Efforts to address such questions have often stumbled on the methodological challenge of systematically describing the ways in which countries differ from one another. To put this more precisely, descriptions of countries (as powerful or weak, democratic, authoritarian, developed, liberal, or otherwise) are commonplace. But systematic schemes for comparing differences among countries are neither robust nor widely used, even by scholars such as constructivists, who would seem to be most interested in taking account of these differences.

This chapter addresses the methodological challenge of describing the ways in which countries differ and the reasons why techniques for meeting this challenge remain so poorly developed. One reason, no doubt, is that many constructivists fear no general, global answers to such descriptive problems are possible. They expect that while we may investigate the provisional and constantly shifting meanings assigned to specific states or even to the state in general, we should not hope for too much generalization in a world where contingency is important and our interpretive scope is large. In such a world, so the argument goes, our interpretations are best situated in specific historical and cultural contexts.

One of the most cogent and empirically rich studies of state identity in recent years, Ted Hopf's thoughtful comparison of early Soviet identity and post–Cold War Russian identity, makes just this determination from the outset.[1] Hopf begins by acknowledging the paucity of general, socially informed accounts or theories of state identity. Where one does find such accounts, they normally predicate identity on certain specific foundational premises, such as material capabilities or the dualism of self and other. "I have in mind," he explains, "those accounts of identity that assume too much about the social world, making too many a priori foundational claims that both hinder the social context from speaking for itself and often put words in its mouth."[2] After considering and dismissing several candidates for a "foundational" theory of identity—based, for example, on material conditions, deep-seated national or ethnic motives, self/other binaries, and the pure politics of identity manipulation—Hopf resumes his call for a new, "thick" inductivism.

> So what are we left with once we reject such assumptions as materialism, innate drives, dangerous Others, and strategic choice? The answer is a thin cognitive account of identity that is thickly inductive and empirical. Society is assumed to consist of a social cognitive structure within which operate many discursive formations. Identities constitute these formations. Individuals have many identities; they participate in a variety of discursive formations; and their daily social practices constitute both themselves and Others, and the identities and discursive formations that constitute the social cognitive structure in which they live.[3]

Identity as a discursive formation has a cognitive structure because it is, after all, a perceptual or phenomenological construct. Yet it is also social, and not purely individual, because it is a discursive phenomenon.

Hopf returns often to the theme that we lack sufficient empirical grounds for making any systematic theoretical assumptions about state identity. Several distinct groups of scholars might object that the terrain of state identity research is not entirely unplowed.[4] Beginning with Kal J. Holsti's innovative study of national role conceptions and extending to the work of, among others, Stephen G. Walker and Cameron Thies, role theorists have made a particularly impressive effort to canvass the possibilities of conceivable state roles.[5] Foreign policy image theorists have also made use of Richard Cottam's typology of state images—resting on judgments about orientation, capabilities, and cultural difference—to investigate the ways in which foreign policy strategies depend on images of other states.[6] In addition, a number of constructivists apart from Hopf have explored possible formulations of state identity, although perhaps less systematically than role and image theorists.[7] Still, Hopf remains unpersuaded that social strictures or other external conditions limit expressions of state identity to any great degree.

> I suggest that the most important mechanism for the reproduction of identity is not role and norm but rather habit and practice. I do not assume that individuals consciously understand their roles through social context and so deliberately abide by the appropriate norm. . . . This conceptualization is too constraining theoretically; it narrows the social world of identity to a small number of positions and an even smaller number of expectable behaviors. Ontologically it is too crabbed; it assumes too few meaningful entities in its theoretical field.[8]

Existing research is simply too narrow, Hopf objects, and it lacks a sufficient empirical basis to justify reliance on its analytical schemes.

This chapter accepts the premise that Hopf's characterization of the state of identity research is apt, but it maintains that the conclusions he draws are unwarranted. There are multiple theoretical traditions of great relevance to the phenomenology of the state. Yet there is no general agreement on the contours of what must be explained and predicted. It is as though we have come to a construction project with an assortment of powerful tools but without any consensus on what should be built. In these circumstances, it is hard to say whether a reciprocating saw or an acetylene torch is needed. Hopf's reticence to embrace any specific theoretical perspective a priori is thus understandable.

An Analogy to Personality: Ontology Meets Methodology

A suitable analogy can be found in the field of personality research. If anything, *personality* is an even more amorphous construct than national role or state identity. At the level of the individual, it may subsume both role and identity, as well as many other characteristics, ultimately amounting to a laundry list of almost any longitudinally stable trait or generalization that can be offered about human beings.[9] Yet two developments have reduced, if not eliminated, some of the confusion in personality research: (1) the creation of reliable general personality tests and measurement techniques and (2) the emergence of a robust factor model of personality.

The second of these developments depended on the first, and it is in this way that ontology meets methodology. Historically, many personality tests have been based on specific theoretical perspectives. The Myers-Briggs Type Indicator (to take a prominent example) rests on Jung's personality theory that starts with a fundamental assumption about internal or external personal orientations toward the world.[10] But psychologists have also developed more general personality inventories to measure a wide array of personality traits, using a variety of methods. The Minnesota Multiphasic Personality Inventory (MMPI) is an early example of such a test, intended to diagnose personality and psychopathology independent of any specific personality theory.[11] The California Psychological Inventory (CPI) resembled the MMPI and even shared many of the same items, but the CPI was intended to measure personality using ordinary concepts understandable to a layperson.[12] The author of the CPI, Harrison Gough, also developed the simpler Adjective Check List (ACL), permitting an even easier scoring method of selecting from a list those adjectives that are characteristic of oneself or another subject.[13] Other, modified ACLs rate adjectives on a Likert scale, from most to least characteristic of the individual being described.[14]

As this array of general personality inventories was developed—those listed above are only a small sample—factor analysis began to reveal a common structure to responses on these tests. This factor structure emerged as early as 1949, when Donald Fiske identified five factors in an analysis of data on twenty-two personality variables developed by Raymond Cattell, and it became the foundation of the five-factor model (FFM) of personality.[15] The personality factors known as the Big Five—conventionally labeled *neuroticism*, *extraversion*, *openness* (to experience), *agreeableness*, and *conscientiousness*—might be thought of as basic clusters of personality variables. As the FFM became widely accepted, additional general personality tests were developed to reflect its factor structure.[16] The most visible of these is the Revised NEO Personality Inventory (NEO PI-R).[17]

The FFM does not purport to be an ideal framework for the study of every aspect of human personality, and the NEO PI-R is not the only suitable method for measuring a particular trait of interest. The virtue of the development of such models and techniques, however, is that they permit general assessments of personality with a confidence that was previously impossible. They have also given psychologists new puzzles to address: why, for example, is there an apparently common basic factor structure in human personality across regions, cultures, and languages? The assessment method and the personality model evolved together through a process of moving back and forth from inductive generalization to deductive model building. Arriving at the "construction site" of contemporary personality research, psychologists today have a better sense of what to do and how to do it and have even more (rather than fewer) questions to answer.

The current status of efforts to study state images, roles, and identities in IR suggests that scholars would benefit from similar, systematic attention to differences among countries. As in psychology, the necessary first step is a general measurement system tied to no theoretical orientation in particular. Induction is the order of the day for this step, and Holsti's early efforts were an important step forward.[18] Holsti coded a total of 972 general foreign policy statements made between 1964 and 1968 by national leaders of seventy-one different countries, with a minimum of at least ten sources per country.[19] Holsti's coding of these statements revealed seventeen distinct national role conceptions, including roles such as regional leader, faithful ally, protectee, bastion of the revolution, mediator, and independent.

Holsti's work was an important step forward but had certain limitations. By relying on the statements of prominent national leaders, Holsti already constrained expressions of national role to those of a very specific (powerful, well-educated, typically male) subset of the general population. Moreover, Holsti's coding and analysis of the data subjectively assigned each statement to a category derived from a first-stage inductive study of seventy-five sources drawn from eighteen countries—not a very extensive foundation for his coding scheme. Holsti offered no formal statistical analysis of factor groupings in his data, an analysis that might have provided revealing evidence of the structure of national role conceptions and the number of role categories that would suffice to account for most national roles.

Holsti's study was pathbreaking. He provided the first major empirical and inductive approximation of the sorts of roles states adopt. Yet scholars studying national role and state identity still lack a reliable scheme for classifying states. The first step in developing such a scheme is to do what Holsti did not: to develop a set of state descriptors that is extensive (not limited arbitrarily to key attributes identified in a particular study or by just one group of scholars), general (not limited to descriptions offered by only certain groups of people), and extensively tested (for internal and external validity).

Developing a General Descriptive Test

It is not difficult to construct a test measuring differences among countries. There are many such differences. One has only to describe some of them and ask people to evaluate countries accordingly. Is a country "powerful"? Is it "developed"? Is it "secure"?

A more difficult challenge is devising a test that encompasses a wide variety of country descriptors, including characteristics widely discussed in the foreign policy literature (e.g., *democratic* or *powerful*); characteristics more often discussed in the popular literature (e.g., *arrogant* or *God-fearing*); and characteristics that may have been previously ignored. A general test, analogous to general personality tests like the MMPI or CPI, should describe many qualities or characteristics of countries, without too much overlap in test items. The lengthier the test is, the more likely it is to include redundant items, and the more cumbersome it is to use. The shorter the test is, the more likely it is to miss important items. The test should also have both internal and external validity. That is to say, the items it includes should not be flawed as measures of what they purport to measure (they should be understandable to a variety of audiences, avoid double-barreled meanings, etc.), and they should provide reliable measures of these qualities in real countries (which might be tested against independent measures of these qualities).[20]

This section describes my own efforts to construct a reliable and general test measuring differences among countries using a two-phase iterated procedure typical of the best practices for constructing personality tests: first expanding the list of descriptors using several techniques, then refining the list to reduce overlap and improved validity, and repeating the entire process one or more times. Compared with a test that employs phrases or questions (e.g., "Is this country capable of influencing other countries?"), Gough's Adjective Check List (ACL) approach is faster and easier to administer while maintaining reliability.[21] It is a good candidate for a general test of country differences.

The ACL consists of a list of descriptive adjectives that can be rated on a Likert scale or, even more simply, checked or selected if they describe the object of the test. My first task in test construction, therefore, was to identify an extensive list of adjectives describing countries. Because countries are often treated as agents, equivalent to people but acting on an international stage, I began with lists of adjectives describing people.[22] Combining adjectives from the Big Five ACL and another ACL developed by the Canadian Alliance of Life Skills Coaches and Associations yielded a list that was long but that contained many items, such as *gregarious* or *punctual*, that were not obviously useful as country descriptors.[23] After I removed the less relevant adjectives and added others that have been prominent in the literature on national roles and state images —such as *powerful*, *isolated*, and *democratic*— the resulting prototype ACL consisted of 132 items.

To further expand the range of potential adjectives, and as a first test of external validity, I drew on popular descriptions of countries recorded in English-language newspapers published in different parts of the world. I drew a sample of five articles of at least one hundred words from the Lexis-Nexis Academic database (which indexes major US and world newspapers) for each UN member state whose population exceeded one million persons. In all, 155 countries met this criterion, ranging from China (the largest) to East Timor (with a population just over one million). Swaziland, Qatar, Estonia, and Gabon all exceeded this threshold, whereas Monaco, Liechtenstein, the Bahamas, Bahrain, and Fiji did not. An assistant conducted searches for articles that were published during a five-month span in 2010 and that mentioned each country. From the resulting pool of articles, we selected the first five articles that dealt with each country as a subject of the article (i.e., not articles that simply mentioned a country or an event that took place within it).[24] Difficulties identifying suitable articles for two countries resulted in a final sample of 770 articles describing 154 countries, and this sample yielded 1,304 adjectives and adjectival phrases in all, roughly 1.7 per coded article.

Comparing this adjective list with the prototype adjective list based on personality descriptors suggested several ways to improve the prototype list. In general, regional descriptors (*Southern*, *European*, etc.) were not part of the original list but were strongly represented in the adjective list derived from the newspaper articles. Religious descriptors (*Buddhist*, *Christian*, etc.) were also well represented in the articles but missing from the prototype list, as were some economic (e.g., *industrial*) or security-related (e.g., *war-torn*) adjectives. Adding adjectives that appeared multiple times in the newspaper articles and removing those that seemed obviously redundant yielded a second prototype ACL of 199 items.

To refine this broad list of adjectives, I next recruited a subject pool of 264 undergraduate students in an introductory IR course, to participate in a survey.[25] The student subjects were asked to describe a country other than the United States in which they had lived and which they knew well, using the 199-item prototype ACL. Subjects who had not lived abroad were asked to describe the United States. Subjects also provided demographic data about themselves and, after completing the survey, were given the opportunity to suggest adjectives not present on the list. Seventy subjects availed themselves of this opportunity, suggesting adjectives such as *lawless*, *patriotic*, *educated*, and *tolerant*.

For purposes of statistical analysis, 58 surveys were removed from the dataset because of missing data, resulting in a final sample of 206 surveys.[26] The final subject pool included 96 women and 110 men. Most were pursuing a major in either IR or political science. The majority were US citizens, but citizens of twenty-nine other countries were also represented. In addition to US citizens, Latin Americans were also over-represented in the sample, which is unsurprising given the survey location at a university in Miami. Forty-five respondents reported holding dual citizenship, and one reported triple citizenship (in the United States, Colombia, and Argentina). The dataset was almost evenly divided between subjects describing the United States (104) and those describing other countries (102). Overall, the dataset contained at least one description for thirty-seven different countries, ranging from Argentina, Bangladesh, and Burkina Faso to the United States and Venezuela.

A primary objective of this survey was to refine the 199-item prototype ACL by removing items that were either redundant or not discriminant. Redundant items are those exhibiting a response pattern that correlates highly with that of other items in the survey. Non-discriminant items are those with a response pattern that is simply invariant: items on which nearly all subjects rate nearly all countries in the same way. This may happen because an item is not seen as relevant (in which case, it would often be ranked 3 on a five-point scale, neither characteristic nor uncharacteristic of the country being described), or it might happen for an item seen as characteristic (or uncharacteristic) of nearly all countries (e.g., *sovereign*). If the goal is to create a test capable of describing and discriminating among countries in general, items characteristic of only one or a very few countries are not good candidates for inclusion.

Because roughly half of the 206 surveys described the United States, analyzing the entire dataset would cause descriptions of just one country to dominate the results. I therefore drew a sample of up to two surveys for each country represented in the dataset, yielding a sample of fifty-six surveys describing thirty-seven countries.[27] I then examined the response patterns in two ways: (1) checking response patterns for each of the 199 test items and (2) checking the correlation of each item with the other 198 items in the test. Studying the subject ratings of each item revealed several prominent response patterns. Most desirable was a pattern of responses ranging from low to high. Such items function well to distinguish some countries from others. On items such as *authoritarian, central, efficient,* or *reckless,* for example, some countries were ranked low and others high. Items on which nearly all countries were ranked high (e.g., *unique*) or low (e.g., *innocent*) were not discriminant. As a rule of thumb, items on which fewer than 10 percent of the countries were placed at the scale's bottom (ranked 1 or 2) or top (ranked 4 or 5) were candidates for elimination.[28]

One other group of items exhibited a more specific response pattern that deserves special mention. As a group, many of these items described a region or religion. For these items, a high percentage of subjects gave scores of either 1 or 3—73 percent for *African* and *Arab,* 68 percent for *Asian,* and 79 percent for *Buddhist.* Some other items, such as *childish* (64 percent) and *imperialistic* (66 percent), also exhibited this pattern. One interpretation of the pattern is that these items, as a group, consist of categorical adjectives rather than adjectives whose meaning suggests a polar opposite and a scale between the two poles (i.e., scalar adjectives). Items such as *efficient* or *powerful* are scalar. Presumably, countries that are inefficient or weak can be ranked 1, efficient and powerful countries can be ranked 5, and other countries fall somewhere in between. A country that is not seen as *Asian* or *Buddhist* poses a scoring dilemma, however, since the opposite of these terms is unclear.[29] Should such countries be scored as 3 (neither Asian nor "anti-Asian") or as 1 (not at all Asian)? It is likely that subjects were unsure how to respond, and the inter-item correlations for categorical adjectives such as regional or religious descriptors support this explanation. Some subjects gave such countries a score of 1 (the item was "not at all characteristic"), whereas other subjects gave such countries a score of 3 (the item was "neither characteristic nor uncharacteristic"). Since each subject presumably followed a similar logic in ratings of other categorical adjectives, a spurious correlation emerged among these items. Subjects who rated a country (e.g., Venezuela) as 1 on *Asian* also rated it as 1 on *African* and *Middle Eastern.* Subjects who ranked it as 3 on one of these items tended to do so on the others. Thus, these test items were highly correlated. In fact, *Buddhist* actually correlated more highly with *Middle Eastern* (0.57) than with *Asian* (0.52). Although such items may be important as descriptors of certain countries, therefore, they are poor candidates for inclusion in a general ACL describing countries, given the likelihood that subjects will be confused about how to interpret them. If such items are included, a factor analysis will identify them as part of a common factor, when their covariance is more likely the result of differences across subjects in question interpretation. The resulting "factor," in other words, will depend on how subjects read the question rather than on what countries are like.

Checking the correlation matrix (Pearson's *r*) for each item against every other item in the test was useful for other reasons as well. Focusing on correlations of 0.70 or greater simplified the process of evaluating 39,601 inter-item correlations. Items with strong intercorrelations (e.g., *appealing*, *good*, and *positive*; μ Pearson's *r* = 0.73) indicated overlapping meaning. The items exhibiting such correlations with several other items were candidates for elimination, although at least one of the overlapping adjectives was always preserved. On the other hand, some items that one might have expected to correlate did not, such as *feminine* and *masculine* (0.06). In such cases, both items should be preserved in the test. Items were also reviewed for double meanings and other difficulties of interpretation. *Occupied*, for example, was rated 4 or 5 by 47 percent of subjects. This suggests that subjects may have been thinking not of military occupation (the intended meaning) but simply that the country was occupied by a (large) population. Another problematic class of items involved those whose placement at the low end of the scale involved a conceptual double negative. Rating a country as low on *indispensable* or *unknown* meant that it is "not indispensable" or "not unknown." Such potentially confusing double negatives made these items good candidates for removal. In general, for the same reason, positive items were preferable to negative items (e.g., *powerful* rather than *weak*).

After once completing this process of searching for items (expanding the ACL) and refining the list (contracting the ACL), I repeated the entire process, asking an even larger pool of 789 subjects to complete the survey in 2011 and 2012, using the same procedure as in the first round.[30] Removing surveys with missing data yielded a final pool of 675 surveys (330 from men and 343 from women, with two respondents not reporting gender). Of this pool, 325 surveys described the United States, and 350 described one of sixty-six other countries. As in the first round, Latin American countries (along with the United States) were overrepresented in the sample. In the second round, I sampled up to 5 surveys per country, yielding a final sample of 179 surveys and sixty-seven countries in all (including the United States). In this sample, nearly two-thirds (62 percent) of the surveys were completed by subjects who were either citizens of or born in the country surveyed. This sample is the basis for the principal components analysis and descriptive analysis reported in the next section.

The final result of this multistep procedure for test refinement is a 130-item General Country Adjective List (GCAL). As this terminology implies, the purpose of the GCAL is to provide a set of general descriptors for variations among countries. The list is ordered alphabetically, and responses are recorded, as noted earlier, using a five-point Likert scale. As with the development of any such test, it is important to be clear about what is being measured, and the term *country* is chosen with this need in mind. In this case—following in the tradition of research such as Hopf's and, more generally, scholarship on foreign policy images and role theory—the intent is to describe characteristics of the state as a corporate entity (including image, role, identity), not the characteristics of citizens or of entire peoples who constitute the populations of states and who may also constitute nations.[31] This is not a "national identity" checklist, therefore, if the term *nation* is understood as referring primarily to *people* or *citizens*. It might be considered a *state* identity checklist, but to name it such would invite confusion over whether only characteristics of governments are being measured or something more inclusive. Because the intent is more general, the term *country* seems most appropriate.

Preliminary Results

The remainder of this chapter applies the GCAL to two tasks—generalization about the key dimensions of difference among countries and descriptive observations about the image of selected countries—as a proof of concept, to illustrate the method's potential. Many other tasks could be imagined. In general, the GCAL might be used to explore people's image of their own country or of other countries. It might be used to compare the images held by different populations (different ethnic groups, different economic strata, etc.) or the ways in which such images change over time. And, in experimental settings, it might be used to investigate the ways in which people form images of countries (e.g., how different kinds of information or different information sources affect country images).

The analysis offered in this section is provisional for several reasons. First, the number of surveys (179) and the number of countries (67) are still too small to permit confident generalization (although a separate pool of 325 surveys is more than sufficient for the purpose of describing the United States).[32] Second, version 1 of the GCAL is still provisional. Ongoing efforts at test refinement will eventually lead to an improved version. Third, the demographic basis of the surveys is limited (to a sample of US undergraduates in Miami). In the future, translation of an instrument such as the GCAL into other languages and application to a wider variety of cultural, ethnic, and national settings will permit more robust generalizations about how people, in general, see differences among countries.

With these caveats in mind, however, the GCAL is already sufficiently developed to illustrate several of the uses to which it can be put. Some of the findings from this analysis appear to converge with the arguments advanced by role theorists concerned with foreign policy, image theorists, and constructivists exploring state identity. This convergence suggests that a factor solution to the dimensionality of country images is a real possibility, as with the emergence of the five-factor model of human personality.

Dimensions of Country Images

As a first step toward generalization about national differences, I performed a principal component analysis of the 179-case dataset describing sixty-seven countries from the second survey refinement round. Principal component analysis (PCA) resembles factor analysis—both are variable reduction techniques using matrix algebra to calculate eigenvectors—and yield similar results for many statistical purposes. Some scholars prefer PCA, however, for exploratory designs.[33]

Table 5.1 presents the results of a principal component analysis with a varimax-rotated factor solution. *Components* are clusters of variables that move together (covary), and the extent of this covariance is represented by the correlation of each item with the component.[34] *Eigenvalues* indicate the total amount of variance accounted for by each component (each axis of multidimensional variance identified by the PCA). Components with an eigenvalue greater than 1.0 are typically reported. In this analysis, however, twenty-five components exhibit eigenvalues greater than 1.0. Only five exhibit eigenvalues over 2.0. A *scree test* (a plot of components against their eigenvalues) shows a fairly straight line after component 5, indicating that the amount of variance accounted for by each additional component is gradually and smoothly declining. Table 5.1 shows the percentage of variance accounted for by each component (not the raw eigenvalues), as well as the correlations of selected GCAL items with each of these five components. Component 1 dominates the analysis and accounts for 21.7 percent of the total variance in the varimax-rotated solution. The next four components combined account for a further 18.5 percent of the variance, for a total of roughly 40 percent of the variance in survey responses. Although this leaves another 60 percent of variance unaccounted for by these first five components, it is useful to keep in mind that there are another 125 variables (items) in the GCAL. After the first five components, only a few items in the survey correlate highly with any other component. Put differently, countries can vary in many different ways, but there are only a few important clusters of covariance. These are shown, with tentative identifying labels, in table 5.1.

Labeling these clusters (components) necessarily involves a process of interpretation. Component 1 includes items such as *good, helpful, responsible, civilized, cooperative, fair,* and at the negative end *corrupt.* These items suggest a generally positive (or, at the other end of the scale, negative) orientation toward a country. Component 1 is thus labeled *Orientation.* High placement indicates a country toward which the subject is positively disposed (the country is seen as good, helpful, and fair), and low placement indicates a negative orientation toward the country. Overall, no fewer than fifty-five survey items correlate with component 1 (positively or negatively) at the 0.5 level or higher. At the 0.65 level, eighteen items correlate positively or negatively with component 1 (these are listed in table 5.1).[35] That *Orientation* emerges first in the PCA and that it accounts for so much of the variance suggests that it is the most important dimension of our judgments about other countries. This is unsurprising. We start by deciding whether we like or dislike another country.

Ten items correlate with component 2 at the 0.5 level or higher, including *dominant, powerful, competitive, aggressive, assertive,* and *forceful.* These items reflect aspects of state power or capacity, suggesting *Capabilities* as a label for component 2. High placement appears to indicate a country with considerable power or capacity to exert its will (some items associated with component 2—such as *assertive, angry,* and *arrogant*—seem to refer to this will). In general, component 2 appears to serve as a general metric of state power. The items *large* (0.435), *important* (0.396), and *developed* (0.335) also correlate positively with component 2; *poor* (–0.282) and *vulnerable* (–0.254) correlate negatively. Again, this seems unsurprising. Power is widely discussed in the literature on foreign policy images, and in the general literature on IR, as a crucial dimension of differences among states. For many realists, it is *the* crucial dimension of state difference.

Only two items correlate with component 3 at the 0.5 level or higher: *vibrant* and *emotional.* Items correlating at the 0.4 level or higher include *religious, warm, impulsive,* and *revolutionary.* Component 3 is harder to interpret than the first two components. The largest negative correlation (–0.255) is with *stable,* which suggests one interpretation: that component 3 distinguishes more volatile or unstable countries from those that are stable.

Table 5.1. Principle Component Analysis of GCAL Survey, Round 2 Data

Component	Item	Correlation	Item	Correlation
Component 1—"Orientation" (21.7% of variance)				
	048 Good	.793	098 Respected	.682
	051 Helpful	.743	033 Efficient	.675
	099 Responsible	.738	064 Loyal	.670
	013 Civilized	.724	028 Developed	.667
	104 Secure	.722	108 Stable	.660
	019 Cooperative	.711	052 Honest	.660
	039 Fair	.700	046 Generous	.651
	086 Peaceful	.699	027 Devastated	–.650
	121 United	.682	020 Corrupt	–.661
Component 2—"Capabilities" (7.7% of variance)				
	031 Dominant	.665	043 Forceful	.566
	089 Powerful	.649	005 Angry	.554
	015 Competitive	.626	004 Ambitious	.534
	003 Aggressive	.578	014 Complex	.534
	007 Assertive	.577	006 Arrogant	.509
Component 3—"Traditionalism" (5.0% of variance)				
	123 Vibrant	.515	037 Exotic	.431
	035 Emotional	.505	100 Revolutionary	.425
	096 Religious	.440	117 Traditional	.411
	128 Warm	.440	049 Grateful	.404
	055 Impulsive	.435	108 Stable*	–.255
Component 4—"Maturity" (3.0% of variance)				
	071 Naive	.509	060 Lazy	.416
	084 Passive	.473	072 Negligent*	.387
	058 Jealous	.428	093 Rational*	.057
Component 5—"Potential" (2.8% of variance)				
	030 Diverse	.535	125 Growing*	.389
	070 Multicultural	.499	130 Young*	.307
	034 Emerging	.414	117 Traditional*	–.357

Note: Varimax factor rotation; n = 179 (67 countries, maximum 5 cases per country); table includes components with eigenvalues greater than 2.0; table includes items with correlations ≥ .650 and ≤ –.650 (component 1), ≥ .500 (component 2), and ≥ .400 (components 3–5); asterisk (*) indicates item with correlation outside specified range, shown for illustrative purposes.

Volatile also correlates with component 3 at the 0.313 level. On the other hand, the items *religious* (0.440) and *traditional* (0.411) suggest a second interpretation: that component 3 distinguishes countries that have resisted modernity. Since the survey was conducted with subjects who were undergraduate students at a US university, items such as *vibrant* (0.515) and *exotic* (0.431) may be related to this interpretation, suggesting a contrast between the American university setting and the "exoticism" of countries that are not advanced, industrial, secular, and Western. Characterized by a traditional or religious orientation, warmth or vibrancy, and volatility, these states are premodern. It is hard to decide on the most appropriate label for such states, since it is easy to imagine several variants: countries that are deeply religious but also Western (Panama), countries that are poorly integrated into the modern state system (Papua New Guinea), countries characterized by religious conflict and volatility (Sudan), and so on. A larger study, carried out in different cultural and national settings, may lend greater clarity to component 3.[36] Provisionally, in table 5.1, it is labeled *Traditionalism*.

Four survey items correlate with component 4 at the 0.40 level or higher: *naïve*, *passive*, *jealous*, and *lazy*. The strongest correlation (0.509) is with *naïve*, suggesting a perceived lack of maturity or sophistication. *Negligent* (0.387) correlates with component 4 and, along with *naïve*, suggests that one might interpret this component as reflecting more or less *rational* countries. Certainly, there is precedent in the foreign policy literature for such distinctions: rogue states are often alleged to exhibit a deficit of just this quality.[37] Yet *rational* is an item in the GCAL and exhibits essentially no correlation (0.057) with component 4. If rationality is a quality that a country (or its leadership) may be perceived to have or lack, component 4 seems to reflect the extent to which a capacity for thoughtful and sophisticated action has been developed. This quality might be labeled *Maturity*.[38]

Finally, three items correlate with component 5 at the 0.40 level or higher: *diverse*, *multicultural*, and *emerging*. The first two of these play an important role in descriptions of the United States, as the next section will show, but *emerging* does not. Component 5 also describes states that are growing (0.389), young (0.307), and untraditional (−0.357 correlation with traditional). As with component 3, component 5 permits multiple interpretations: it may distinguish states that are comparatively young and multicultural, such as the United States, and those that are emerging and diverse, such as China, India, or Brazil. The modest positive correlation between *large* (0.235) and component 5 suggests that states such as these may have served partially as archetypes for this component, and size itself is likely to be associated with cultural diversity. Again, a larger study carried out in different settings may help to tease apart the "emergent" and "multicultural" qualities of states described by component 5. Provisionally, however, this combination of cultural diversity and capacity for growth might be labeled *Potential.*

Among the conclusions we might draw from this principal component analysis, two seem especially important. First, there is an evident family resemblance among several of the components in the analysis reported here, the dimensions identified in the literature on foreign policy images, and the dimensions implicit in foreign policy role theory. The first two dimensions identified by the PCA—*Orientation* and *Capabilities*—are essentially the same as Cottam's first two dimensions (*motivation* and *capabilities*).[39] Similarly, many of Holsti's national role conceptions could easily be arrayed along two dimensions reflecting state strength and orientation.[40] Cottam's third dimension, *decisional style*, also bears a strong resemblance to component 4, *Maturity*. And Cottam's fifth dimension, *domestic forces interaction*, which indicates tolerance and ideological pluralism, seems related to the qualities of diversity and multiculturalism within component 5, *Potential.* That there is a certain convergence among the PCA results and these other models is a hopeful indicator of scholarly progress.

Second, more generally, the emergence of readily interpretable components or factors from the PCA and their convergence with existing models of foreign policy images suggest that there is a certain underlying structure or dimensionality in our judgments about countries, just as in judgments about people. The key to the identification of the Big Five personality traits in psychology was not merely the identification of five factors, however, but their extensive replication across various tests and subject populations. Only time and additional research will tell whether or not a stable factor solution characterizes differences among countries as it does with people.

Profiling Countries

An instrument for measuring the various, general differences among countries, such as the GCAL, is indispensable to the task of determining whether or not there is an underlying structure or dimensionality to our judgments about countries. Yet a good general instrument can also be put to other uses, such as identifying the most salient qualities of a particular country image or comparing the images of selected countries. This section illustrates the latter sort of application, beginning with the image of the United States.

To derive a description of the United States using the GCAL, I employed another sample of the dataset consisting of all 325 survey responses describing the United States in round 2. Table 5.2 lists the GCAL items that subjects judged to be *most* characteristic of the United States (twenty-two items, scoring one standard deviation or greater above the mean) and those items judged to be *least* characteristic of the United States (another twenty-two items, scoring one standard deviation or greater below the mean). They can be grouped together, broadly, into four categories.

First, many of these items—for example, *developed, powerful, competitive, large, capable, important, dominant, leading, wealthy,* and *assertive*—suggest comparisons in terms of national capabilities and influence, ranking the United States high on the dimension *Capabilities*. The United States ranked at the low end of the scale for the items *vulnerable, exploited, subordinate, devastated,* or *poor*. This is not particularly surprising, since *Capabilities* emerged as one of the two most important dimensions of differences among countries in the PCA, and because of the status of the United States as the world's most powerful country economically and militarily.

Table 5.2. Items Most and Least Characteristic of the United States

Characteristic items (μ score ≥ 4.20)	μ score	Standard deviation	Uncharacteristic items (μ score ≤ 2.80)	μ score	Standard deviation
030 Diverse	4.79	0.55	101 Rural	2.73	1.13
028 Developed	4.78	0.63	072 Negligent	2.70	1.13
089 Powerful	4.74	0.60	094 Reckless	2.70	1.19
015 Competitive	4.72	0.62	071 Naive	2.68	1.23
059 Large	4.69	0.64	042 Feminine	2.68	1.07
009 Capable	4.69	0.59	074 New	2.67	1.38
054 Important	4.67	0.59	060 Lazy	2.66	1.33
070 Multicultural	4.67	0.71	073 Neutral	2.63	1.10
031 Dominant	4.65	0.71	023 Dangerous	2.57	1.29
004 Ambitious	4.63	0.66	037 Exotic	2.53	1.14
001 Active	4.61	0.64	127 Vulnerable	2.52	1.20
061 Leading	4.57	0.66	010 Careless	2.46	1.17
013 Civilized	4.46	0.75	038 Exploited	2.45	1.22
044 Free	4.33	0.94	106 Simple	2.41	1.10
032 Dynamic	4.33	0.82	102 Sacred	2.40	1.17
025 Democratic	4.32	0.90	111 Subordinate	2.37	1.06
098 Respected	4.24	0.97	058 Jealous	2.29	1.17
116 Tough	4.24	0.85	084 Passive	2.28	1.10
129 Wealthy	4.23	0.88	082 Outcast	2.18	1.14
007 Assertive	4.23	0.79	057 Isolated	1.90	1.17
021 Courageous	4.22	0.86	027 Devastated	1.82	0.99
056 Independent	4.21	1.18	088 Poor	1.79	1.00

While there was general agreement that the United States ranks high in terms of capabilities (component 2), it is noteworthy that comparatively few items in table 5.2 pertain to *orientation* (component 1). In fact, only one item that appears in table 5.1 as a constituent element of component 1 also appears in table 5.2: *civilized*. Other possibly relevant items in table 5.2 include *free*, *democratic*, *respected*, *courageous*, and *dangerous* (an uncharacteristic item). These items do correlate with component 1, but several (*free*, *democratic*, and perhaps *courageous*) seem specifically related to how the subject feels about US governmental institutions. In fact, since *Orientation* is a positional indicator of valence (describing how the subject feels about a given country, seen from the subject's own perspective), it is not surprising that component 1 figures less prominently in table 5.2.[41] Respondents may have different attitudes toward the United States, though presumably most will agree that it has high *capabilities*.

Two other components from the PCA (table 5.1) are also well represented in table 5.2: *Maturity* and *Potential*. With low scores on *naïve*, *lazy*, *jealous*, and *passive*, the United States is seen as relatively *mature*. A low score on *reckless* and a high score on *active* seem relevant to this dimension of the US image as a mature and rational state. High scores on *diverse* and *multicultural* describe a country with high cultural *potential* (component 5). As noted earlier, high placement of *large* may also relate to another aspect of US potential (or perhaps simply to its power and capabilities). That *diverse* and *multicultural* are so highly placed suggests, however, that subjects focused on a particular aspect of American potential, associated with its cultural diversity. Other descriptors relevant to potential—such as *young*, *growing*, or *emerging*—do not figure prominently in this profile of the United States, and *new* is one of the least characteristic items, even though the country might still be described by some as young.

The remaining component from the PCA, *Traditionalism*, is represented only by one item, *exotic*. That item is placed low rather than high, indicating a modern country rather than a traditional one. Low placement of *rural* and *sacred* also suggests an interpretation of the United States as secular and modern.

To this point, I have used the GCAL data to describe the United States in terms of the five components that emerged in the PCA: *Orientation*, *Capabilities*, *Traditionalism*, *Maturity*, and *Potential*. Yet we need not adhere slavishly to a five-factor framework, any more than personality theorists would argue that there are only five important distinctions among people. The PCA-derived model (tentatively) represents an underlying structure in judgments about countries, not an exhaustive list of every important way in which countries can differ. Paying less attention to the PCA, it seems evident that "cultural diversity" emerged as a salient characteristic of the United States for many subjects. Descriptions of US power, wealth, and institutions (democratic) also figure prominently. More generally, the overall pattern of item placement constitutes a profile of the United States that might be compared with profiles of other countries, to suggest the ways in which they resemble or differ from one another. The US profile offered in table 5.2 is also a profile based on responses from a subject pool composed overwhelmingly of US citizens. It might be compared, therefore, to profiles based on responses from citizens of other countries. One virtue of this approach, compared with more traditional public opinion surveys (e.g., those that ask about feelings toward a list of other countries), is that while the GCAL generates data that facilitate comparison, it permits respondents far greater subjectivity in identifying the points of comparison that they believe are important.

As a final example of how the GCAL can be applied, we might compare the profile of the United States in table 5.2 with a profile of another country. Because the survey was conducted in Miami, several Latin American countries were highly represented in the sample. One of these—Colombia—makes a good candidate for comparison. Colombia was described by sixty-three subjects, making it the most frequent object of the survey after the United States. Respondents included Hispanic US citizens of Colombian birth, non-Hispanic US citizens of US birth, Colombian citizens of Colombian birth, those holding dual or multiple citizenship (including Colombian citizenship), and non-Colombian citizens of non-Colombian birth. The data can be disaggregated, therefore, to show not only a contrast with the profile of the United States but also a contrast in the perspectives of Columbia held by, for example, Hispanic individuals of Colombian descent and non-Hispanic US citizens. Table 5.3 presents an abbreviated profile of Colombia from the perspective of Colombian citizens of Colombian origin; table 5.4 presents a profile from the perspective of US citizens of non-Hispanic US origin.

It is immediately apparent that whereas items referring to power and capabilities (component 2) dominated the US profile, these items are almost entirely absent among the most salient items (high or low) in the Colombian profile. Only one item, *secure*, appears partially relevant. Component 1 is represented by such items as *creative*, *friendly*, and *likeable*. *Authoritarian* and *outcast* are also placed low, reflecting the more institutional dimension of *Orientation* that was apparent in the US profile. Unsurprisingly, Colombian citizens thus express a positive *orientation* toward Colombia (table 5.3).

US citizens also express a positive *orientation* toward Colombia, placing *friendly* and *likable* high and *authoritarian* low, perhaps as a result of the two countries' comparatively good relations and close cooperation in the "war on drugs."

Component 3 is much better represented in tables 5.3 and 5.4, describing Colombia, than in table 5.2, describing the United States, with such items as *traditional, vibrant, religious,* and *exotic* placed high by both Colombian and US citizens. In this case, unlike component 1, respondents appear to see a sharp contrast between a more traditional and religious Colombia and a more modern and secular United States. Component 4, *Maturity,* is also well represented. In fact, the same four items that were ranked low indicating American *maturity*—*naïve, passive, lazy,* and *jealous*—were also ranked low by both Colombian and US citizens in their descriptions of Colombia. Respondents see both states as *mature.* Finally, whereas component

Table 5.3. Items Most and Least Characteristic of Colombia according to Colombian Citizens of Colombian Origin (n = 18)

Characteristic items (μ score ≥ 4.50)	μ score	Uncharacteristic items (μ score ≤ 2.30)	μ score
040 Familiar	4.67	104 Secure	2.28
022 Creative	4.61	060 Lazy	2.17
045 Friendly	4.61	082 Outcast	2.17
037 Exotic	4.56	010 Careless	2.06
096 Religious	4.56	074 New	2.06
123 Vibrant	4.56	008 Authoritarian	2.00
063 Likable	4.50	057 Isolated	1.72
081 Original	4.50	058 Jealous	1.72
117 Traditional	4.50	006 Arrogant	1.67

Table 5.4. Items Most and Least Characteristic of Colombia according to US Citizens of US Origin (n = 11)

Characteristic items (μ score ≥ 4.30)	μ score	Uncharacteristic items (μ score ≤ 2.50)	μ score
050 Growing	4.91	071 Naive	2.45
096 Religious	4.64	112 Superficial	2.45
079 Optimistic	4.55	008 Authoritarian	2.36
117 Traditional	4.55	084 Passive	2.36
123 Vibrant	4.55	060 Lazy	2.27
034 Emerging	4.55	010 Careless	2.09
045 Friendly	4.55	006 Arrogant	2.00
063 Likable	4.55	058 Jealous	1.81
014 Complex	4.36	057 Isolated	1.64

5, *Potential,* figured in Americans' descriptions of the US as *diverse* and *multicultural,* US citizens saw the other aspect of *potential,* represented by the items *growing* and *emerging,* in Colombia. Interestingly, Colombian citizens themselves did not place such items as high. This divergence might reflect somewhat greater pessimism on the part of Colombians themselves about their country's prospects for continued growth. Conversely, it may reflect a somewhat patronizing attitude on the part of US citizens or perhaps simply a lack of awareness of how much Colombia's internal security situation has improved since 2002, with the decline of the FARC (Fuerzas Armadas Revolucionarias de Colombia) and the ELN (Ejército de Liberación Nacional).[42]

The GCAL has considerable heuristic value in illuminating differences among countries and in providing a mechanism to translate subjective expressions of these differences (through a ranking of a general adjective checklist) into data that facilitates comparisons. Moreover, it also facilitates exploration of the ways in which different groups of people see different countries. There are doubtless far sharper contrasts to be found than in how Colombian citizens and US citizens see Colombia. It would be interesting, for example, to explore how US and Chinese citizens see their two countries or the ways in which South Korean images of Japan are evolving over time, with potentially dangerous consequences for their joint alliance with the United States.

Conclusion

As the study of country imagery has progressed from Kal Holsti's pathbreaking inductive studies to the development of Richard Cottam's deductive cognitive model of foreign policy images and then to more recent constructivist research on state identity, such as that popularized by Alexander Wendt and Ted Hopf, the field has gradually moved away from general models of roles or identity and toward contextually specific, historically bounded accounts of state identity, on one hand, and formalized models of state images, on the other.[43] Scholarship on the characteristics of the state has undoubtedly become more sophisticated. Like the well-worn parable of the blind men and the elephant, however, it has become more adept at describing the parts (national roles, state identities) without becoming appreciably more skilled at describing the creature in general.

In presenting several claims about how countries differ in general, along with a five-component framework for thinking about these differences, this chapter has sought to bring some order to the profusion of scholarship on state identity and images. Tracing the evolution of this scholarship suggests a certain convergence on judgments about capabilities and orientation, in particular, as being crucial to the images we form of other countries. Ultimately, however, whether people converge in the sorts of judgments they make about countries is an empirical matter, and this chapter outlines a broad strategy for investigating perceptions of countries. It does so out of two convictions: that methodology and ontology are productively bound up with each other in the study of such problems and that our perceptions of countries matter a great deal to the sorts of policies we advocate for our own country in its relations with others.

Notes

1. Ted Hopf, *Social Construction of International Politics: Identities and Foreign Policies, Moscow, 1955 and 1999* (Ithaca: Cornell University Press, 2002).

2. Ibid., 2.

3. Ibid., 3–4.

4. For an extended overview of research on state identity, see Rawi Abdelal et al., "Identity as a Variable," *Perspectives on Politics* 4.4 (2006): 695–711; Paul A. Kowert, "Foreign Policy and the Social Construction of State Identity," in *The International Studies Encyclopedia*, ed. Robert Denemark et al. (Oxford: Wiley-Blackwell, 2010), 2479–98.

5. See Kal J. Holsti, "National Role Conceptions in the Study of Foreign Policy," *International Studies Quarterly* 14.3 (1970): 233–309; Stephen G. Walker, "National Role Conceptions and Systemic Outcomes," in *Psychological Models in International Politics*, ed. Lawrence S. Falkowski (Boulder, CO: Westview, 1979), 169–210; Walker, *Role Theory and Foreign Policy Analysis* (Durham, NC: Duke University Press, 1987); Walker, *Role Theory and the Cognitive Architecture of British Appeasement Decisions: Symbolic and Strategic Interaction in World Politics* (New York: Routledge, 2013); Cameron G. Thies, *The United States, Israel, and the Search for International Order: Socializing States* (New York: Routledge, 2013). See also, *inter alia*, Lisbeth Aggestam, "Role Theory and European Foreign Policy: A Framework of Analysis," in *The European Union's Roles in International Politics: Concepts and Analysis*, ed. Ole Elgström and Michael Smith (London: Routledge, 2006), 11–29; Cristian Cantir and Juliet Kaarbo, "Contested Roles and Domestic Politics: Reflections on Role Theory in Foreign Policy Analysis and IR Theory," *Foreign Policy Analysis* 8, no. 1 (2012): 5–24; Martha Cottam and Chih-yu Shih, eds., *Contending Dramas: A Cognitive Approach to International Organization* (New York: Praeger, 1992); Sebastian Harnisch, Cornelia Frank, and Hanns Walter Maull, eds., *Role Theory in International Relations: Approaches and Analyses* (Abingdon: Routledge, 2011); David McCourt, "The Roles States Play: A Meadian Interactionist Approach," *Journal of International Relations and Development* 15, no. 3 (2012): 370–92; Naomi Wish, "Foreign Policy Makers and Their National Role Conceptions," *International Studies Quarterly* 24, no. 4 (1980): 532–54.

6. See Richard Cottam, *Foreign Policy Motivation: A General Theory and a Case Study* (Pittsburgh: University of Pittsburgh Press, 1977); Richard Herrmann, *Perceptions and Behavior in Soviet Foreign Policy* (Pittsburgh: University of Pittsburgh Press, 1985); Richard Herrmann and Michael Fischerkeller, "Beyond the Enemy Image and Spiral Model: Cognitive-Strategic Research after the Cold War," *International Organization* 49, no. 3 (1995): 415–50. Although Cottam does not cite Kenneth Boulding, the latter's classic study of images, or *eiconics,* is an important precursor to Cottam's work; see Kenneth Boulding, *The Image: Knowledge in Life and Society* (Ann Arbor: University of Michigan Press, 1956).

7. See Erik Ringmar, *Identity, Interest, and Action: A Cultural Explanation of Sweden's Intervention in the Thirty Years' War* (Cambridge: Cambridge University Press, 1996); Iver Neumann, *Uses of the Other: "The East" in European Identity Formation* (Minneapolis: University of Minnesota, 1999); Alexander Wendt, *Social Theory of International Politics* (New York: Cambridge University Press, 1999); Richard Ned Lebow, *The Politics and Ethics of Identity: In Search of Ourselves* (Cambridge: Cambridge University Press, 2012).

8. Hopf, *Social Construction of International Politics,* 10.

9. Cf. Gordon Allport, *Personality: A Psychological Interpretation* (New York: Holt, Rinehart, and Winston, 1937).

10. Carl G. Jung, *Psychological Types* (New York: Harcourt Brace, 1923). See also Isabel Briggs Myers, *Gifts Differing* (Palo Alto, CA: Consulting Psychologists Press, 1980); S. K. Hirsch, *Using the Myers-Briggs Type Indicator in Organizations: A Resource Book* (Palo Alto, CA: Consulting Psychologists Press, 1985).

11. S. R. Hathaway and J. C. McKinley, "A Multiphasic Personality Schedule (Minnesota): I. Construction of the Schedule," *Journal of Psychology* 10, no. 2 (1940): 249–54.

12. Harrison G. Gough, *California Psychological Inventory* (Palo Alto, CA: Consulting Psychologists Press, 1956).

13. See Harrison G. Gough, "The Adjective Check List as a Personality Assessment Research Technique," *Psychological Reports* 6, no. 1 (1960): 107–22; Harrison G. Gough and A. B. Heilbrun, *Adjective Check List Manual* (Palo Alto, CA: Consulting Psychologists Press, 1965).

14. See, e.g., Lewis R. Goldberg, "The Development of Markers for the Big-Five Factor Structure," *Psychological Assessment* 4, no. 1 (1992): 26–42.

15. See Donald Fiske, "Consistency of the Factorial Structures of Personality Ratings from Different Sources," *Journal of Abnormal and Social Psychology* 44, no. 3 (1949): 329–44; Paul T. Costa and Robert R. McCrae, "Age Differences in Personality Structure: A Cluster Analytic Approach," *Journal of Gerontology* 31, no. 5 (1976): 564–70; Robert R. McCrae and Oliver John, "An Introduction to the Five-Factor Model and Its Applications," *Journal of Personality* 60, no. 2 (1992): 175–215.

16. Goldberg, "Development of Markers"; Brent W. Roberts et al., "A Lexical Approach to Identifying the Lower-Order Structure of Conscientiousness," *Journal of Research in Personality* 38, no. 2 (2004): 164–78.

17. Paul T. Costa and Robert R. McCrae, *The NEO Personality Inventory Manual* (Odessa, FL: Psychological Assessment Resources, 1985).

18. Holsti, "National Role Conceptions."

19. See ibid., 256–60. Holsti drew on statements from the early 1960s in a few cases and from as early as 1957 in one case, Liberia.

20. Pursuing reliability in test construction does not entail a commitment to the argument that countries have any particular real or essential qualities or to positivism or scientific realism more generally. The qualities or images that we impute to countries may be socially constructed and historically contingent, but we may still wish to measure such subjective, socially embedded images.

21. Gough and Heilbrun, *Adjective Check List Manual*; Stephen H. Miller et al., "Factor Structure and Scale Reliabilities of the Adjective Check List across Time," *Journal of Consulting and Clinical Psychology* 46, no. 1 (1978): 189–91.

22. On countries as "people," see Alexander Wendt, "The State as Person in International Theory," *Review of International Studies* 30, no. 2 (2004): 289–316.

23. Roberts et al., "Lexical Approach"; Canadian Alliance of Life Skills Coaches and Associations, "Adjective Checklist," updated October 7, 2009, http://calsca.wordpress.com/adjective-checklist/.

24. I am deeply indebted to my graduate student, Saziye Burçu Giray, for her superb work performing this analysis. We sampled articles with titles suggesting that they pertained to the countries themselves and that were published between May 10 and October 15, 2010. We included news stories, letters to the editor, and opinion articles, omitting those of less than one hundred words and coding only the first two thousand words for long articles. In general, this sampling technique resulted in a large pool of articles for each country. The challenge, particularly for countries that are frequently in the news, was identifying articles about a country amid unrelated articles that simply happened to mention the country or events taking place within it. In one case, Australia, the sampling technique did not yield any usable articles. Overwhelmingly, the search results for Australia produced articles dealing with sports and local news but not with the country itself. For similar reasons, only four articles were obtained in one other case, Japan. In all other cases, if a given article contained no relevant adjectives, a replacement article was obtained, and this process was repeated until a total of five articles per country could be coded. We coded the content of these articles in the following manner. For each text, we compiled a list of all adjectives (the country is "small") and metaphors (the country is a "fighter") describing the country itself. Descriptions explicitly referring to the people, the government, or other specific aspects of the country were omitted, as were references to other countries (the country is "like Portugal"). We recorded only the first appearance of an adjective in a given article and did not record adjectives referring to countries other than the subject of the article.

25. This study was carried out in 2010 at Florida International University, an urban research university in Miami, Florida, with a student body of about fifty thousand. The student body is roughly 60 percent Hispanic and includes many international students, particularly from Latin America and the Caribbean.

26. Although the survey instructions asked subjects to rate adjectives about which they were unsure as 3 (the midpoint on a five-point Likert scale), fifty-eight subjects nevertheless failed to provide a response for one or more of the 199 items.

27. For the sample, I selected, by survey number, the dataset's first two surveys describing each country. Eighteen countries appeared only once in the resulting dataset, whereas nineteen countries appeared twice.

28. As a criterion for identifying nondiscriminant items, the 10 percent threshold was useful but not applied slavishly. For example, some items, such as *masculine* or *feminine,* seemed important to retain even though relatively few countries in this sample scored high or low on these terms. The results were not particularly sensitive to the use of different thresholds (e.g., 5 percent or 15 percent).

29. The adjective *pregnant* provides a good analogy. There is no scale meaningfully describing various degrees of "unpregnancy." Like *pregnant, Buddhist* does not lend itself to interpretation on a scale ranging from most to least characteristic.

30. Subjects were recruited in the same fashion as in round 1, from a pool of students in an introductory survey course on international relations at a large public university in Miami, Florida. Subjects were given the same instructions as in round 1, to describe a country (other than the United States) with which they were familiar (in which they had lived or to which they traveled frequently). They were asked to describe the United States if there was no alternative. Procedures for recording subject demographic data were updated to improve the accuracy of data on race, ethnicity, and citizenship.

31. Hopf, *Social Construction of International Politics.* For an early example of a similar technique, using adjective lists to describe characteristics of citizens, see D. Katz and K. Braly, "Racial Stereotypes of One Hundred College Students," *Journal of Abnormal and Social Psychology* 28 (1933): 280–90. See also, more recently, Nick Hopkins and Neil Murdoch, "The Role of the 'Other' in National Identity: Exploring the Context-Dependence of the National Ingroup Stereotype," *Journal of Community and Applied Social Psychology* 9, no. 5 (1999): 321–38.

32. There are various guidelines for the necessary number of cases, but two hundred is widely regarded as a desirable number, and fifty is sometimes suggested as an absolute minimum; see W. A. Arrindell and J. van der Ende, "An Empirical Test of the Utility of the Observations-to-Variables Ratio in Factor and Components Analysis," *Applied Psychological Measurement* 9, no. 2 (1985): 165–178. The subject-to-variable (STV) ratio is also used as a guideline for sample size, although a wide variety of STV ratios are reported in the literature, according to R. K. Henson and J. K. Roberts, "Use of Exploratory Factor Analysis in Published Research: Common Errors and Some Comment on Improved Practice," *Educational and Psychological Measurement* 66, no. 3 (2006): 393–416. Costello and Osborne find that roughly 85 percent of articles employing factor analysis and indexed by PsychINFO in a two-year period use a ratio of at least 2:1; see A. B. Costello and J. W. Osborne, "Best Practices in Exploratory Factor Analysis: Four Recommendations for Getting the Most from Your Analysis," *Practical Assessment Research and Evaluation* 10, no. 7 (2005): 1–9. This suggests a minimum sample size of 260 for a 130-variable test.

33. Whereas principal component analysis analyzes variance, exploratory factor analysis analyzes covariance; see James Dean Brown, "Principal Components Analysis and Exploratory Factor Analysis—Definitions, Differences, and Choices," *Shiken: JALT Testing and Evaluation SIG Newsletter* 13, no. 1 (2009): 26–30, http://jalt.org/test/PDF/Brown29.pdf. Follow-up research employing factor analysis is desirable, to produce better estimates of latent variables (factors).

34. In factor analysis, these correlations (with factors rather than *components*), are known by convention as *factor loadings.*

35. The levels of correlation necessary for inclusion in table 5.1 are indicated in the table legend and chosen to provide a manageable number of items for analysis. The fifty-five items correlating with component 1 at the 0.5 level or greater would be cumbersome to report and interpret. Only ten items correlate with component 2 and the 0.5 level or greater, only two items with component 2, and only one item each with components 4 and 5. In the latter cases, it makes sense to consider items correlating with the component at the 0.4 or even 0.3 levels. In PCA or factor analysis, correlations of over 0.7 are generally considered "high." Correlations above 0.4 or 0.5 are commonly reported in applied studies.

36. The relatively high percentage of Latin American countries in the survey may help to explain why component 3 blends religious traditionalism, volatility (or even revolutionary character), and perceived warmth or vibrancy.

37. K. P. O'Reilly, "Perceiving Rogue States: The Use of the 'Rogue State' Concept by U.S. Foreign Policy Elites," *Foreign Policy Analysis* 3, no. 4 (2007): 295–315.

38. The *Maturity* scale is reversed: high item scores indicate immaturity, and low scores indicate maturity.

39. Cottam, *Foreign Policy Motivation.* Richard Herrmann and Michael Fischerkeller later reformulated Cottam's two dimensions, as *orientation* and *capabilities*; see Herrmann and Fischerkeller, "Beyond the Enemy Image." Kenneth Boulding also identified essentially the same two dimensions in his study of state images (hostility vs. friendliness and strength vs. weakness); see Kenneth Boulding, "National Images and International Systems," *Journal of Conflict Resolution* 3, no. 2 (1959): 120–31.

40. Roles such as *regional leader*, *regional protector*, and *liberator* suggest high capabilities and a positive orientation. *Protectee* and *regional collaborator* suggest lesser capabilities. *Bastion of the revolution* and *anti-imperialist agent* may, at least from a Western perspective during the Cold War, suggest a more critical orientation toward the other. See Holsti, "National Role Conceptions."

41. On valence as a crucial element of constructivist theory, see Paul A. Kowert, "Completing the Ideational Triangle: Identity, Choice, and Obligation in International Relations," in *Psychology and Constructivism in International Relations: An Ideational Alliance*, ed. Vaughn P. Shannon and Paul A. Kowert (Ann Arbor: University of Michigan Press, 2011), 30–53.

42. On improvements in Colombia's internal security, see Audrey Kurth Cronin, *How Terrorism Ends: Understanding the Decline and Demise of Terrorist Campaigns* (Princeton, NJ: Princeton University Press, 2009).

43. Holsti, "National Role Conceptions"; Cottam, *Foreign Policy Motivation*; Wendt, *Social Theory of International Politics*; and Hopf, *Social Construction of International Politics.*

PART 2

Formal and Computational Methods

CHAPTER 6

Computing Narratives

Assemblage Relations in Diplomatic Conversations

DAVID SYLVAN

My purpose in this chapter is to propose a formal methodology for analyzing diplomatic conversations. That methodology, which, different from much other social science work on sequences, involves computing the ways in which narratives are assembled, is particularly appropriate for the kinds of constitutive questions asked by constructivist scholars in International Relations (IR). My specific research proposition is that conversations have discernible narrative features and that we can formalize those features (building on existing work in the field of conversation analysis) to shed light on significant aspects of the social relation between interlocutors. I apply this proposal to diplomatic conversations, giving a "who influences whom" analysis of two such conversations involving US presidents and UK prime ministers. The chapter concludes with brief thoughts on the potential benefits for scholars of IR in using this methodology.

Narrative Analysis and Assemblage

A striking characteristic of social life is that it both unfolds and is recalled in sequential form. By this, I mean not simply that events are indexed temporally (e.g., A happened at 9.00 and B at 11.00) but that they seem to exhibit a necessary ordering: either A's occurrence is necessarily followed by B's, or B's occurrence implies that A's must necessarily have already happened.[1] Moreover, B is not usually the end of the story, so the A-B sequence will customarily be part of a longer sequence involving events C, D, and so forth. Such sequences are not only considerably easier to remember than collections of events unordered temporally but are arguably one of the principal means by which participants recount—and perhaps even understand at the moment—the events in which they are involved.

The Specificity of Narratives

Many sequences are ordered far more than as a set of before-and-after relations between pairs of events. When we say that a sequence is made up of more than two events, we are saying something about a feeling of incompleteness if the sequence were to be terminated after the second event. Much in the way that melodies in Western tonal music are expected to resolve, sequences being recounted are expected to arrive at a natural ending point. Of course, life goes on, and other events will follow, but those later events represent some sort of a shift to a new (or expanded) sequence. Sequences, in other words, are quite often apprehended as narratives.[2]

The difference between sequences in general and narrative sequences in particular can best be seen by a stylized example. Take a five-element nonnarrative sequence S: A-B-C-D-E, and a five-element narrative sequence N: U-V-W-X-Y. Both of these sequences display necessary ordering relations, so that any two consecutive elements will be linked: C, for example, might only occur if B did earlier, and D might occur only if C did. What N has that S does not is a sense of completeness, or closure: there can be no sixth element Z, at least not without turning N into something else. By the same token, there can be no element T preceding U, again not without turning N into something else. Thus U is an opening element, and Z is a closing one (e.g., "there was once a king whose wife gave birth to a son" and "the son blinded himself"); this is one of the ways in which N is a structured whole.[3]

In effect, I am proposing a distinction between three types of sequences: (1) temporally indexed arrangements, in which the order of events matters but in which the elements are not related to each other in a causal or entailment fashion; (2) historical sequences, in which events cause subsequent events or are entailed by preceding ones; and (3) narrative sequences, in which the arrangement of events evokes a sense of closure. This distinction corresponds roughly to Hayden White's tripartite division of historical representation into annals, chronicles, and "proper" histories.[4]

A note on terminology is needed before proceeding further. Much work in sociology and, separately, in political science often goes under the heading of narrative analysis. Accepting the above distinction, these otherwise disparate approaches should be characterized as the analysis of historical sequences. Thus the pioneering studies by Andrew Abbott, Peter Abell, and David Heise and his colleagues are each concerned, in different ways, with causal entailment relations between consecutive pairs of events.[5] Similarly, political science work on "analytic narratives" and on conflict "trajectories" is primarily concerned with causal entailment relations.[6] Sociologists and political scientists who use the term *narrative* in their work mostly do not study narratives as structured wholes, analyzable as assemblage relations (see below).[7]

Narratives and Computation

What are some of the characteristics of narratives, as events arranged to evoke a sense of closure, that is, as structured wholes? There are a number of possibilities, ranging from the types of agents (characters) to the topics dealt with over and over (themes). We can, à la Aristotle, talk about plot trajectories (e.g., *peripeteia*) or genres; alternatively, we can, à la Labov, talk about evaluation (akin to point of view). Regardless of which characteristics we focus on, that focus can be exemplified in a narrative label, with the apprehending of the label used to reproduce at least the main lines of the narrative. In other words (to anticipate the argument below), narrative closure (as a well-formed and self-contained sequence) implies that sequential relations can be put into correspondence with a label, much as a mathematical function brings into correspondence arguments and a value.

Interestingly, many labels are actually components of narratives. A classic example comes from the frames of Marlow's story about Kurtz in Joseph Conrad's *Heart of Darkness*. The inner frame begins,

> The sun set; the dusk fell on the stream, and lights began to appear along the shore. The Chapman lighthouse, a three-legged thing erect on a mud-flat, shone strongly. Lights of ships moved in the fairway—a great stir of lights going up and going down. And farther west on the upper reaches the place of the monstrous town was still marked ominously on the sky, a brooding gloom in sunshine, a lurid glare under the stars.
>
> "And this also," said Marlow suddenly, "has been one of the dark places of the earth."

The final paragraphs of the novella conclude,

> "I heard a light sigh, and then my heart stood still, stopped dead short by an exulting and terrible cry, by the cry of inconceivable triumph and of unspeakable pain. 'I knew it—I was sure!' . . . She knew. She was sure. I heard her weeping; she had hidden her face in her hands. It seemed to me that the house would collapse before I could escape, that the heavens would fall upon my head. But nothing happened. The heavens do not fall for such a trifle. Would they have fallen, I wonder, if I had rendered Kurtz that justice which was his due? Hadn't he said he wanted only justice? But I couldn't. I could not tell her. It would have been too dark—too dark altogether. . . ."
>
> Marlow ceased, and sat apart, indistinct and silent, in the pose of a meditating Buddha. Nobody moved for a time. "We have lost the first of the ebb," said the Director, suddenly. I raised my head. The offing was barred by a black bank of clouds, and the tranquil waterway leading to the uttermost ends of the earth flowed somber under an overcast sky—seemed to lead into the heart of an immense darkness.

Marlow both starts and ends his account with the word *dark*, and the unnamed narrator of the outer frame does the same, glossing first London and then the sea as marked by "brooding gloom" and "the heart of an immense darkness." In this way and with great artistry, Conrad furnishes a label that adumbrates and summarizes the novella's theme.[8]

It might be objected that we are dealing here with high art and that people simply do not bother including labels in their narratives in everyday life. That view, I think, is mistaken. Consider a narrative elicited and reproduced by William Labov in his famous early work on narrative analysis.

> (Did you ever have a feeling, or a premonition, that something was gonna happen, and it did happen?) Yes I did. (Tell me about it.)
>
> I was goin' with a girl, one time; we were layin' on a bed—we weren't doin' anything, we were talkin'—and, I don't know, I looked into her face, and I saw, like, horns coming out of her head. You know. You know—like—I said, "You look like the devil!"
>
> She said, "What do you mean, I look like the devil? Don't kid around."
>
> I said "I'm not kiddin'. I saw horns comin' out of your head."
>
> And the girl got very angry, and walked out. But we got together, and we went together about four months.

> And, like, this girl tried to put me in a couple of tricks. Like she tried to get some boys to hurt me. You know. And she was a devil.
>
> So, now, anything I see I believe it's gonna happen.[9]

Labov supplies a label in his question, and the respondent not only recounts a narrative but finishes it off quite nicely with exactly the same label ("gonna happen"). Arguably, only the very shortest stories, recounted by the very youngest children (e.g., the one analyzed by Sacks),[10] lack such labels.

The presence of a label suggests that a particular sequence is a narrative; but it does not, in itself, shed any light on how the individual elements in the sequence are connected to each other. In fact, as indicated above, the mode of connection will depend on which aspect of the narrative, as a whole, is of interest. If the focus is on a presumed goal of the plot (as is the case in many of Propp's folktale types), successive elements must move in the direction of the goal, provide impedances that are overcome, or perhaps provide information (on character, say) that will help move toward the goal. If, instead, we focus on a narrative's theme or point of view, successive elements must each illustrate a hitherto unmentioned dimension of the theme or point of view. Notice that none of these modes of connection is causal in nature; without denying that some of the consecutive elements in a recounted narrative are connected causally,[11] they are not—and cannot be—what gives the narrative its status as a complete whole.[12] Rather, we are looking for consecutive elements to share both the hypothesized overall aspect of the narrative and some situational semantics (e.g., if the narrative is posited to have a theme of, say, self-sacrifice, an element describing a mother sacrificing her life to save her child would not be seen as connected to a following element of a man giving his dining companion his dessert—unless, of course, the overall aspect of the narrative is authorial irony).[13]

I am claiming that the way in which a narrative is put together on a microlevel—the way in which particular elements are linked to preceding or following ones—mirrors the narrative's overall aspect. Here, two points are worth making. First, we are speaking about two types of relations: (1) the linkage between elements and (2) the relation between the linkages and the overall aspect. The linkage between elements is, as pointed out above, not a relationship of causality; rather, it is a mode of assembly. Similarly, the mirroring of linkages and overall aspect is one of wholeness, not one of cause and consequence: a narrative whose linkages are at odds with its claimed label is at best a poorly constructed narrative. In this sense, the relationships that give a narrative its sense of closure are constitutive: they define those specific elements, related to each other in that specific way, as a specific narrative.

Second, the *constitutive relations* by which narratives are composed can be thought of as akin to mathematical functions that take component elements as "arguments" (think, crudely, of inputs) and, by bringing those elements into some type of arrangement (this is the "structure," whether sequential or otherwise), generate as a "value" (think, crudely, of an output) the particular phenomenon of interest, whether that phenomenon is an algebraic term or a *social fact*, such as a fair election.[14] Note that when functions are calculated for particular instances of the arguments (e.g., $y=x^2$ for $x=3$ or a fair election when only a handful of people vote), the calculation involves engaging in a specific, predefined action. That action, in turn, is mechanical, involving the manipulation of symbols, whether by a person or a machine; as such, it is a "computation."[15] In fact, any constitutive relation can be represented as a function that, in turn, can be "evaluated" computationally.[16] Thus, for narratives, we can cast the aspect of a narrative (e.g., goal, theme, point of view) as a function of multiple assemblage relations between individual elements; by evaluating assemblage relations for a specific candidate narrative,[17] we can make empirical claims about the existence of evidence of a particular aspect of the candidate. For example, if we hypothesize that particular sequential elements are key parts of a narrative in which an important aspect is the hero's accomplishing of almost impossible tasks, we should find numerous paired elements along these lines (task + accomplishment), as well as a general label about the hero accomplishing tasks. Indeed, by coding each pair of elements in the candidate narrative, we can check not only whether the elements jointly compose a narrative of that sort but when the narrative proper begins and ends.

Narratives and Constructivism

Since the assemblage relations by which narratives are constituted are a particular type of structured social facts, it follows that the computation of those assemblage relations could be of relevance to constructivists. I make this claim not so much because constructivist theories spend much time on narrative analysis[18] but, rather, because a key claim for many constructivist writers is that social facts are structured—that is, arranged in a patterned fashion, with the patterns having important generative implications for interactions between the units being studied. As Wendt put it, a structure is "a set of internally related elements," with the internal relations of a structure comprising one or more "possible transformations or combinations of its elements."[19] One of the most frequently cited instances of this structured quality of social facts is "anarchy"; the claim made by some of the early constructivists is that the absence of an explicitly acknowledged central authority is compatible with more than one set of interaction relations among states.[20] In the terminology introduced above, we could rewrite this claim as a functional relationship between alternative sets of interaction patterns, on the one hand, and the social fact "anarchy," on the other.

The focus on social facts as structured goes back to at least one of the antecedents of the early constructivists, the work of British "new social realists" such as Roy Bhaskar, Anthony Giddens, and Rom Harré (although less often cited, Harré's work profoundly influenced both Bhaskar and Giddens).[21] As Bhaskar put it in a review article published at a time when the new social realists had been taken on board in the United Kingdom but before IR constructivism had really gotten off the ground, "society itself is a social product"; that is, "social forms" (equal to particular social structures) are dependent on activity and relational in character.[22] Because, as we have seen, narratives are one ubiquitous type of social form, the study of their assemblage could be a constructivist project.

Research Proposition: Conversations as Narratives

When one thinks of narratives, particularly in IR, one thinks of the stories recounted by statesmen in speeches and memoirs, as well as the histories crafted by political scientists, biographers, and historians to explain state interactions, policy decisions, and the creation of international institutions. I propose, however, that we cast the net further afield and compute the assemblage relations of a very different type of verbal product, diplomatic conversations. A priori, since conversations unfold in real time between at least two interlocutors, they would not seem to be good candidates for narrative analysis. In this section, I argue the contrary.

When Harvey Sacks began the systematic study of conversations some fifty years ago, he quickly realized that even though they were unscripted and involved actors with quite different agendas who often jumped from one topic to another, they were, nonetheless, highly structured.[23]A recent textbook on the subject glosses the issue by beginning with a snippet of conversation held between a husband and wife after two old friends, who had stayed the night, left.

01 Ann: That was fun,
02 (0.4)
03 Jeff: mm
04 Ann: ish.[24]

Ann begins the conversation with an evaluative description. Jeff, who might be expected to respond with a phrase or sentence, is silent for almost half a second, then produces a noncommittal sound, which leads Ann to modify her statement significantly.

The conversation between Ann and Jeff has several notable characteristics. First, it is collaborative. Even though the participants do not necessarily agree, each works with the other. Ann, as the first speaker, is silent while Jeff is supposed to respond; Jeff, needing to respond, finally makes a sound, to which Ann, in turn, responds by a new utterance. Each conversationalist, in his/her sounds and his/her silences, opens a space for the other to respond and does not (normally) intrude on the other when it is his/her turn for the response. Second, the conversation involves semantic and pragmatic connections between the utterances, with responses having to be locally (at that moment) relevant: Jeff could have said no or yes, but if he had instead started talking about the cat or a bank loan, it would likely have been apprehended by Ann as an attempt to avoid coming down on one side or the other of her opening characterization. Conversational turns therefore point both forward and backward (every utterance or silence is linked pairwise to its predecessor and its successor; the term for such linked elements is *adjacency pair*), and the conversation can only be sustained as long as each participant keeps up that pointing. Third, the conversation is highly indexical: no one besides the participants would know, merely on reading the transcript, that the word *that* referred to the friends' visit rather than to something else (a film? dinner?), which is why conversational continuity—of necessity, unscripted—is a genuine, if unremarkable, achievement.[25]

This continuity has aspects of structural wholeness. For example, in the Ann-Jeff conversation, Ann's "ish" comment not only is a response to Jeff's immediately preceding silence and noncommittal sound but modifies her initial characterization—now separated from the modification by Jeff's turn. Similarly, all three turns are about the same topic, the evaluation of the friends' visit. It could be objected that the snippet is so short that its wholeness is not much of an achievement, but participants often construct much longer conversations as wholes through various sequential mechanisms.[26] One particularly noteworthy way of tying together conversations is via closings, that is, deliberately bringing conversations to an end by such means as recapitulation or bounding of earlier topics.[27] Some of these closings strongly resemble labels as that term was used above for narratives. Computationally, this implies that one can specify various whole-creating assemblage relations across a conversation's adjacency pairs and then assess the apprehension of that generated whole by the participants' labels for what they had just gone through.

Obviously, brief conversations or brief conversational segments may not occasion the explicit closings in which participants label what they have just been going through. Sometimes, the closings may be nonverbal, such as a gesture or a nod of the head; at other times, they may be too short to contain a detailed label ("OK"; "Well"). Nonetheless, to a very significant degree, participants in even brief, unscripted conversations, whether between strangers or old friends, often provide labels that arguably summarize the microassemblage relations in which they have just been engaged. For this reason, in line with the spirit, if not the letter, of much work in conversation analysis, a computational approach to conversational assemblage relations seems warranted.[28] If the conversations are high-level diplomatic interactions, which presumably are scripted for each participant (though without guarantees that the interlocutor will abide by the script), then labeling (and hence my proposal on computing assemblage in a way akin to narratives) seems quite plausible. To see if it is, I now turn to some examples.

Diplomatic Conversations

One of the virtues of electrical means of voice communication is that they permit third parties to listen in (perhaps at the time, perhaps to a recording) and thereby produce a fairly accurate and detailed transcript of what was said. As an information source, this is far superior to the memoranda of conversation regularly produced in foreign ministries and embassies. Moreover, and luckily for the scholar, top leaders tend to be sufficiently paranoid that they routinely make it possible for their conversations to be transcribed (e.g., both Richard Nixon and Henry Kissinger regularly had their phone conversations, including with each other, listened to and transcribed by their subordinates), which has meant that an enormous cache of materials has now begun to make its way into the public domain.

It might immediately be objected that such transcripts are next to worthless as a report on what policies leaders actually followed. The standard putdowns of this sort are "lies" or "cheap talk,"[29] and there is certainly a kernel of truth to that criticism—even if these conversations are behind closed doors and even if saying something that turns out to be untrue reduces a leader's credibility in the eyes of his/her peers. (For that matter, documents can be classified, misplaced, redacted or destroyed; conversations can be not committed to paper; and journalists can be spun, if not downright lied to. In other words, there is no privileged access point to a knowledge of *wie es eigentlich gewesen*.) However, the point of analyzing conversations is not to get a better idea of a government's secret policies but to understand what leaders were agreeing or disagreeing on and how much one deferred to another. By analyzing conversations, one might shed some light on such phenomena as partnership, adversarial relations, or power.

In the following examples, I summarize a "who influences whom" analysis of two diplomatic conversations. For each conversation, I begin by briefly giving the background, then a transcript of the actual words. That transcript includes, in square brackets, the results of a manual parse of illustrative portions of the conversation, with conversational turns labeled as argumentative speech acts.[30] I then count the number of argumentative speech acts used by each interlocutor, calculate the most common pair(s) of those acts in the conversation, and see whether that most common pair is, as per the above research proposition, reflected in the label of the conversation as a whole.

In this method, identifying the assemblage relations constitutive of a conversation's narrative and, computing the conversational label from those relations are straightforward tasks: the most common pair of speech acts is taken as the function's input and matched against the label for the conversation as a whole.[31] Of course, we can imagine far more complicated assemblage relations, but in the case of diplomatic conversations, where at least one of the leaders has clear points that she/he wants to make, a focus on the most frequent speech acts is reasonable, especially as a way to start analyzing who influences whom.

Example 1: Reagan and Thatcher, Grenada, 1983

My first example is drawn from a conversation between Ronald Reagan and Margaret Thatcher a day after US troops intervened in the former British colony of Grenada. Reagan had cabled Thatcher on the eve of the intervention, indicating that he was thinking of sending troops; a few hours later, he sent her a follow-up cable saying that he had decided to intervene. Thatcher, who had been working on a draft reply after the first cable, immediately reworked it and dispatched it after receiving Reagan's second message. In her telegram, she argued that intervention was both unjustified and likely to have negative consequences. She then followed up her cable with a phone call to Reagan (by then, it was shortly after midnight in London), urging him to take seriously her written message. Reagan promised to do so but was fairly clear that he had reached the point of no return, a position he reiterated in another cable sent some half a dozen hours later. The day went on, fighting occurred, and the next day, in the afternoon, Reagan telephoned Thatcher, starting their conversation by joking that if he were there, he would throw his hat in the door before he entered. He then stated that he regretted any embarrassment US actions had caused to the British government because of the secrecy of US military planning. After a somewhat lengthy recitation of events, the conversation continued as follows:

01 Prime Minister Thatcher: I know about sensitivity, because of the Falklands. That's why I would not speak for very long even on the secret telephone to you. Because even that can be broken. I'm very much aware of sensitivities. The action is underway now and we just hope it will be successful. [CHALLENGE]

02 President Reagan: We're sure it is. It's going beautifully. . . . They turned out to be a military command and the opposition that still remains, as the last word we have here—in about three spots on the Island—is led by these Cubans. They are the leading combat forces, not the Grenadian forces. We have captured 250 of them already. [RESPONSE TO CHALLENGE; INVERSION OF EVALUATION]

03 Prime Minister Thatcher: Well let's hope it's soon over Ron, and that you manage to get a democracy restored. [REITERATION; INVERSION OF EVALUATION]

04 President Reagan: We're very hopeful that it is going to be short and then your role is going to be very critical, as we all try to return Grenada to democracy under that constitution that you left them. [REVISION OF RESPONSE TO CHALLENGE; RESPONSIBILITY SWITCH] . . .

05 President Reagan: . . . We know that you and through the Queen's Governor General there—all of us together—can help them get back to that constitution and a democracy. [RESPONSIBILITY SWITCH]

06 Prime Minister Thatcher: I just hope Ron, that it will be very soon and that they will manage to put together a government which can get back to democracy. [REITERATION; RESPONSIBILITY SWITCH]

07 President Reagan: Those people on those other islands are pretty remarkable. [PARTIAL AGREEMENT; RESPONSIBILITY SWITCH] . . .

08 President Reagan: . . . We want to put them out ahead in helping with the restoration of a government, so there will be some taint of big old Uncle Sam trying to impose a government on them. [RESPONSIBILITY SWITCH]

09 Prime Minister Thatcher: There is a lot of work to do yet, Ron. [SIDESTEP; RESPONSIBILITY SWITCH]

10 President Reagan: Oh yes. [PARTIAL AGREEMENT; TRYING TO CLOSE]

11 Prime Minister Thatcher: And it will be very tricky. [REITERATION; CHANGE IN EVALUATION]

12 President Reagan: We think that the military part is going to end very shortly. [TOPIC SHIFT; TRYING TO CLOSE]

13 Prime Minister Thatcher: That will be very, very good news. And then if we return to democracy that will be marvellous. [REITERATION; INVERSION]

14 President Reagan: As I say, I'm sorry for any embarrassment that we caused you, but please understand that it was just our fear of our own weakness over here with regard to secrecy. [TOPIC SHIFT; APOLOGY]

15 Prime Minister Thatcher: It was very kind of you to have rung, Ron. [COURTEOUS NONACCEPTANCE][32]

For Reagan, the most common speech act in this conversation is RESPONSIBILITY SWITCH (four instances; he carries out no other speech act more than twice); for Thatcher, it is REITERATION (five instances; she carries out no other speech act more than twice). The closing (which, per the argument above, is presumed to be the label given by the interlocutors to the conversation as a whole) is APOLOGY (Reagan), COURTEOUS NONACCEPTANCE (Thatcher).[33] Although this is not an exact match to the pair RESPONSIBILITY SWITCH (Reagan), REITERATION (Thatcher), it is compatible with it: in both cases, we see Reagan proposing something to Thatcher (for most of the conversation, Reagan is attempting to get the British to help out or at least to sympathize with the US action), only to be rebuffed by her. Indeed, what is interesting about the conversation is how a superpower, dominant in its own region and able to take the military initiative, is nonetheless unable to persuade a supposedly close ally to lend it support, a finding reflected in a lopsided Security Council vote the next day.[34] Formal analysis of the conversation thus sheds light on limits to international power relations, limits usually scanted in the scholarly literature.

Example 2: Blair and Bush, G-8, 2006

A second example comes from a conversation held during the G-8 meeting in the summer of 2006. It was captured by an open microphone when Tony Blair walked over to where George Bush was eating lunch. My focus here is on the portion of the conversation that bore on the Middle East: the summit issued a statement in support of Kofi Annan's efforts; Blair, who wanted more to be done, proposed dealing with the Israel-Hezbollah conflict by sending an international force, then offered himself as an envoy. In the press commentary (see below), Blair was widely ridiculed for the way he stood behind Bush (who was munching on a roll at the time) and was spoken to by the latter (Bush began the conversation, "Yo, Blair. How are you doing?" Bush later mentioned his presumption that Blair himself had picked out a gift sweater for Bush, which led to a gushing response by Blair).

1 President Bush: What about Kofi? [inaudible] His attitude to ceasefire and everything else . . . happens. [PROPOSAL]

2 Prime Minister Blair: Yeah, no I think the [inaudible] is really difficult. We can't stop this unless you get this international business agreed. [DISAGREE; ALTERNATIVE]

3 President Bush: Yeah. [NONCOMMITTAL; WAITING]

4 Prime Minister Blair: I don't know what you guys have talked about, but as I say I am perfectly happy to try and see what the lie of the land is, but you need that done quickly because otherwise it will spiral. [REITERATION; PROPOSAL]

5 President Bush: I think Condi is going to go pretty soon. [NONCOMMITTAL; ALTERNATIVE]

6 Prime Minister Blair: But that's, that's, that's all that matters. But if you . . . you see it will take some time to get that together. [PARTIAL DISAGREEMENT; REITERATION]

7 President Bush: Yeah, yeah. [NONCOMMITTAL; WAITING]

8 Prime Minister Blair: But at least it gives people . . . [PARTIAL DISAGREEMENT; REITERATION]

9 President Bush: It's a process, I agree. I told her your offer to . . . [NONCOMMITTAL; TRYING TO CLOSE]

10 Prime Minister Blair: Well . . . it's only if I mean . . . you know. If she's got a . . . , or if she needs the ground prepared as it were. . . . Because obviously if she goes out, she's got to succeed, as it were, whereas I can go out and just talk. [PARTIAL DISAGREEMENT; REITERATION]

11 President Bush: You see, the irony is that what they need to do is to get Syria, to get Hezbollah to stop doing this shit and it's over. [SIDESTEP; ALTERNATIVE]

12 **Prime Minister Blair:** [inaudible]
13 **President Bush:** [inaudible]
14 **Prime Minister Blair:** Syria. [REITERATION]
15 **President Bush:** Why? [QUESTION; WAITING]
16 **Prime Minister Blair:** Because I think this is all part of the same thing. [PARTIAL DISAGREEMENT; REITERATION]
17 **President Bush:** Yeah. [NONCOMMITTAL; WAITING]
18 **Prime Minister Blair:** What does he think? He thinks if Lebanon turns out fine, if we get a solution in Israel and Palestine, Iraq goes in the right way . . . [BUTTRESSING OPINION; REITERATION]
19 **President Bush:** Yeah, yeah, he is sweet. [NONCOMMITTAL; TOPIC SHIFT]
20 **Prime Minister Blair:** He is honey. And that's what the whole thing is about. It's the same with Iraq. [PARTIAL AGREEMENT; REITERATION]
21 **President Bush:** I felt like telling Kofi to call, to get on the phone to Assad and make something happen. [SIDESTEP; ALTERNATIVE][35]

For Blair, the most common speech act is REITERATION of his proposal to visit the Middle East as an envoy (eight instances); second is PARTIAL DISAGREEMENT with Bush's alternative of Condoleezza Rice going to the region (five instances); Blair carries out no other speech act more than once. For Bush, the most common speech act is NONCOMMITTAL with respect to Blair's proposal (six instances); second is WAITING for Blair to give better arguments or give up on his idea (four instances); third is ALTERNATIVE of sending Rice (three instances); Bush carries out no other speech act more than twice. Since the conversation was cut off, there is no closing supplied by the interlocutors; instead, we need to look at press accounts to label the conversation as a whole. In fact, there is unanimity on the label (REITERATED PROPOSAL [Blair], REITERATED NONACCEPTANCE [Bush]), with media commentary emphasizing Blair's self-imposed and serial humiliation.[36] Although this is not an exact match to the pair (REITERATION [Blair], NONCOMMITTAL [Bush]) or to some other pairing of the top two or three instances by each speaker, it again is compatible with the top pairing and most of the other combinations.

To say that Blair's inability to influence Bush is simply part and parcel of a more general weakness of junior partners as compared with senior ones, particularly superpowers, somewhat misses the local dynamics of the conversation between the two leaders. Bush never flat out says no to Blair (just as Thatcher never explicitly rejects Reagan's ideas); Blair, who was of course a very skilled politician, takes advantage of Bush's reaction to push his idea over and over again, each time putting a slightly different spin on it. In the end, that Blair was a close ally of Bush and loyally supported him, including on the Israel-Hezbollah conflict, meant that Bush at least had to listen to Blair, an action that foreshadowed the drafting of an eventual cease-fire resolution the following month. In this sense, once again, formal analysis illuminates more of the subtleties of international power relations than either structural accounts or press commentary.

So What?

The computations summarized for the two conversations above lend support to the proposal made earlier that diplomatic conversations, at the very least, display modes of assemblage strongly akin to narratives. But what does this gain for us either substantively or theoretically? Why go through an intricate coding and aggregating procedure, when one can simply eyeball transcripts? Why even study conversations, when, as everyone knows, strong states push around their allies? To start with, the reason to engage in systematic coding is that "eyeballing" texts is practically a guarantee of overemphasizing certain passages and scanting or ignoring others. Similarly, explicitly coding on several possible adjacency-pair dimensions and calculating the frequency with which each dimension appears is a good way of counteracting biases and preconceptions (e.g., the British press reaction to the "Yo, Blair" conversation) as to the overall tenor of a given conversation.

More generally, without bothering to repeat the arguments made earlier against the "cheap talk" objection, the computations summarized above show that the US leader has the upper hand, substantively speaking, in both conversations, even though, in both cases, he makes more concessions to his British counterpart than IR theory would suggest. This is why both the clearly prescripted talking points that Reagan had been given and the equally clearly preset position that Bush had on the Middle East had to be fuzzed even as they were insisted upon. However, the conversations also show what we might call "first-mover disadvantage." In the Grenada case, Reagan was the requester, Thatcher the refuser; in the G8 case, those roles were played by Blair and Bush, respectively. If the person who is being asked a favor by an ally feels some pressure not to say no directly, the person who is asking the favor is in a structurally disadvantaged position: the interlocutor only needs to avoid saying yes. That the favor seeker is the superpower in one of my examples and the junior partner in the other makes this first-mover disadvantage particularly striking. This is a concrete demonstration of how power involves consent, not just imposition; as Reagan and Bush (but not Thatcher and Blair) might have put it had they ever read Gramsci, hegemony is always more pleasant when it is swaddled in compliments.

Conclusion

This short analysis, though both partial and preliminary, is promising. It suggests that whether social facts are assembled in a temporally indexed fashion, as narratives, or as conversations, they are constitutive relations akin to functions. As such, they can be modeled computationally, a task that involves bringing into correspondence their nature as a specific phenomenon and the assemblage of their elements.

We have also seen that despite the necessarily improvised nature of most conversations, they are every bit as structured as narratives or typical social objects. This, I think, has three implications for future constructivist work. Methodologically, it would be worthwhile to learn computational techniques, particularly from linguistics. Theoretically, it would be of value to become better acquainted with microsociological work, particularly in the field of conversation analysis. This is a well-established domain, with its own vocabulary and coding techniques; its emphasis on locally produced forms of order is a useful complement to the fascination many constructivists have for macrosociological theories. Microsociological work does not ignore issues of power or identity; it grounds them in concrete, routine practices. Finally, it would be of considerable interest for constructivists to become better acquainted with diplomatic conversations and other traces of the nuts and bolts of day-to-day global politics. It would give us many more phenomena to theorize about, provide a built-in series of checks for empirical assessment, and, last but not least, help us be better able to compare and also contrast the world we live in with other, earlier historical eras.

In addition, constructivists and other IR scholars are able to contribute a certain theoretical depth that until now has been lacking in the analysis of diplomatic conversations. Until recently, of course, there were few real-time conversations available for analysis (comparison with "memoranda of conversations" or telegrams summarizing conversations shows just how inexact most official summaries are); in the last two decades or so, such conversations have mostly been studied by biographers and diplomatic historians. Their intellectual hobbyhorses—whether about personality, the role of individuals, or the significance of chance, are well-known, and both the systematic quality of social science methods and the institutionalized cynicism of IR scholars, whether constructivist or otherwise, offer the possibility of bringing to the study of diplomatic conversations significant theoretical and substantive insights.

Notes

1. This requirement is at the core of sequence analysis as it is used to study phenomena such as careers and life cycles; for applications to political science and more specifically to international relations, see Philippe Blanchard, Felix Bühlmann, and Jaques-Antoine Gauthier, eds., *Advances in Sequence Analysis: Theory, Method, Applications* (Cham, Switzerland: Springer, 2014), chaps. 9–11; Valerie M. Hudson, Philip A. Schrodt, and Ray D. Whitmer, "Discrete Sequence Rule Models as a Social Science Methodology: An Exploratory Analysis of Foreign Policy Rule Enactment within Palestinian-Israeli Event Data," *Foreign Policy Analysis* 4, no. 1 (2008): 105–26.

2. In "The Narrative Construction of Reality," *Critical Inquiry* 18, no. 1 (1991): 1–21, Jerome Bruner argues that narratives are not only (locally, at least) complete but have a point to them and that, for that reason, scripts of the Schank-Abelson type are not really narratives. I think that this view is a bit too literary (and a bit insufficiently sociological): yes, executing a restaurant script does not usually involve Propp-type complications, but a disruption in the script (e.g., the waiter failing to bring a dish, the customer walking out without paying, or the customer asking for dessert before the main course) not only is likely to be seen as a break (or, in effect, a switch to a different script) but carries with it a sense of norm violation, which might well be gist for a new narrative. Cf. Livia Polanyi, *Telling the American Story: A Structural and Cultural Analysis of Conversational Storytelling* (Norwood, NJ: Ablex, 1985).

3. In "Some Further Steps in Narrative Analysis," *Journal of Narrative and Life History* 7, no. 1 (1997): 359–415, William Labov enumerates a number of other features of narratives; one that would be particularly interesting to explore is point of view.

4. Hayden White, "The Value of Narrativity in the Representation of Reality," *Critical Inquiry* 7, no. 1 (1980): 5–27.

5. Andrew Abbott, "Event Sequence and Event Duration: Colligation and Measurement," *Historical Methods* 17, no. 4 (1984): 192–204; Abbott, "Conceptions of Time and Events in Social Science Methods: Causal and Narrative Approaches," *Historical Methods* 23, no. 4 (1990): 140–50 (cf. Abbott, "On the Concept of Turning Point," *Comparative Social Research* 16, no. 1 [1997]: 85–105; the concept of "turning point" that is presented there is not really followed up); Peter Abell, "Comparative Narratives: Some Rules for the Study of Action," *Journal for the Theory of Social Behaviour* 14, no. 3 (1984): 309–31; Abell, "Causality and Low-Frequency Complex Events: The Role of Comparative Narratives," *Sociological Methods and Research* 30, no. 1 (2001): 57–80 (in "Narrative Explanation: An Alternative to Variable-Centered Explanation," *Annual Review of Sociology* 30 [2004]: 301–2, Abell touches on the topic of "generative structuralism"); Larry J. Griffin, "Narrative, Event-Structure Analysis, and Causal Interpretation in Historical Sociology," *American Journal of Sociology* 98, no. 5 (1993): 1094–1133; David R. Heise and Alex Durig, "A Frame for Organizational Actions

and Macroactions," *Journal of Mathematical Sociology* 22, no. 2 (1997): 95–123. Heise has a useful piece of software guiding the researcher through the specification of causal structure for historical sequences: see http://www.indiana.edu/~socpsy/ESA/.

6. See Robert H. Bates et al., *Analytic Narratives* (Princeton, NJ: Princeton University Press, 1998), introd.; Thomas Schmalberger and Hayward R. Alker, "A Synthetic Framework for Extensible Conflict Early Warning Systems" and "Exploring Alternative Conflict Trajectories with the CEWS Explorer," in *Journeys through Conflict: Narratives and Lessons*, ed. Hayward R. Alker, Ted Robert Gurr, and Kumar Rupesinghe (Lanham, MD: Rowman and Littlefield, 2001), chaps. 11–12; cf. Hayward R. Alker, "Historical Argumentation and Statistical Inference: Towards More Appropriate Logics for Historical Research," *Historical Methods* 17, no. 3 (1984): 164–73. I find it particularly striking that neither in the original introduction by Bates et al. nor in the debate that their volume touched off (*Social Science History* 24, no. 4 [2000]) is there any mention of what had, by that time, become an extensive literature on the sociological applications of causal event sequences.

7. An extremely partial exceptions is the work by Roberto Franzosi and his colleagues on the features of the most commonly occurring events in certain recurring sequences: see Roberto Franzosi, Gianluca De Fazio, and Stefania Vicari, "Ways of Measuring Agency: An Application of Quantitative Narrative Analysis to Lynchings in Georgia (1875–1930)," *Sociological Methodology* 42, no. 1 (2012): 1–42; see also the description of "composition analysis" on Heise's website cited in n. 5 above.

8. Other classic examples of labels from literature include the following openings: "It was now lunch time and they were all sitting under the double green fly of the dining tent pretending that nothing had happened" "This is the saddest story I have ever heard," and "Nel mezzo del cammin di nostra vita / mi ritrovai per una selva oscura, / ché la diritta via era smarrita." Examples of closings are "His soul swooned slowly as he heard the snow falling faintly through the universe and faintly falling, like the descent of their last end, upon all the living and the dead," "But I reckon I got to light out for the Territory ahead of the rest, because Aunt Sally she's going to adopt me and sivilize me, and I can't stand it. I been there before," and "Il fait une clientèle d'enfer; l'autorité le ménage et l'opinion publique le protège. Il vient de recevoir la croix d'honneur."

9. William Labov and Joshua Waletzky, "Narrative Analysis: Oral Versions of Personal Experience," in *Essays on the Verbal and Visual Arts, ed. June Helm* (Seattle: University of Washington Press for the American Ethnological Society, 1967).

10. Harvey Sacks, "On the Analyzability of Stories by Children," in *Directions in Sociolinguistics: The Ethnography of Communication*, ed. John J. Gumpers and Dell Hymes (New York: Holt, Rinehart and Winston, 1972).

11. Cf., though, the famous *Seinfeld* segment in which two of the characters discuss the possibility of a television show "about nothing": "'No story?' 'No, forget the story.' 'You gotta have a story.' 'Who says you gotta have a story?'"

12. This statement may seem surprising, at least as regards wholeness through typical plot or plot trajectory. Are the motivational or causal linkages between consecutive elements not what drive the plot forward? Maybe so, but that has nothing to do with the narrative as a whole, even as a plot with a particular arc. If a hero overcomes various obstacles, then loses hope, and finally finds the strength to win out over all, we

cannot say that a particular accomplishment along his trajectory is the cause of the next obstacle. Rather, the obstacles may be arranged in order of difficulty, which is a magnitudinal quality of the narrative as a whole and not a set of interlocked plot elements. This is why it is important to distinguish between narratives as recounted or recalled and the causal sequences about which narratives are constructed.

13. Cf. David R. Heise, "Narratives without Meaning?" *Journal of Mathematical Sociology* 18, nos. 2–3 (1993): 183–89.

14. Cf. Alonzo Church, *The Calculi of Lambda-Conversion*, Annals of Mathematics Studies 6 (Princeton, NJ: Princeton University Press, 1941), 1.

15. A. M. Turing, "On Computable Numbers, with an Application to the Entscheidungsproblem," *Proceedings of the London Mathematical Society*, 2nd ser., 2 (1936): 230–66.

16. This involves the use of the calculus of λ-conversion, which, as Post showed, is tantamount to string editing operations (Emil L. Post, "Formal Reductions of the General Combinatorial Decision Problem," *American Journal of Mathematics* 65, no. 2 [1943]: 197–215). The argument here is drawn in a highly compressed fashion from Stephen Majeski and David Sylvan, "Modeling Theories of Constitutive Relations in Politics" (unpublished manuscript, Feb. 19, 2000, Microsoft Word file); for an application, see Majeski and Sylvan, "How Foreign Policy Recommendations Are Put Together: A Computational Model with Empirical Applications," *International Interactions* 25, no. 4 (1999): 301–32.

17. The researcher will also need to specify threshold criteria for how many assemblage relations of a given type are representative of the narrative.

18. In constructivist writings, one finds occasional references to "narrative" but, to the best of my knowledge, no analysis of assemblage relations by which narratives are constituted. Cf. Audie Klotz and Cecelia Lynch, *Strategies for Research in Constructivist International Relations* (Armonk, NY: M. E. Sharpe, 2007), chap. 3.

19. Alexander Wendt, "The Agent-Structure Problem in International Relations Theory," *International Organization* 41, no. 3 (1987): 357. See also Wendt, *Social Theory of International Politics* (Cambridge: Cambridge University Press, 1999), 249; Nicholas Greenwood Onuf, *World of Our Making: Rules and Rule in Social Theory and International Relations* (Columbia: University of South Carolina Press, 1989), 158; Onuf, "Constructivism: A User's Manual," in *International Relations in a Constructed World*, ed. Venduka Kubálková, Nicholas Onuf, and Paul Kowert (Armonk, NY: M. E. Sharpe, 1998), 63.

20. The principal target cum cynosure of Wendt and other early constructivists was Kenneth Waltz. Note that although early constructivists' work followed hot on the heels of post-structuralist writings, the key "post" aspect of the latter—namely, that there are multiple possible structures possible in any set of elements, with the dominance of one particular structure being a historical artifact—was largely left by the wayside.

21. Roy Bhaskar, *The Possibility of Naturalism: A Philosophical Critique of the Contemporary Human Sciences* (Atlantic Highlands, NJ: Humanities Press, 1979), chap. 2; Anthony Giddens, *A Contemporary Critique of Historical Materialism, Vol. 1, Power, Property, and the State* (Berkeley: University of California Press, 1981), chap. 1; Rom

Harré, *Social Being: A Theory for Social Psychology* (Totowa, NJ: Littlefield, Adams, 1979), chap. 2. Cf. David Sylvan and Barry Glassner, *A Rationalist Methodology for the Social Sciences* (Oxford: Blackwell, 1985), chap. 4.

22. Roy Bhaskar, "Beef, Structure, and Place: Notes from a Critical Naturalist Perspective," *Journal for the Theory of Social Behaviour* 13, no. 1 (1983): 84.

23. Sacks was a student of Harold Garfinkel, the sociologist who coined the term *ethnomethodology* for his work on mechanisms of social order that are locally produced, in situ, and bottom-up (all synonyms). Sacks, who died in a car accident in 1975, did not publish most of his work, but his students tape-recorded his lectures, and transcripts of those lectures had a profound influence on the new field of conversation analysis. The transcripts were subsequently published in *Lectures on Conversation*, 2 vols., ed. Gail Jefferson (Oxford: Blackwell, 1992). Numerous overviews of conversation analysis now exist; one I have found useful for teaching purposes is Jack Sidnell's *Conversation Analysis: An Introduction* (Chichester: Wiley-Blackwell, 2010). Recent work is published in a number of places (e.g., *Human Studies*, *Journal of Pragmatics*), but the journal *Research on Language and Social Interaction* is, in effect, the official periodical of the International Society for Conversation Analysis.

24. Sidnell, *Conversation Analysis*, 2.

25. Cf. Paul Seedhouse, "Conversation Analysis Methodology," *Language Learning* 54, no. S1 (2004): 1–54. One of the hallmark papers in conversation analysis concludes similarly that the key aspect of conversations—their turn-taking character—is structured as "locally managed, party-administered, interactionally controlled, and sensitive to recipient design [orientation and sensitivity of parties to each other]" (Harvey Sacks, Emanuel A. Schegloff, and Gail Jefferson, "A Simplest Systematics for the Organization of Turn-Taking for Conversation," *Language* 50, no. 4 [1974]: 696. The terms *indexical* and *achievement* (which I use in the text) are fetish terms in ethnomethodology: the former signifies that many of the phrases used in social interaction are specific to time and place (e.g., "now" and "here") and thus that the produced order is genuinely bottom-up; the latter points to the fact that the order in question involves effort and is not a matter of mechanically applying generic rules.

26. Emanuel A. Schegloff, *Sequence Organization in Interaction: A Primer in Conversation Analysis*, vol. 1 (Cambridge: Cambridge University Press, 2007).

27. Emanuel A. Schegloff and Harvey Sacks, "Opening Up Closings," *Semiotica* 8, no. 4 (1973): 289–327.

28. Several points should be noted here. First, although the entire point of conversation analysis is to adduce patterns of, and test hypotheses about, the microassemblage relations between interlocutors, little work in the field explicitly analyzes conversations as narratives (there is work on stories told in the course of conversations, but up to now, that work has mostly been on how such stories are announced or recounted if they are lengthy or on how they are distinguished from other conversational elements; see, e.g., Sidnell, *Conversation Analysis*, chap. 9). Second, by the same token, despite the extremely technical nature of much work in conversation analysis, computational approaches have only recently begun to be used (see the references below about adjacency pairs). Third, as I touch on below, the mechanics of coding adjacency pairs to evaluate assemblage relations is presently a lengthy process involving numerous passes through a conversational transcript; although there are numerous functional forms

that assemblage can involve, the actual computation is, at least given current limitations in parsing technology, much less involved a task than the prior one of coding pairs.

29. However, cf. Gavan Duffy and Evelyn Goh, "Testing Sincerity: Henry Kissinger's February 1973 Encounter with the Chinese Leadership," *Journal of Language and Politics* 7, no. 1 (2008): 1–30.

30. The parses are manual for two reasons. First, there are large numbers of indexical expressions, which make the use of standard parsing corpora (many of which are drawn from newspaper articles) of only limited use in identifying both the coreferential terms ("he," "it") that permit adjacency pairs to be identified and the argumentative speech acts that indicate what is going on in the backward and forward chaining in each adjacency pair (e.g., seeing "they," in the first conversation, as a responsibility switch from "all of us together"). Second, the usual way of "training" automated parsers—namely, hand-correcting initial parses—is only feasible with large textual corpora, which obviously is not the case for isolated conversations lasting perhaps fifteen minutes. For further discussion and references on these points, see David Sylvan, "Automated Detection of Political Rejoinders: Identifying Adjacency Pairs in Diplomatic Conversations" (paper presented at the Fifth Annual Conference of the European Political Science Association, Vienna, June 26, 2015).

31. Writing the actual computer code for the counting and matching is straightforward; trickier is setting the threshold for "most common," particularly when each interlocutor frequently resorts to two or more specific speech acts. Neither the literature on narratives nor that on conversations says much about this issue.

32. Memorandum of a telephone conversation between Ronald Reagan and Margaret Thatcher, October 26, 1983, http://www.margaretthatcher.org/archive/displaydocument.asp?docid=109426. Note that most turns are labeled with two speech acts: the first points back to the turn that, together with the current turn, makes up the preceding adjacency pair; the second points forward to the next turn (the following adjacency pair). The exceptions to this are the start of a passage or the end of the conversation as a whole, in which cases there is only one speech act.

33. Additional evidence of this label comes from press commentary years later, when the Ronald Reagan Presidential Library released the actual audiotapes: see, e.g., the following articles from November 10, 2014: "Reagan Apologised to Angry Thatcher over Grenada, Tapes Reveal," *Guardian*, http://www.theguardian.com/politics/2014/nov/10/reagan-apologise-angry-thatcher-grenada-white-house-tapes; "Reagan's Apology to Thatcher over Grenada Revealed," BBC News, http://www.bbc.com/news/uk-29986729; "Reagan Apologized to Thatcher for Grenada Invasion," *Time*, http://time.com/3576221/ronald-reagan-margaret-thatcher-new-tapes/; "Listen: When Reagan Apologized to Thatcher for a U.S. Invasion," *Washington Post*, https://www.washingtonpost.com/news/worldviews/wp/2014/11/10/listen-when-reagan-apologized-to-thatcher-for-a-u-s-invasion/.

34. UN Security Council resolution S/16077/Rev.1, condemning the invasion of Grenada by US troops, received eleven votes (including from three US allies) and three abstentions (including from the United Kingdom) and had to be vetoed by the United States.

35. "Transcript: Bush and Blair's Unguarded Chat," BBC News, July 18, 2006,

http://news.bbc.co.uk/2/hi/5188258.stm. The conversation ends here abruptly (which is why there are two speech acts, rather than one, as a closing would involve) because Blair figured out that the microphone was live and tapped it, and the technician presumably flipped the switch off.

36. "It Wasn't the 'Yo' That Was Humiliating, It Was the 'No'," *Guardian*, July 23, 2006, http://www.theguardian.com/commentisfree/2006/jul/23/comment.politics; "'Private' Chat Heard by World Caps Disastrous G8 Summit for Blair," *Independent*, July 17, 2006, http://www.independent.co.uk/news/world/politics/private-chat-heard-by-world-caps-disastrous-g8-summit-for-blair-6095108.html. Geoffrey Wheatcroft wrote that Bush treated Blair "like a put-upon valet, a part Blair played very convincingly": *Yo, Blair: Tony Blair's Disastrous Premiership* (London: Politico's Publishing, 2007), 6.

CHAPTER 7

Thinking Counterfactually and with Discipline

Agent-Based Models for Constructing and Deconstructing the Future

IAN S. LUSTICK

The Future: Gaining Traction on a Great Unsolved Problem

The chief purpose of knowledge, according to Niccolò Machiavelli, is to control one's life—not the life one has already lived, but the life to be lived, with all its dangers and opportunities. In other words, the purpose of pursuing knowledge systematically (i.e., the purpose of science) is to solve the problem of knowing as much as possible about the future, a place impossible to visit, filled not only with danger and risk but also perhaps with opportunity. Contemporary social science remains powerfully committed to this ethos. Grant applications promise the prince that science can help effectively defend against potential threats and exploit possible opportunities.

The key difficulty is that the future does not exist and so cannot be directly studied. Neither can it be predicted exactly in all its dimensions. But implicit in the recommendations of Machiavelli, as well as in the studies advanced by policy analysts and in the practices of political scientists who think their work is of value to those who practice politics, is that rational action requires assessments of what will happen that depend on decisions taken in the present; that is, rationality entails assessments of that which cannot be directly examined. Accordingly, a surrogate of some sort must be provided as the target of investigation. These surrogates are stories constructed, with more or less self-consciousness, about what the future could look like. To construct these surrogates, Machiavelli used the past and theories about how the world works to construct stories about the future. Machiavelli produced the past he used for this purpose by selective retrieval and narration of various sources about the past, including heavy reliance on Livy and Tacitus. Whether drawing on historians of ancient Rome, cable traffic from relevant embassies, specialized monographs, field research, casual reading of newspapers, or personal prejudices, the traditional and still standard method of both social scientists and policy analysts is to tell stories about how the future could unfold along dimensions selected as relevant or interesting. The technical term for this procedure is *scenario analysis.*

Scenarios are stories, imagined as plausible depictions about what could happen (or would have happened, if attention is directed to retrodiction) and why. Each of these stories is an elaborate counterfactual account. Normally—in the worlds of business and government—a small number (three to five) of such accounts are developed, compared, and analyzed, usually by asking individuals or groups to imagine plausible and interesting futures in a domain in which they are presumed to have some expertise. This process, highly informal but sometimes partially structured, is commonly referred to as BOGSAT (Bunch of Guys Sitting Around Talking). In academia, the sources of these stories can sometimes be explicitly theoretical. For example, a game theorist could describe outcomes by imagining key players interacting according to payoff structures associated with different kinds of games. Aggregate data analysts could accomplish the equivalent task by inferring patterns in the future similar to those measured along relevant dimensions in the past. But since outcomes of interest are commonly too rare to have been observed as categories of aggregate measurement, even aggregate data analysts must use their imagination and judgment to guide the production of their stories about the future.[1] However these scenarios are produced, they constitute, as a set, the basis for analyzing the implications of present policy choices for future outcomes. To talk about how one's actions might affect the future, one must first *construct* an image or a set of images of what the future would be absent one's own contribution. These images, cast dynamically and in emplotted form as "narratives," are thus treated as surrogates for what the analyst (looking forward from the present) hopes that he or she has—a collection of representations of the most plausible futures or kinds of futures that could unfold.

When we direct attention to how these surrogate futures are constructed and deployed as the database for making decisions about probabilities and courses of action, we are engaging in a deconstructive enterprise. In a fundamental sense, this enterprise is the core element of a critical approach. In the context of thinking about the future, constructivism means recognizing that scenarios represent interpretations of the future that are built out of assumptions, theories, purposes, and selected data. A critical approach to the subject matter means identifying and fostering awareness of the limitations of the (interpretive) constructions that result from our engagement with questions of interest about the future. Since claims about events in the present and past involve assessments of the implications of events and patterns prior to them, we cannot logically claim knowledge of the past or present without implying the possibility of knowledge of the future. This does not entail belief in the ability to prophesy what actually will happen in detail, but it does imply the expectation that disciplined analysis will be able to distinguish between credible and less credible forecasts about the ways events may materialize.

In this chapter, I illustrate the use of computer-assisted agent-based modeling as a formal technique for both constructing and critically evaluating our interpretations of the future.[2] Since the assumptions of the model must be explicit and consistent for the computer program to operate, every batch of histories that is produced (i.e., constructed) can legitimately be interpreted as illuminating the implications of the specific assumptions and theories operationalized within the model. Moreover, because every trajectory of the model (i.e., every virtual future) can be subjected to process tracing in exquisite detail, opportunities exist for every future and every batch of futures to be critically assessed—indeed, to be deconstructed into the chains of mechanisms that produced individual outcomes and into the propensities of different theoretical judgments or parameter settings to produce futures with particular features.

To appreciate the advantage of computerized simulation as a generator of accounts of the future, we should first recall that all scenarios—that is, all depictions of the future—are "virtual" in that they exist as or at least are translated from images in the minds of their producers. For even the best analysts, "transition rules" within the domain of their expertise (i.e., the laws of social behavior at all levels of analysis) are, at best, only very partially understood. Thus every story about what the future may hold and every judgment about the relative likelihood of a kind of event under particular conditions must include large doses of arbitrary, even idiosyncratic decisions about what dimensions and variables will dominate, in what combinations, in what sequence, and with what consequences. These are the crutches that human minds require when facing the immense cognitive problem of imagining the implications of what they know or believe about the present for discerning the future of a complex state of affairs. Contemporary cognitive psychology understands these crutches, these departures from strict Bayesian rationality, as a vast array of heuristics or "psychologics" that trump or simply replace cognitively onerous and informationally demanding processes of evidence-based and probability-based inference.

Which scenarios are produced or endowed with credibility is also affected by political preferences and the structuring of choice, standardly by bracketing a "preferred" scenario with two "extreme" and fairly clearly wrong or distasteful alternatives. Given our cognitive inadequacies and political prejudices, how can moderately credible theory be combined with computerization for systematic understanding of the future? The problem becomes even more daunting when we acknowledge how much of the future is shaped by "accidents" or "random events," that is, by effects of below-the-analytic-horizon events that we can never aspire to know.

We can usefully approach this problem by translating what has been said so far into the language of "counterfactuals."[3] Since the future has not occurred, all claims about it are counterfactuals—conditional statements about something that could or will happen under conditions that have not yet obtained. Since most errors about the future cannot be identified definitively as such until the actual future becomes the past, a critical stance toward claims about the future cannot rest on assertions of truth over falsehood. Such a stance must instead rest on a more sophisticated concept of what is entailed by thinking about the future, that is, on a disciplined approach to the evaluation of counterfactuals. That, in turn, requires being able to think not about the likelihood of individually imagined trajectories within what is assumed to be a normal or near-normal distribution but about differently shaped distributions of trajectories of different types. Needed, in other words, is a map of the space of the future that affords some sense of how uncertainty is distributed within it.

Consider the debate over the catastrophic failure by policy makers to anticipate the financial collapse of 2008. The problem was not that policy makers did not succeed in predicting the exact consequences of the closure of Lehman Brothers but that they failed to understand the shape of the distribution of the state space of the future. From the bursting real estate bubble and the associated collapse of financial markets that inaugurated the Great Recession of 2007–9, we learned that treating an underlying distribution as normal when it is not is immensely dangerous. In their prescient book published four years prior to that event, *The Misbehavior of Markets*, Benoit Mandelbrot and Richard L. Hudson explain that the modern financial theories used by brokers to confidently recommend investment strategies seemed to offer virtually guaranteed returns, which, the authors forecast, would result in economic disaster. The brokers' strategies were based on the expectation that certain extreme fluctuations in market prices were so unlikely that they could not even be considered "rare" and could be relegated to a category of events that were theoretically possible but so improbable as to be disregardable for all practical purposes. Of the (relatively minor) crash of the stock market on October 19, 1987, the authors wrote, "On one day, the Dow plunged 29.2 percent. Something was wrong; The academics said that the fall should not have happened, that it was a once-in-an-eon event."[4]

By looking closely at the "volatility of volatility" in data describing market fluctuations over the previous century, the authors demonstrated that types of events that "should not have happened at all" were better described as implausible, perhaps, and as unpredictable, but certainly not as effectively impossible. The fundamental flaw in modern portfolio theory, the capital asset pricing model, the Black-Scholes equation, and other reigning financial theories was the assumption that the relevant universe of cases has attributes distributed according to a normal, "bell" curve. The underlying distributions driving market behavior are not normal but Cauchian, subject to the regular intrusion of "rare" events of enormous impact that are not common enough to be expected at any particular point in time with any confidence at all but that are plausible enough, given both the shape of the underlying distribution and their magnitude, to warrant taking them into consideration as decisive factors when planning for the future.

The overall point to note for my purpose here is that forecasting in politics means focusing, first at least, on the shape of the distribution of the possible, rather than on whether any particular event or discrete kind of event that is thought to be possible will occur. The strength of the analyses of Mandelbrot and others, such as Nassim Taleb, is that they are able to show emphatically and convincingly that we should expect many more "rare events" to occur across a wide array of domains than our natural inclinations to expect a "bell-shaped" world suggest. The problem is that their conclusions are pitched at such a high level of analysis that their policy prescriptions are extremely limited. Taleb takes an extreme view, that "almost everything in social life is produced by rare but consequential shocks and jumps."[5] But planning is effectively impossible if, as he further claims, "a small number of Black Swans explain almost everything in our world."[6] Indeed, such a view implies not only that planning is impossible but that surprise is inevitable and that protection against maximum loss, rather than organizing to exploit opportunity, is the only rational course of action. But policy makers, including those charged with devising foreign and national security policies pertaining to a wide array of specific but complex issues, experience considerable variation in the "Cauchiness" of underlying distributions. On occasion, they may even confront domains within which the most important underlying distributions *are* normal. That state of affairs puts a premium on the *a priori* ability of planners to gauge the relative character of the distribution of possible outcomes in their domain of responsibility or with respect to a particular question within that domain.

As noted above, there are good reasons why experts relying on their brains and imagination alone cannot produce a set of scenarios large enough or systematic enough to depict the state space of the future of a complex social system. Yet BOGSAT is still, in one form or another, the standard technique for producing the basis for thinking about the future. To appreciate how agent-based modeling (ABM) can be used to radically improve the way this problem is addressed, let us take a closer look at the distinction between the "actual" future and the space of possible futures.

From any time labeled the "present," we can only imagine or visualize the "future" correctly as a large set of multidimensional trajectories. These trajectories travel through an enormous, though not boundless or totally disorganized, state space of the possible worlds that could evolve from the world that we experience as the present. In other words, looking forward from the present, we can imagine many ways, along many dimensions (some important and some not), in which the actual set of events of our world can vary. Uncertainty about what trajectory will be followed is not only a function of the weakness of our theories. For any complex system, a salient but unanticipatable fraction of the explanation of what actually happens will emanate from causes located below what I have called the analytic horizon of any of our theories. We may treat these factors as random; for most purposes, they are. Still, the deep meaning of chaos theory is that although order may exist in the apparently random intrusions of factors operating outside our theoretical purview, that order is present at a vast remove from our sensors and is therefore irrelevant to an effort to improve the particulars of a forecast.

With these considerations in mind, we can better understand why the process of forecasting political events of interest in a particular setting entails tracing the contours of the space of possible futures along relevant dimensions, rather than searching for the one actual trajectory that our world will follow through that space. "Point predictions" are fool's gold. For complex social problems, systematic analysis cannot produce them, and attempts to do so encourage a fundamentally misleading construction of the problem. What we can achieve are informed judgments about probabilities, associations, and dynamic nonlinearities within distributions of outcomes.

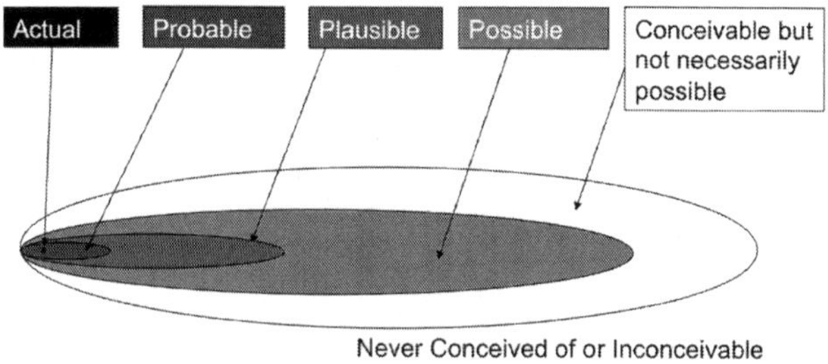

Fig. 7.1. Categories of worlds. The dot indicates the actual future, with all possible outcomes depicted.

Figure 7.1 highlights the irrationality of seeking to predict the actual future, by locating that future as a nearly imperceptible dot in a schematic depiction of intersecting spaces of the conceivable, the possible, the plausible, and the probable.[7] The diagram depicts all possible outcomes as a subset of all those that are conceivable, all plausible outcomes as a subset of those that are possible, all probable (or not improbable) outcomes as a subset of those that are plausible, and the actual outcome as located within the realm of the probable. Except for the dot representing the actual, all other descriptions of the future world in this diagram can be classified as "counterfactuals"—accounts contrary to what the world actually was or what it became.

Although we might prefer to imagine or construct the landscape of the future to be as orderly as is suggested in the depiction in figure 7.1, it is likely to be considerably messier and more complex. Taking a critical stance toward this attractive construction leads us to note, for example, that the ratio of the possible to the conceivable may be substantially greater than we think. Some of the outcomes that we might consider probable may be not only implausible but downright impossible. The "actual" world that emerges may be one of the variants considered not "probable" but only "plausible." Even some of those possibilities we consider relatively probable may be merely possible or actually impossible. For illustrative purposes, figure 7.2 incorporates these potential misconceptions.

Despite the difficulty of producing a reasonably accurate surrogate for the contours of what should be considered "possible," precisely that surrogate is required for any forecasting tool to be consistent with what the "future" actually "is." Whatever technique modelers use to accomplish this task with respect to a domain as complex as international politics, it must be governed by principles or be based on assumptions that enable what is produced to be treated as not only logically but also empirically possible.

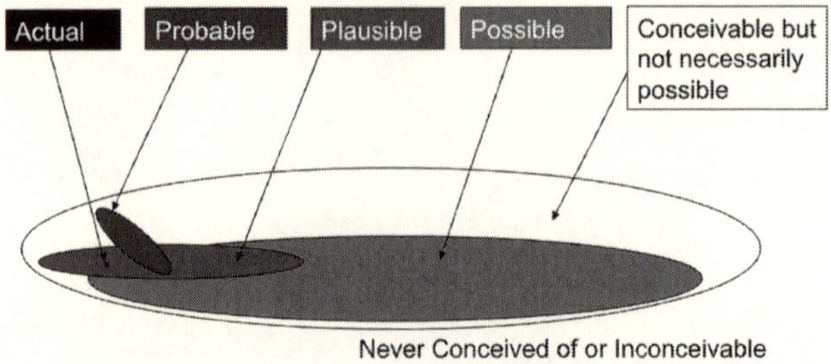

Fig. 7.2. Categories of worlds if imagined incorrectly. The dot indicates the actual future, with possible outcomes depicted with real-world messiness.

The technique must also be capable, at very low marginal cost, of generating large numbers of empirically realizable multidimensional trajectories or chronologies.

ABM and Computer Simulation: Constructing Deconstructible State Spaces of the Future

A large flock of birds traces a trajectory through the sky that is as distinctive as it is unpredictable. One could extravagantly explain this combination of orderliness and unpredictability as the result of a dictatorial leader bird whose whims govern the direction and speed of every other bird in the flock. A better explanation is achieved by using a computer to endow each bird with a simple set of algorithms requiring it to stay near, but not too near, the birds in its immediate vicinity. Numerous computer models of such "boids" show how precisely such an agent-based model can produce flocking behavior, thereby explaining it parsimoniously and in strict conformance with what we know about the information-processing capacities of birds.

Any one run of a boid model, perturbed randomly by the virtual presence of tasty bugs in the line of sight of some boids, traces a flock's trajectory that will be unique among the trajectories the flock could follow. Similarly, each interpretation of the future offered by an agent-based model is a trajectory through an immense space of possible trajectories whose boundaries are established by the interactive implications of the theoretical assumptions of the model, its initial conditions, and the exogenous random stream of tiny perturbations that affect it. Built from and decomposable into identifiable theoretical claims, the model is stylized to conform, at $t = 0$, to a target political system at the present or some stipulated point in the past. By changing parameters and/or algorithms to reflect adjustments in the theories that we wish to include in the model and by repeating the production of batches of trajectories, we can criticize our own expectations about the future and critically assess the credibility of different theories (once future outcomes can be compared, systematically, to outcome probabilities as registered by model output).

The algorithms that comprise the model's transition rules animate masses of interactions among agents instantiated in ways that condense the limited but high-confidence knowledge available from theoretically and ideographically sophisticated experts and their work. But once the model is animated, the massive interaction effects that arise produce emergent processes of dynamic change across the entire "landscape" of agent behavior, processes that cannot be derived, inferred, or predicted from the algorithms themselves. As individual agents update their state and behavior, the entire array of agents moves forward through time. By collecting data on stochastically perturbed repeated runs of an appropriately assembled model, we can identify outcomes that are typical, plausible, and just possible. Each outcome is consistent with the assumptions, data, and theoretical operationalizations used to build and instantiate the model but is impossible to infer from them. From a constructivist perspective, these algorithms express agentive motivations and have consequences shaped by circumstances, that is, social structure. ABM thus allows a modeling of agent-structure coevolution in ways that both require and exploit contemporary computational power.

Applications of this kind of technology are prevalent in many disciplines, including molecular biology, oncology, archaeology, natural resource management, pharmacology, climatology, immunology, transportation, marketing, and city planning.[8] The approach is now also well established in the social sciences. One of the earliest and still most influential studies animated by this approach was published in 1978 by Thomas C. Schelling, who demonstrated ABM's in-principle fecundity with an agent-based model of segregation.[9] To be sure, Schelling made his key contributions without using a computer and even emphasized the importance of doing necessary calculations manually, but he subsequently developed interest in and spent considerable time investigating how computer programs for exploring his ideas could be designed. Indeed, Schelling-style models run on computers have been used to greatly extend his thinking, by experimenting with different rules that individuals might follow, different patterns of interaction among neighbors, and different tastes for living in integrated or segregated areas.[10]

In political science and other social sciences, computational, bottom-up, or agent-based modeling is a generalization of this method, using computer simulation to explore the often nonlinear relationship between inputs at the unit level, interaction networks, and outputs at the collective level.[11] ABM has been particularly attractive to researchers in domains where intractability problems make algebraically solvable techniques of formal analysis impossible or when either the complexity of conjectures about macropolitical relationships or the openness of systems involved precludes relying on regression or natural experiments. Among the political science domains where ABM techniques have been successfully deployed are collective mobilization, norm and strategy evolution, constructivist identity theory, secessionism, power sharing, party competition, political communication, national state formation, institutionalization, international treaty making, and the relationship between the structure of the international system and state behavior within it.[12]

Agent-based models are most sensibly deployed to investigate problems that are too complex to be captured algebraically, because of large numbers of relevant dimensions, large numbers of interacting "bodies," or both. Accordingly, there is a strong elective affinity between ABM and computerization, This is because the effects of ABM emerge from the algorithmic behavior and simple interactions of masses of autonomous agents, yielding an otherwise-impossible-to-perform multitude of calculations at each time step—calculations that are straightforward at the agent level but overwhelming if approached as an integrated set. Given the immensity of the possibility space, it is almost certain that building an analytically suitable surrogate for the state space of the future will require computerization. Indeed, the automaticity of computer technology itself helps impose the discipline required for the production of this surrogate, by translating initial conditions and a stable set of theoretical propositions into very large numbers of individually distinctive trajectories.

Each trajectory—that is, each run of a stochastically perturbed ABM—constitutes a distinctive "story," in the sense that every event is fully traceable to the state of the world prior to its occurrence. Since the "laws" governing behavior of types of agents and interactions between types of agents are known, the range of possible outcomes is fully determined (though unknowable). Good computational models, in other words, are capable of combining opportunities for process-tracing, and the distinctiveness and granular, multi-dimensional complexity that traditionally attract constructivist and critical theorists to ideographically oriented research, with the standardization, control, and large *n*'s that enable rigorous testing of nomothetic propositions about a world rightly treated as both orderly and unpredictable.

Mapping the State Space of the Future for Bangladesh

In the late 1990s, I used a rather simple modeling platform known as ABIR (Agent-Based Identity Repertoire) to produce working models of a generic Middle Eastern semiauthoritarian country, to explore the contours of the state space of the future for the Middle East as a whole over a thirty-year period.[13] Substantially refined and elaborated techniques were used in 2002, with a more advanced modeling platform known as PS-I (Political Science–Identity).[14] In response to requests from the US government, this platform was used to produce models and to conduct experiments analyzing prospects for different kinds of stability and instability in Pakistan between 2002 and 2005 and to evaluate repeated cycles of Israeli-Palestinian violence and/or war in the region, considering their implications for stability and the fate of US-friendly regimes in the Middle East.[15] This work was the background for the approach taken by Lockheed Martin's Advanced Technology Laboratories team that participated in a competition sponsored by the Defense Advanced Research Projects Agency (DARPA) and begun in 2005, known as the Integrated Crisis Early Warning System (ICEWS).[16] The competition required modeling teams to reach relatively high levels of accuracy, recall, and precision for forecasts of "events of interest" (e.g., rebellions, insurgencies, domestic political crises, and outbreaks of ethnoreligious violence) in dozens of countries. Forecasts generated automatically from models ingesting data from the late 1990s and early 2000s were tested against what actually happened in those countries in subsequent years.

Most of the modeling effort undertaken by these competing teams used variations of data mining and statistical correlation or pattern-matching techniques. But ABM models produced with PS-I, which passed minimum requirements for forecasting while complementing the ATL team's statistical models, were judged to be especially valuable for the depth and richness of their output and for their potential to assist with option analysis. The result was a separate stand-alone project known as the Virtual Strategic Analysis and Forecasting Tool (V-SAFT), developed under contract from the Department of Defense via the Human Social Cultural Behavioral Modeling Program and the Office of Naval Research. Data presented below are drawn from the array of monthly updated models produced by V-SAFT for a small but growing number of countries.

Bangladesh is one of the nine countries for which monthly updated models were available in 2013. The Bangladesh model's forecast results, which looked forward one year from February 2013, vividly exemplify the technique of using a theoretically informed, computer-assisted, agent-based model of a real and complex political system to construct an analyzable surrogate for the state space of the future. The presentation of the results here will be followed by a brief account of how the state space that was constructed by running a virtual Bangladesh model was then deconstructed for critically assessing US policy options toward a political crisis threatening the real Bangladesh in late 2013. The published summary forecast of the model looking forward one year in February 2013 reads,

> V-SAFT's Bangladesh model forecasts a somewhat less than 75% probability of a sustained domestic political crisis between March 2013 through February 2014 and only a 10% probability of avoiding any sort of domestic political crisis during this period. Insurgent activity and incidents of rebellion have a roughly 75% probability of appearing in this period, but the likelihood of these activities sustaining themselves for three months or more is very low (below 3%). These probabilities remain more or less the same across the entire forecast period. Nor do probabilities vary widely depending on the complexion of the governing coalition. Under a broad-based nationalist government, a business dominated coalition, or one based on Bengali appeals that is yet not dominated by the Awami League, Bangladesh has the best chance of enjoying a year relatively free from instability or severe instability. But the model shows a wide variety of different coalitions capable of emerging, most of which are associated with some significant instability or severe instability. Probabilities for at least one of these coalitions range from a low of 15% in governments dominated by non-partisan nationalists or business elites, to a high of nearly 65% under governments oriented toward narrow civic and technocratic appeals. Compared to last month's forecasts, a Muslim dominated government is no longer evaluated as plausible, while a business dominated government is to be considered plausible, and not merely possible. V-SAFT's overall assessment for the coming year is that governing elites in Bangladesh will likely face higher than average amounts of illegal and violent political mobilization over the coming year. This represents a substantial trend across the last five months of V-SAFT forecasts for Bangladesh. Keeping in mind what is normal for Bangladesh, this month's forecast registers not just an increasing probability of instability, but an increasing probability of severe instability.[17]

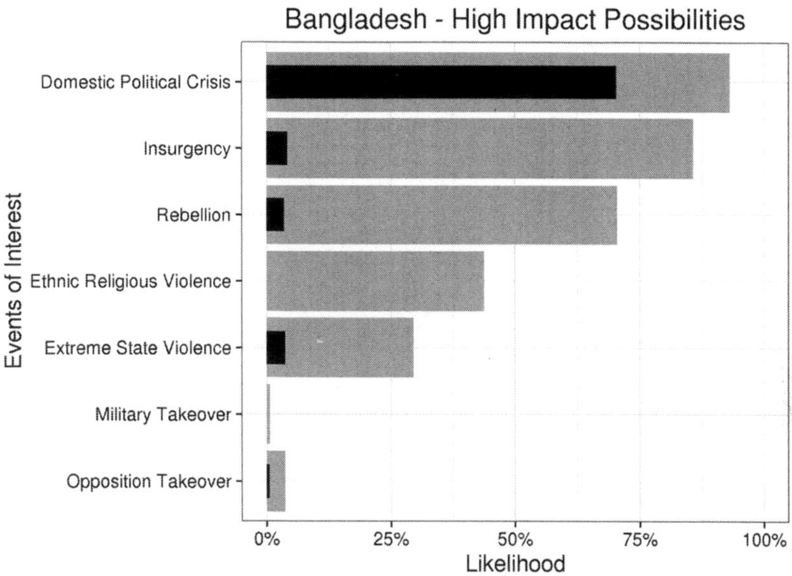

Fig. 7.3. Probabilities for key EOIs of historical importance in Bangladesh, such as the 75 percent chance of a sustained domestic political crisis

Probabilities attached to specific forecasts were calculated directly from proportions of the event space produced by the model exhibiting particular kinds of behavior. Most of the probabilities cited appear in the visuals displayed in this section. For example, the "somewhat less than 75%" likelihood of a sustained domestic political crisis (DPC) over the forecast year and the unlikelihood of Bangladesh avoiding any period of DPC during that time frame are read off the "high impact possibilities" chart (fig. 7.3). The gray "occurs" bar for "domestic political crisis" shows that nearly 90 percent of the weeks comprising all one thousand simulated years of possible Bangladesh futures in the model contain behavior coded as corresponding to the definition of a DPC: organized, mostly nonviolent opposition to the government, significant enough to threaten the integrity of the ruling coalition.[18] The black portion of the bar, extending to roughly 70 percent, shows the probability of a sustained DPC. Precisely, it shows the size of the subset of those weeks featuring DPC and including parts of episodes lasting at least three months. The summary forecast also draws attention to the likelihood of at least some insurgent activity or rebellion. However, in view of the very small size of the black bars in those categories, the forecast notes that sus-

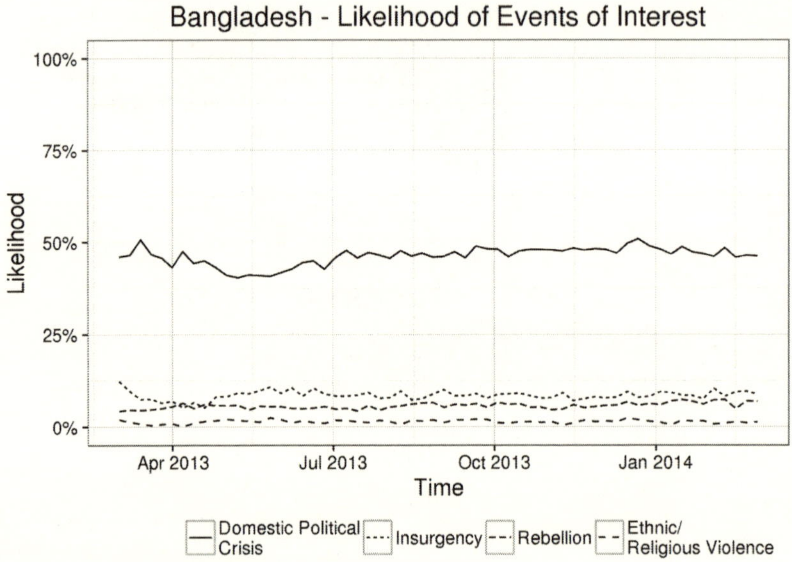

Fig. 7.4. Probabilities for key EOIs in Bangladesh over the forecast year, with DPC relatively stable at 50 percent

tained insurgencies or periods of ethnoreligious violence occurred so rarely in this set of trajectories that they should be considered implausible—in other words, possible but extremely unlikely.

How are probabilities for specific events of interest (EOIs) distributed over the forecast year? Figure 7.4 shows, on the *x*-axis, the months of the coming year and, on the *y*-axis, proportions of futures in the state space, registering EOI activity. As noted in the summary forecast, we see that "these probabilities remain more or less the same across the entire forecast period," with a slight trend toward increasing risk after April 2013.

The summary forecast indicates that instability, including severe instability, is associated with many different constellations of political power that are anticipated as plausible within the forecast year. In figure 7.5, different groups or political appeals that the model identifies as plausibly able to play a dominant and organizing role in Bangladesh governing coalitions over this time period are arrayed on the *x*-axis. The width of the columns associated with political dominance by different groups signifies the proportion of weeks when they are dominant, within all one thousand trajectories; the width of the bars within each column indicates how that amount of the state space is divided into periods (shaded from lightest to darkest) of

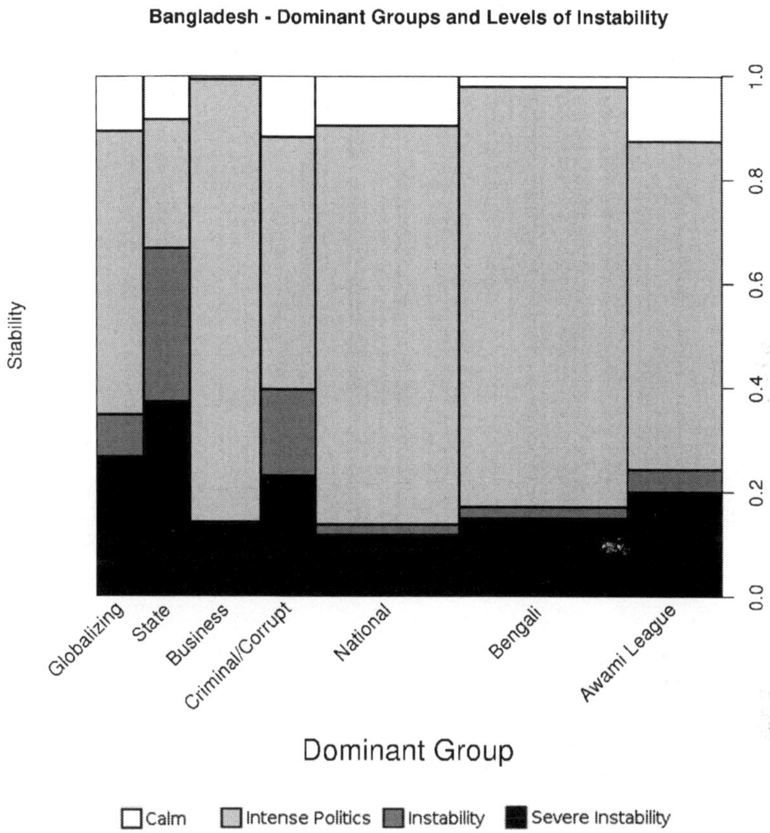

Fig. 7.5. Dominant groups and levels of instability in Bangladesh

calm (white), intense politics (light gray), instability (dark gray), and severe instability (black). Going somewhat beyond the explicit statements in the summary forecast, we can observe that the most likely coalitions—those dominated by nationalist, Bengali, or Awami League ideas and elites—hold out a nearly 80 percent chance of avoiding instability or severe instability, but no government that the model deems plausible has more than a 15 percent likelihood of enjoying calm throughout the year. A government based on alliances led by bureaucratic state elites faces the greatest likelihood of both instability and severe instability.

To probe more deeply, we could see which groups are allies, opponents, or radical opponents of the government when bureaucratic state elites domi-

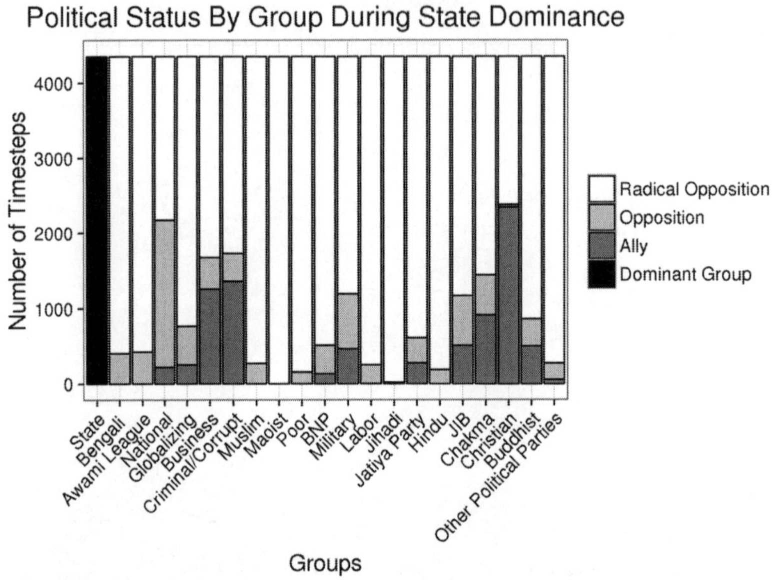

Fig. 7.6. Domestic political hierarchy levels during state dominance

nate the coalition (fig. 7.6) or when "globalizing, Western-oriented" elites dominate (fig. 7.7). We see that these types of governments, when they have significant allies at all, tend to rely on corrupt and criminal elements and on the (highly corrupt) business community.[19]

The *y*-axis of figure 7.6 is the number of model time steps (within the total number) that featured the "state" identity group as dominant. The *y*-axis of figure 7.7 is the number of model time steps (within the total number) that featured the "globalizing" (Western-oriented) identity group as dominant. The shaded bars comprising the columns report the proportion of state-dominant model time (fig. 7.6) and globalizing-dominant model time (fig. 7.7) during which each group was categorized within the DPH as either ally, opponent, or radical opponent.

Again, as noted in the summary forecast, in the relatively unlikely, but still plausible, circumstance that business itself organizes a governing coalition—relying on state bureaucrats, globalizers, and criminal or corrupt networks—prospects for intense politics, if not calm, appear to improve considerably. We can see why this occurs by considering the display in figure 7.8, which shows that when business dominates, the largest groups in Bang-

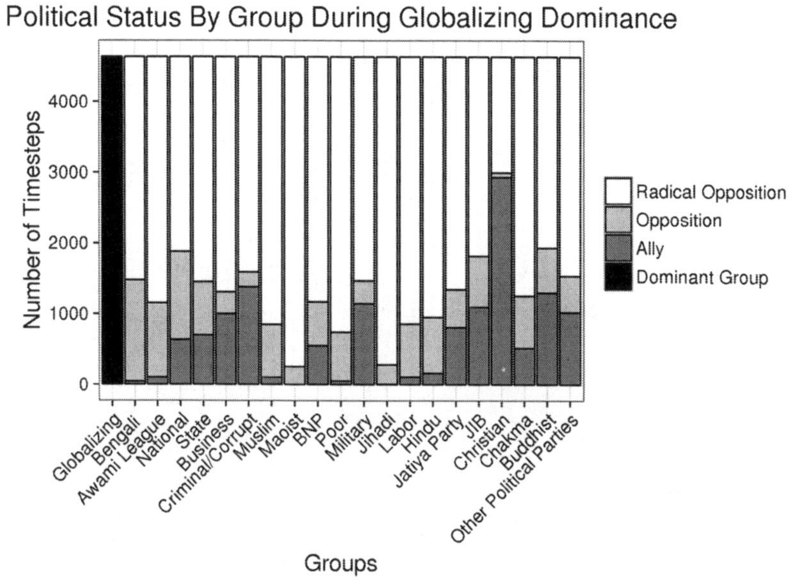

Fig. 7.7. Domestic political hierarchy levels during globalizing dominance

ladesh are much less likely to adopt a radical oppositionist posture toward the government (the white portion of columns on the left of the display) than when state bureaucrats, globalizers, or criminal or corrupt networks (not shown) dominate.

Comparing the state space mapped by running V-SAFT's Bangladesh model for the year beginning March 2013 to mappings produced in earlier months can help identify general trends. For example, in Bangladesh, Islamist-dominated governments appeared prominently enough in the state space to justify treating that outcome as plausible in each of the six previous months' forecasts (meaning that it appears in at least 3 percent of the space of the future). For the year beginning in March 2013, however, the likelihood of Islamist governments dropped below the 3 percent threshold. Accordingly, although such regimes appear in fig. 7.9 in the display on the left, for the year beginning February 2013, they do not appear in the display on the right—the year beginning March 2013. By noting the thin black line at the bottom of the column marked "Muslim" in the "political status by group" display in figure 7.10, we can see that V-SAFT still charted a Muslim-dominated government as possible, just not as "plausible" by the

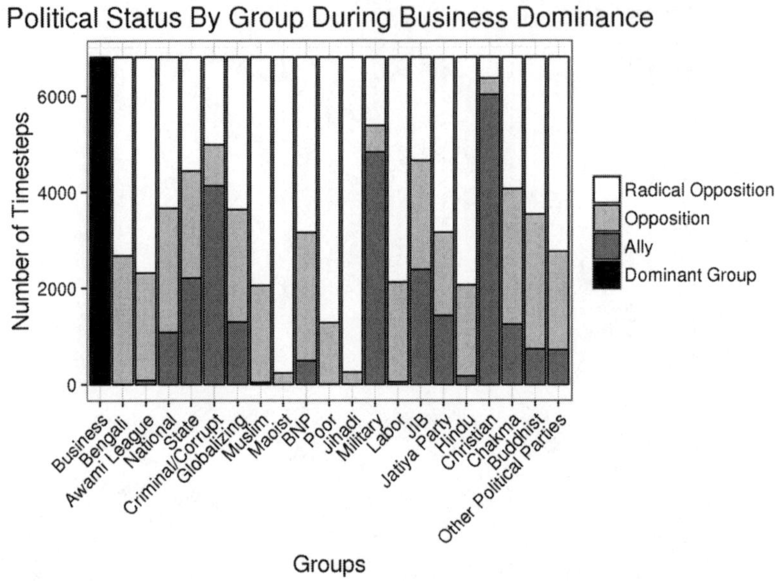

Fig. 7.8. Domestic political hierarchy levels during business dominance

3 percent rule. Along the *x*-axis in figure 7.9 are the dominant groups, the first *y*-axis is stability, and the second *y*-axis is the percentage of the space in which the forecast holds.

The final portion of the summary forecast focuses on the trend toward an increasing likelihood of instability, particularly severe instability. This trend is most easily discerned by considering the group of six sequence plots displayed in figure 7.11—beginning with the forecasts made for the October 2012–September 2013 year and ending with forecasts made for the March 2012–February 2014 year. V-SAFT produces these sequence plots by stacking all one thousand trajectories. Each week in each trajectory, traced horizontally by a single line, is shaded to represent either calm (white), intense politics (light gray), instability (dark gray), or severe instability (black). Determining the order of the stacking is the condition present at the beginning of the run and, within that group, the length of time before that condition changes. Different horizontal patterns register different sequences of stabilization or destabilization. By noting the changing prominence of shading horizontally, we can gain a quick sense of time trends toward stabilization (becoming more white or light gray) or toward destabilization (becoming more dark gray or black). By noting the changing prominence of shades

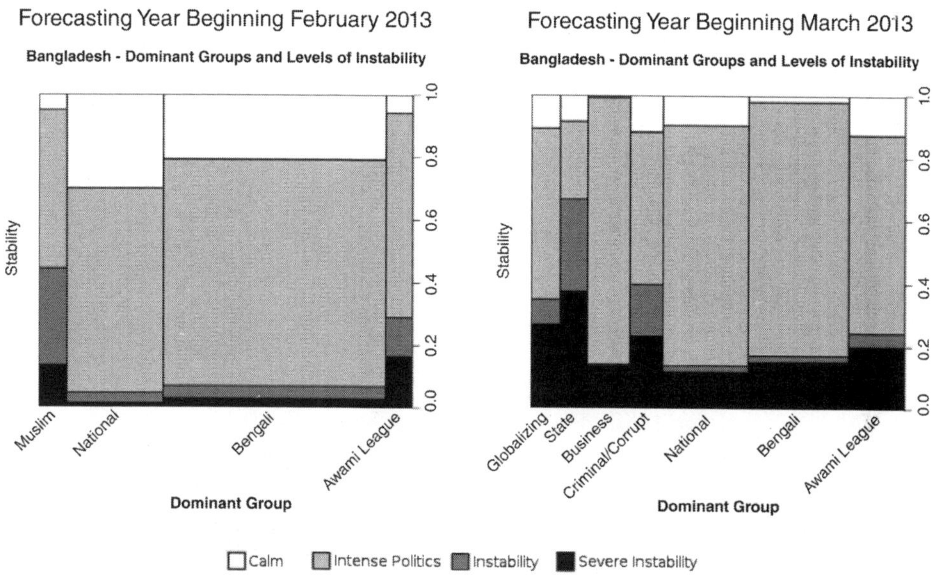

Fig. 7.9. Dominant groups in Bangladesh

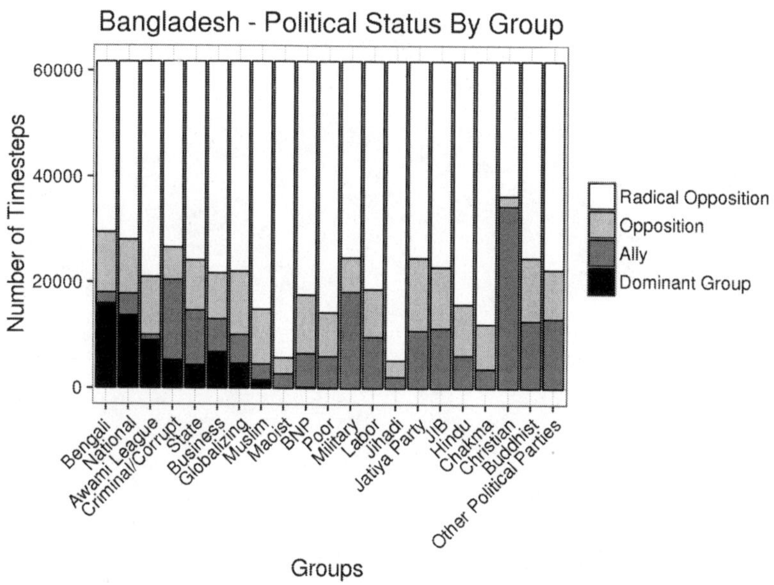

Fig. 7.10. Political status by group in Bangladesh

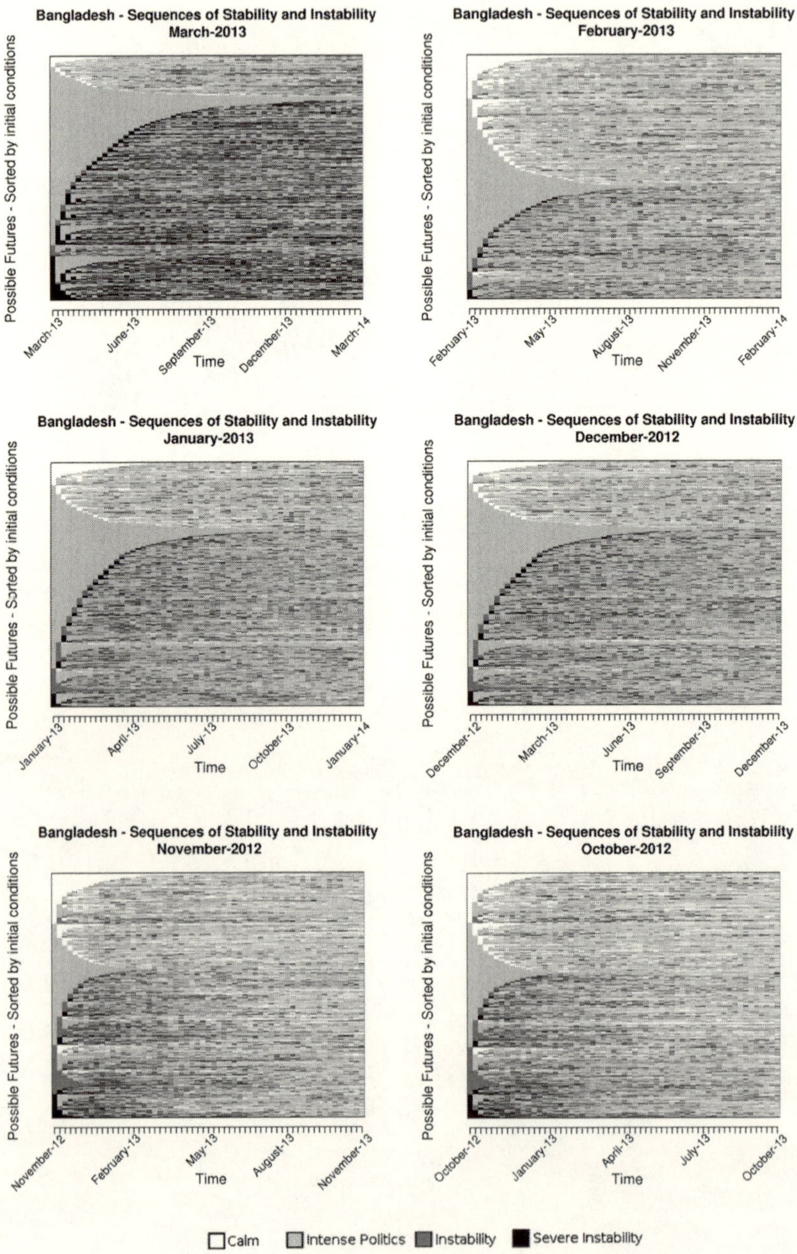

Fig. 7.11. Six sequence plots with forecasts for October 2012 until February 2014. Each of one thousand trajectories is traced horizontally by a single line to represent either calm (black), intense politics (dark gray), instability (light gray), or severe instability (white).

vertically, we can gain a sense of how much of the state space of the future—taking into account all one thousand trajectories—is relatively stable or unstable across the entire square. In the case of Bangladesh forecasts for the year beginning with October 2012 through the year starting in March 2013, we see a trend toward a pronounced shrinkage in the areas of light gray and white and expansion in the areas of dark gray and especially black, suggesting not just a decreasing probability of calm but an increasing probability of either intense political competition or severe instability.

Precisely how productive is this approach to thinking about the future compared to others? How productive might it become? These questions are unanswerable in the context of this chapter, but some evidence for the validity of the results of V-SAFT's depiction of the space of Bangladesh's future can be considered. If we set aside "internal validity" or "verification" questions, considering that—in principle, at least—computer models do offer certain assurances about consistency of propositions and transparency of operations, we can consider the more challenging question of "external validity." How good was the modeling effort as a guide to the future of Bangladesh? This is a daunting question, since once the future is understood as a distribution of possible trajectories, with the actual future understood as but one of them, it is difficult to learn about the model's validity from the failure to forecast correctly in a particular case. But models can be faulted and perhaps improved, if they fail to include outcomes as possible when events show that they actually were. A more systematic and demanding form of validation is to require very large numbers of forecasts from such models—forecasts made with various levels of confidence or with various probabilities attached. The distribution of these forecasts can then be compared to the distribution of actual outcomes for evidence that the contours of the spaces of the future produced by the model resembled the contours of the actual spaces of the future from different points in the past.

Using a technique known as a "separation plot" (developed by Greenbill, Ward, and Sacks),[20] V-SAFT accumulated an archive of forecasts of four EOIs by country and compared them to "ground truth" with respect to whether and when those events occurred. Figure 7.12 displays a separation plot reporting data about EOIs in Bangladesh from October 2012 to November 2013 and V-SAFT forecasts of those EOIs. For each event-month combination listed across the *x*-axis, the shade of each bar represents whether the event occurred and how intense it was according to a review of relevant online sources. The black line represents our forecasted likelihood of each event one month prior (ranging from 0 percent to 100 percent likely). The most accurate forecast would only have shaded bars to the far right, and

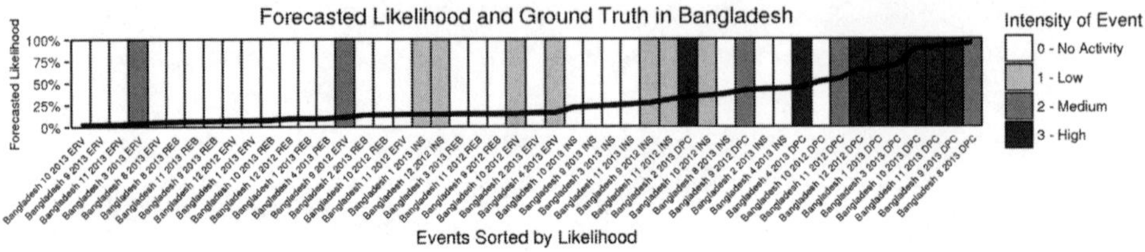

Fig. 7.12. Forecasts arrayed by increasing forecasted probabilities of events plotted against their nonoccurrence, occurrence, and intensity

all of the bars to the far left would be white. Simple visual inspection suggests an encouraging interpretation, since, despite errors, the white columns, where events did not occur, are strongly clustered to the left, where low probabilities were forecasted, while dark columns, where events did occur, are strongly clustered to the right, where high probabilities were forecasted.

V-SAFT models, including virtual Bangladesh, have been used repeatedly to conduct "what-if" experiments, counterfactual experiments that seriously treat questions that scholars have often discussed as whimsy. What, it has often been asked, would have happened if Hitler had been killed in the trenches in World War I, if the asteroid that made the Chicxulub crater had narrowly missed the Earth rather than plunging into the Yucatan, if the battle of Salamis had been fought without the brilliance of Themistocles, and so on? What, as Steven J. Gould put it, would have been the case if the "tape of life" could be "replayed" under slightly different conditions?[21] With the sort of capacity described here, this kind of question is no longer whimsy, and answers provided to it can be evaluated, at least in principle, against criteria much more reliable than rhetorical seductiveness.

In the fall of 2013, Bangladesh was headed toward elections. The opposition party, the Bangladesh Nationalist Party (BNP), fully cognizant of the way it had manipulated past election outcomes when it was in power, demanded that the Awami League dominated government turn over the management of the elections to a neutral caretaker government—one run by the judiciary and the state bureaucracy. A law had been passed requiring this arrangement, but the government argued that progress made to rid Bangladesh of corruption was sufficient to justify the government's direct management of the election, without a caretaker regime. The BNP began a campaign to delegitimize the elections, which threatened to destabilize the country, potentially involving intervention of the military. The United

States, wishing to preserve Bangladeshi democracy while insuring the country's stability, was faced with the problem of deciding whether to push the government to acquiesce in the demands of the Islamist-leaning BNP and the apparent requirements of the law or to maximize prospects for the stability of the country under the rule of leaders Washington favored. By closely analyzing the distribution of futures produced by the virtual Bangladesh model, it was possible to discern a pattern that yielded nonintuitive but compelling insights into the implications of this decision.

We proceeded by identifying a subset of futures produced by the model, in which the election period featured either a caretaker government or a government dominated by the Awami League. Comparison of patterns of instability within those two types of futures (each comprising approximately 17 percent of the entire distribution) suggested that a caretaker government would increase the stability of the election period itself, but at the price of a considerably larger risk of severe instability later. On the other hand, Awami League government management of the election would produce more disturbance during the election period but lower risks of subsequent severe instability. The model also suggested that the risks of subsequent severe instability could be significantly reduced if the composition of the Awami League's government was broadened to include representatives of major sectors and groups not directly associated with the BNP.

Military domination of the country did not emerge within the range of "possible" outcomes that our model forecast, but since this counterfactual was much discussed and much worried about, we conducted "what-if" experiments by rerunning the model to produce two additional batches of trajectories. The script governing the running of each experiment punctuated the trajectories, at a point prior to the scheduled election period, with two types of military interventions, each with a precedent in Bangladesh's political history. The first intervention, high-level coup, featured seizure of the government in the capital by high-ranking officers. The other focused on action by low-level officers on a much more diffuse basis, taking over local governing institutions.

The result can be summarized by noting that a military coup was seen to significantly decrease the likelihood of an apolitical caretaker government afterward. A period of military governance following a coup does become possible and, in the case of a high-level coup, even politically stable. However, following either form of military intervention, political polarization increased, signaled by a marked change in the balance of violent versus nonviolent mobilization.

Conclusion: Why Bother with Another Method?

The principles governing the contributions to this volume are that the worlds we experience and analyze are constructed and that understanding those worlds means critically interpreting them by deconstructing the assumptions and frames of reference they reflect. I have argued that ABM offers a theoretically powerful approach to implementing these principles systematically, supporting my argument by offering the "hard" case" of thinking in a disciplined way about the future. One might even consider this challenge an extreme example of the problem of analysis with a small n and many variables (since, technically, $n = 0$). With computer power as cheap as it is and with islands of good theory ready to be applied to real problems, the approach has the potential, at least, to do much better than any other method available in producing outputs closer to the complexity of the worlds inhabited by politicians and policy makers. For younger scholars, accustomed to finding and using apps of various kinds, the intuition that computers could be used for social science research in exciting new ways is probably more natural than for previous cohorts.

To be sure, portions of the learning curve for using the approach can be steep. But acquisition of the necessary skills is less arduous than may be commonly imagined. For one thing, neither advanced algebra nor calculus is required. Indeed, ABM is designed primarily for problems that cannot, even in theory, be solved mathematically. Twenty years ago, working with ABM would require good programming skills, but modeling platforms are now available that do not assume the ability to read or write in a programming language and that enable substantive theoretical knowledge to be quickly and intuitively encoded.

ABM based in computer simulation is dynamic, visually entrancing, rich in data, and formal. In all these ways, it is nifty. But niftiness per se does not itself justify attention, especially for scholars who are masters of other methods still useful for problems yet unsolved. There are deeper reasons why IR scholars should investigate the technique, other than the increased facility they may thereby enjoy for answering questions they already entertain. Specifically, mastery of this method is likely to significantly expand both the number and kind of questions IR scholars are able to address.

Without a systematic method to produce very large numbers of analytically consistent but substantively distinctive scenarios, both researchers and policy-makers are precluded from thinking about what has not happened yet as distributions of what could happen. Instead their attention is confined to tiny zones in the state space of the possible—zones traced by a few strategically or idiosyncratically crafted stories. As emphasized at the beginning of this chapter, thinking in a disciplined way about the future requires the systematic and controlled construction of very large numbers of scenarios. This requires a method capable of exploiting what is now readily available computing power to conduct large numbers of disciplined thought experiments, thereby offering opportunities to ask more appropriate questions about the future than can be asked with conventional techniques. Methods, in other words, should not be seen as only equipment used by those whose ideas and purposes arise independent of method. Methods, such as ABM, can often prime the pump of insight. Indeed, precisely because this method is based squarely on principles of constructivism and critical practices of deconstruction and because it incorporates randomness, it will act as an intuition pump—changing the way researchers think about the social world, expanding the questions they see it proper and possible to address, suggesting approaches to problems that have seemed intractable, and simultaneously imposing discipline on interpretations of what the world was, is, can be, and why.

But just as a new interpretation of the world may shock or confound those whose expectations it contradicts, a new method may produce incredulity and even horror if it seems to entail combining "high-tech" devices with an "interpretivist" posture that usually celebrates itself as antagonistic to misplaced "scientism." Anyway, why bother with a method that requires investment and training, if one does not feel currently available methods have been exhausted of the contributions they could make? Is the only reason to adopt a new method that it provides better ways to achieve established goals or answer standard questions ? For most researchers in most situations, the answer may well be "yes." Afterall, the very meaning of "normal science," in Thomas Kuhn's terms, is that paradigmatic techniques and methods for solving problems are fully agreed on and seen as effective. However, when researchers are unsatisfied with the questions and answers available in their field, then methodological questions can become nearly indistinguishable from substantive ones. In this circumstance progress is likely to require new methods enabling researchers to pose questions impossible to address with familiar techniques.

Herein lies a serious obstacle to scientific progress, or scholarly work in general. Established researchers have outsized influence on what apprentice researchers judge to be the appropriate methods and training to receive. Successful researchers are successful partly because they have mastered technologies to support investigation of the particular kinds of questions the methods associated with those technologies can answer effectively. The role of senior researchers as models, supervisors, or judges of new work thus considerably raises the barriers to entry that methods designed for answering different questions must overcome, even if the answers to those questions might be more rewarding—intellectually or socially. Therefore, despite the crucial role that loyalty to established research programs, paradigms, and methods plays in the ability of communities of experts to share and rigorously critique their work, scientific progress cannot rely only on the questions and methods that scholars who are currently successful find "interesting" or useful. Ultimately, disciplines, as research programs, are threatened and destroyed by the degenerative consequences of narrowing substantive foci and the exclusion of new questions deemed unaddressable—and therefore uninteresting.

Whether via the contingencies of Kuhnian paradigm shifts or mechanisms of Lakatosian competition for resources among rival research programs, science does progress. Substantive innovation in theory and in methods available can constitute the proximate impetus for these shifts—most likely a combination of the two. The crucial point is that from the point of view of the advancement of science in general and of the social sciences in particular, it is a fundamental mistake to view methodology as purely a function of the substantive task at hand or of interest only to methodology "specialists." Across all the arts and sciences, methods that are employed both open and close avenues of investigation, creativity, and discovery. Without new methods of seeing or studying the world, many kinds of new questions could never be posed. Consider how artists expanded their horizons as new methods and materials for drawing and painting became available. Or think of poetry, which, as a method, imposes disciplines on the use of language, such as meter and rhyme. These elements of the poetic method restrict language use, thereby forcing a greater role for imagination and creativity. In the hands of excellent practitioners, the result is new ideas, associations, images, and expressions. Without the rules and limits imposed by the method of poetry, these uses of language would otherwise remain undiscovered and unexpressed. In other words, as a method, poetry allows access to terrains of the human imagination that would otherwise remain unexplored.

In the sciences, there could be no Newtonian theory of gravity without calculus, no theory of general relativity without tensor calculus, no microbiology without the microscope, no modern astronomy without the telescope, no experimental particle physics without particle accelerators, and no sophisticated paleontology or serious cross-cultural archaeology without carbon dating. In the social sciences as well, methods help produce the ideas we have and the questions we pose. In the last fifty years, a number of new methods have transformed what we know of as the social sciences and the practices associated with them. These include Bayesian statistics, natural language processing, mass survey techniques, field experiments, discourse analysis, deconstructionist techniques of textual exegesis, game-theoretic formal modeling, and even word processing. In all fields, new methods that arise in response to unsolved problems and new technological capacities help produce new questions, new ideas, new answers to old questions, and often new sets of questions that themselves become the basis for new subfields and even new disciplines.

Constructivist and critical stances toward domains of interest in the social sciences open the potential for new insights and effective understandings. But only methods capable of exploiting that potential—for systematic elaboration of possibilities and disciplined deconstruction of outcomes—can enable scholars to exploit that potential. I have argued that ABM is such a method, and I have illustrated the plausibility of this claim with a report on the application of one relatively ambitious ABM tool for parsing the space of political futures. V-SAFT's successes with respect to Bangladesh and a range of other countries suggest that deployment of virtualization models of particular political systems can be more effective than standard methods for exploring and evaluating the relationship between variables and past outcomes as well as between policy choices and future outcomes. However, whether V-SAFT is presently developed enough to regularly outperform other techniques should not be the sole or even the primary criterion for giving the kind of investigative tool it represents serious consideration. The real test of a method is not whether it outperforms other methods on traditional tasks but whether it can lead to a level of sophistication and breadth of consideration that lead scholars and scientists to trade traditional tasks for even better ones.

Notes

1. See Gary King and Langche Zeng, "Logistic Regression in Rare Events Data," *Political Analysis* 9 (2001): 137–63.

2. I thank Matthew Reichert for his very helpful and repeated readings of earlier drafts of this essay and Miguel Garces for his critical reading of the text and his expert assistance in the development of data visualizations. Portions of this chapter appeared in "Making Sense of Social Radar: V-SAFT as an Intelligent Machine," in *Sociocultural Behavior Sensemaking: State of the Art in Understanding the Operational Environment*, ed. Jill Egeth, Gary D. Klein, and Dylan Schmorrow (McLean, VA: MITRE, 2014), 317–37.

3. For an extended treatment of the problem of disciplining counterfactual analy-

sis, see Ian S. Lustick, "Tetlock and Counterfactuals: Saving Methodological Ambition from Empirical Findings," *Critical Review* 22, no. 4 (2010): 427–47.

4. Benoit Mandelbrot and Richard L. Hudson, *The (Mis)Behavior of Markets: A Fractal View of Financial Turbulence* (New York: Basic Books, 2004), 77.

5. Nassim Taleb, *The Black Swan: The Impact of the Highly Improbable* (New York: Random House, 2010), xxix.

6. Ibid., xxii.

7. This entire approach is related to "modal logic" and "possible worlds" theory in philosophy, as developed to think about a variety of philosophical problems associated with thinking counterfactually. For an extreme but influential view, see David K. Lewis, *On the Plurality of Worlds* (Malden, MA: Blackwell, 1986). For colorized versions of the figures appearing in this chapter, see Lustick, "Making Sense of Social Radar," 317–37, https://www.mitre.org/sites/default/files/publications/SocioculturalSensemaking.pdf.

8. For details and exemplary studies in each of these fields, see http://www.martinos.org/biosystems/projects.php; S. J. Dean, G. J. Gumerman, J. M. Epstein, R. Axtell, A. C. Swedlund, M. T. Parker, and S. Mccarroll, "Understanding Anasazi Culture Change through Agent-Based Modeling," in *Human and Primate Societies: Agent-Based Modeling of Social and Spatial Processes*, ed. T. A. Kohler and G. J. Gumerman, Santa Fe Institute Studies in the Sciences of Complexity (New York: Oxford University Press, 2000), 179–205; L. R. Izquierdo, N. M. Gots, and J. G. Polhill, "FEARLUS-W: An Agent-Based Model of River Basin Land Use and Water Management" (paper presented at the conference "Framing Land Use Dynamics," Utrecht, April 2003),; Riccardo Boero and Flaminio Squazzoni, "Does Empirical Embeddedness Matter? Methodological Issues on Agent-Based Models for Analytical Social Science," *Journal of Artificial Societies and Social Simulation* 8, no. 4 (2005): 6, http://jasss.soc.surrey.ac.uk/8/4/6.html sections 4.42–4.47; http://www.talkorigins.org/faqs/genalg/genalg.html; http://biosystems.ucsf.edu/research.html; http://www.msysbio.com/; Joshua M. Epstein, *Agent Zero: Toward Neurocognitive Foundations for Generative Social Science* (Princeton, NJ: Princeton University Press, 2014).

9. Thomas C. Schelling, *Micromotives and Macrobehavior* (New York: Norton, 1978).

10. See Rainer Hegselman, "Thomas C. Schelling and the Computer: Some Notes on Schelling's Essay 'On Letting a Computer Help with the Work,'" *Journal of Artificial Societies and Social Simulation* 15, no. 4 (2012): 9, http://jasss.soc.surrey.ac.uk/15/4/9.html.

11. The most convenient and reliable source for surveying the variety of applications of ABM to social science problems is the *Journal of Artificial Societies and Social Simulation* (http://jasss.soc.surrey.ac.uk/).

12. For a survey of political science applications of ABM, see Ian S. Lustick and Dan Miodownik, "Abstractions, Ensembles, and Virtualizations: Simplicity and Complexity in Agent-Based Modeling," *Comparative Politics* 41, no. 2 (2009): 223–44.

13. See Ian S. Lustick, "Locating the History We Have within the Distribution of Counterfactuals: Laws, Stories, and Computer Simulation" Paper prepared for presentation at Columbia's Center for Historical Social Science, for the workshop on "His-

tory, Rationality, and Agency in Social Science," New York, April 16, 2002), http://www.polisci.upenn.edu/ps-i/papers.html.

14. See Ian S. Lustick, "PS-I: A User-Friendly Agent-Based Modeling Platform for Testing Theories of Political Identity and Political Stability," *Journal of Artificial Societies and Social Simulation* 5, no. 3 (2002); Lustick and Miodownik, "Abstractions, Ensembles, and Virtualizations"; Ian S. Lustick, Dan Miodownik, and Roy J. Eidelson, "Secessionism in Multicultural States: Does Sharing Power Prevent or Encourage It?," *American Political Science Review* 98, no. 2 (2004): 209–29.

15. See Ian S. Lustick, "Simulating the Effects of Israeli-Palestinian Violence, Fundamentalist Mobilization, and Regional Disruption on Regime Stability and USA-Friendly Outcomes in Middle East Polity" (paper presented at the workshop "Origins and Patterns of Political Violence 1: Violence in Civil Wars," Santa Fe, January 16–18, 2004), http://www.polisci.upenn.edu/ps-i/publications/Lusticksantafe.pdf.

16. See Sean O'Brien, "Crisis Early Warning and Decision Support: Contemporary Approaches and Thoughts on Future Research," *International Studies Review* 12, no. 1 (2010): 87–104.

17. Slight disrepancies between the original and this discussion are due to the correction of small errors discovered in the process of reformatting the visuals for this publication.

18. These higher-level concepts require precise operationalizations. For example, DPC is operationally defined as existing "in a time-step when the aggregate influence of protesting agents (protest) multiplied by the protest_threshold (6) is greater than the aggregate influence of the dominant identity (data$dominant_activation)." The routine that implements this category as a rule for data collection is dpc_exists = (protest*protest_threshold>data$dominant_activation).

19. In figures 7.6–7.8 and 7.10, groups and identities listed along the *x*-axis are arrayed from left to right in order of decreasing "aggregate influence" during the periods of dominance by the group named under the column on the extreme left. V-SAFT computes aggregate influence for each group for any time step by summing the individual influence of agents activated on that identity.

20. See Brian Greenhill, Michael D. Ward, and Audrey Sacks, "The Separation Plot: A New Visual Method for Evaluating the Fit of Binary Models," *American Journal of Political Science* 55, no. 4 (2011): 991–1002.

21. Concerning the prominence of this meme, implying (incorrectly) that the tape of "history" cannot be rerun, see Lustick, "Tetlock and Counterfactuals," 441–42.

CHAPTER 8

Constructing Rational International Fisheries Governance

J. SAMUEL BARKIN

At first glance, formal models of rational choice theory might seem to be methodologically incompatible with constructivist theorizing. The former is generally used in a manner that is both epistemologically and ontologically individualist, in ways that put it in direct contradiction with the more sociological assumptions of constructivism. In narrow terms of method, a rational choice model by itself will not yield a constructivist analysis. This chapter makes the argument, however, that formal rational choice modeling can usefully inform constructivist analysis. More specifically, formal models used heuristically or counterfactually can identify patterns of strategic behavior that we might expect of actors in a specified social setting. Relating these expectations to observed behavior can shed light on the social structures within which the strategic behavior is located and through which it is being mediated.

To make this case for the methodological compatibility of formal rational choice models and constructivist analysis, I present a (relatively simple) model of international negotiations toward the cooperative management of common pool resources and illustrate the analysis with the example of international fisheries management. Because international fisheries are common pool resources, it makes sense, from an intuitive rationalist perspective, that they are badly overfished. But that perspective cannot explain some of the peculiarities of international cooperation to ameliorate overfishing. In particular, rational cooperation is embedded in a set of norms and discourses—about things as varied as the standards against which to measure fishing effort, the role of fisheries in development, and the international legal structure within which fisheries negotiations happen—that yield outcomes that do not make rational sense. This case, in other words, shows intentionally strategic negotiating behavior that points to a normative and discursive structure with several interesting peculiarities.

Juxtaposing a formal rational choice model with constructivist analysis of the predictive failures of that model can be an effective way of getting at the relationship between these peculiarities and the rational cooperation that state negotiators are ostensibly undertaking. This chapter uses the fisheries case to illustrate one way in which the two modes of analysis can be used together to generate a broader heuristic understanding of specific cases of international politics. A prior step to presenting the model and analysis is to define what I mean by formal rational choice modeling and constructivist analysis and to make the case that they are methodologically compatible. The phrase "formal rational choice modeling" in particular requires some unpacking.

Formal Rational Choice Modeling

There are three components to the phrase "formal rational choice modeling": "formal," "rational choice," and "modeling." Most straightforward to deal with in this context is the first component. "Formal" here means using a formal language, understood as a set of symbols with clearly defined meanings and connected by a syntax with precise rules. In practice, this means a model presented using game-theoretic symbols and syntax rather than presented narratively. The formal aspect of the presentation in and of itself is not really of issue in this discussion; it is a language, rather than a method, methodology, epistemology, ontology, theory, or paradigm. Formal language has the advantage of precision, making it easier to verify logical claims and conclusions drawn from them than is the case with narrative language, at the expense of descriptive richness. Therefore, it is well suited to the drawing of conclusions from postulates but less well suited to the description of complex social structures. The latter observation makes formal language inappropriate for many forms of constructivist analysis but not necessarily to the construction of counterfactual or heuristic models as part of a constructivist analysis.

More complicated than defining "formal" is defining "rational choice theory." At one level, the term is straightforward: it refers to social science analysis that is methodologically individualist and begins with the assumption that agents act in accordance with cost-benefit analyses drawing on exogenously defined transitive utility preferences. But, at another level, it is misleading to speak of a single rational choice theory. Methodologically individualist analysis based on the assumption of economic rationality can be embedded in a variety of understandings of the epistemological meaning of "rational choice theory."[1]

A basic distinction is between what are sometimes called the "domain" and the "as-if" approaches to rational choice theory. The domain approach takes rational choice assumptions to be empirical fact and therefore takes rational choice theory more broadly to be a description of how the world works. In some versions of this reading of rational choice, preferences can be imputed from observed behavior using the tools of formal modeling, because the mechanism connecting preferences and behavior can be assumed to be rational.[2] In other versions, preferences are assumed to be economic and, therefore, measurable in money. These preferences can be connected with observed behavior by assuming imperfections in market structure, particularly the availability of information.[3]

The as-if approach takes rational choice assumptions to be analytically useful tools rather than empirical fact. People are assumed to act "as if" they were rational, because doing so is an effective way of generating hypotheses about likely behavior.[4] Eliding the question of how people actually think, this approach focuses on the utility of rational choice models in generating testable hypotheses. While these two forms of rational choice theory draw on correspondence theories of epistemology, or what Patrick Thaddeus Jackson calls "mind-world dualism," there are versions that use the theory in what Jackson calls an "analyticist" manner, as a heuristic mechanism for understanding the world, rather than predicting it.[5] Many discussions of market theory, for example, are heuristic in this sense; we know that markets cannot be perfect in practice, but the creation of a perfect market as an analytical construct can help us think about the role of market imperfections.[6] This last use of rational choice theory is the one most likely to be compatible with constructivist analysis.

The final component of the phrase I am defining here is "modeling." At its most general, a social science model is a representation of a social system that both simplifies and helps to explain that system. Models can use a variety of syntaxes, including formal, narrative, and graphical. They can be designed to be predictive, explanatory, or heuristic.[7] Different kinds of models hew to different standards of evaluation. Predictive models are generally evaluated on their ability to predict outcomes in a particular category of events. Explanatory models are evaluated on the extent to which they explain particular outcomes within the framework and assumptions of the model. Heuristic models are designed as thought experiments, as exercises in "what would happen if" rather than "this explains why." They can be thought of as Weberian ideal types.[8] The standard of evaluation for heuristic models is therefore necessarily less precise than for the other two kinds of models. Heuristic modeling is useful in helping us to understand the world, rather than in the creation of a specific correspondence with it.

Formal rational choice modeling, then, is the use of a formal symbolic syntax to create a representation of the social world that builds on assumptions of individual rationality. The use to which such models are put depends on the version of rational choice theory to which one subscribes. While this subscription dictates how one uses the model, it does not necessarily dictate the form or content of the model itself; a given model can be used in distinct ways by proponents of different versions of rational choice theory. However, different versions have biases toward particular types of model. There has been a tendency over the past few decades for models published in the IR literature, particularly in journals with a bias toward rational choice and formal modeling, to become increasingly mathematically complex.[9] This is true of work in both the domain and, to a lesser extent, the as-if traditions. It is not clear, however, whether this trend is related to the demands of rational choice theorizing per se or to disciplinary pressures.

In either case, a trend toward increasing mathematical complexity, accompanied by higher barriers to entry into modeling, can be actively counterproductive to the use of formal rational choice models in a methodologically heuristic or counterfactual way. The smaller the number of scholars who can understand the model is, the less broadly useful the model is as a heuristic. Therefore, heuristic models should ideally avoid unnecessary mathematical complexity. In this chapter, I build a heuristic model of international cooperation to address questions of international fisheries management. To this end, I use an analyticist version of rational choice theory and language that is formal but relatively simple.

Constructivist Analysis

How does this version of formal rational choice modeling interact with and serve the purposes of constructivist analysis? The definition of constructivism used here follows that in the introductory chapter to this volume. The analysis that follows later in the chapter uses a relatively thin or neoclassical version of constructivism. But, in principle, the relationship between heuristic rational choice modeling and constructivism should apply as well to thicker or more postmodern versions.[10]

Two ways in which the relationship between rational choice and constructivism have been discussed in the IR literature provide a useful starting point for the discussion here. The first, following March and Olsen,[11] refers to the distinction between a logic of consequences and a logic of appropriateness. In the former, agents act rationally to maximize utility, as per rational choice theory; in the latter, agents act according to social/organizational norms. The second discussion references what Wendt and Fearon call the "two-step process," in which the constructivist study of identity illuminates the interests that rational choice theory takes as exogenous.[12]

The logic of appropriateness, as opposed to the logic of consequences, is often cited as a definitional feature of constructivism. The logics themselves, as assumptions of why people behave the way they do, are in a tension that cannot be reconciled, either theoretically or empirically. Both logics can in fact be read as ultimately tautological. If we assume that people behave as rational maximizers, we can impute from any behavior a motivating set of interests. If we assume that people behave according to social scripts, we can read any behavior as evidence of an underlying script (so that if people behave strategically, it must be the situationally or institutionally appropriate thing to do). This suggests fairly little scope for communication across these two logics and, if the logics are taken as definitional, across rational choice and constructivism as well.[13]

But the logic of appropriateness does not quite work as a definitional element of constructivism. The term *logic of appropriateness* was developed in the context of the study of organizational behavior and is certainly compatible with the constructivist study of organizational behavior in international politics. But constructivist analysis can also be used to study a much broader array of behaviors and, furthermore, to study the effects of those behaviors on institutional structure, whether the institution is a formal organization or a discourse. More specifically, constructivist analysis can be and has been used to study consequentialist behavior and its use in constituting the discourses and institutions that define appropriateness.[14] Since constructivism is broader than the logic of appropriateness and can be used to study consequentialist action, the distinction between the two logics cannot meaningfully serve as the focus of a discussion of the relationship between constructivism and rational choice.

The two-step process, in which the interaction of exogenous interests is studied through rational choice models while those interests are endogenized using constructivist analysis, seems at first a more promising avenue for a discussion of the relationship between rational choice and constructivism. With the relationship framed in this way, the two approaches are defined not in terms of mutually exclusive tautologies but in terms of complementary components of an analysis that is broader than either can provide on its own. This still fails to get the relationship quite right, however, for at least two reasons. First, the relationship is recursive. Agents act consequentially to affect the social structures that, in this view, generate the preferences that drive consequentialist action. Seen as part of a dialectic of co-constitution, this recursive relationship can be difficult to study effectively from a methodological perspective yet is not problematic from an epistemological perspective. But seen as part of a neopositivist two-step process, it generates an infinite regress problem. Preferences cannot be successfully exogenized from the rationalist calculations if the creation of preferences is endogenous to those calculations.

This recursiveness problem suggests a tension between rational choice assumptions and constructivist analysis, pointing to the second reason that the two-step process fails to get the relationship quite right. The process implicitly imports into the discussion a domain theory of rational choice (the as-if version does not fit the process), and the domain theory is itself epistemologically incompatible with constructivist analysis. In a way, the claim that the two-step process makes about human motivation is the opposite of the claim made by the consequences/appropriateness distinction. The former assumes that agents act purely rationally given their (socially constructed) preferences, rather than purely appropriately. But constructivist analysis can cope with a much broader variety of motivations than either assumption allows.

This last observation suggests both a less formalized and a less dichotomized relationship between rational choice theory and constructivism. Given that constructivism is not compatible with the domain version of rational choice theory and its assumption that people necessarily behave instrumentally rationally, a formal model that works methodologically with constructivism would have to make as-if or heuristic rational choice assumptions. These assumptions—that people may or may not act instrumentally rationally but that it is useful, either predictively or heuristically, to assume in some circumstances that they do—lend themselves to a less formalized and dichotomized relationship. They also lend themselves to the sort of heuristic modeling discussed in the previous section.

The assumptions involved in the use of formal rational choice models in constructivist theorizing is not, then, that people always behave rationally or that they never behave as *homo economicus* but, rather, that they may do either sometimes and that drawing a clear line between rational and nonrational behavior may not ultimately be a useful exercise. The latter assumptions are based on a claim that we can learn interesting things about the social structure of international politics by observing action, modeling rational behavior, and navigating the tension between the two. The observed action in the case considered in this chapter is international fisheries negotiations. The model captures some of the features that differentiate this issue from others about which states seek to cooperate with each other.

International Fisheries Politics

International fisheries are those involving either fishing on the high seas—that is, outside of exclusive economic zones (EEZs)—or fishing of straddling or highly migratory stocks, those that swim across EEZs or between the zones and the high seas. These fisheries are a classic example of common pool resources. They are nonexcludable; states cannot (legally) restrict the nationals or ships of other states from fishing in the high seas or from fishing for migratory or straddling stocks in their own waters or EEZs.[15] They are also subtractable. Fishing not only directly reduces the number of fish available to others but, when carried out beyond a certain point, threatens the ability of the fish stock to reproduce and replenish itself in the future.[16]

International fisheries regulation happens mostly under the auspices of a set of intergovernmental organizations called regional fisheries management organizations (RFMOs). These organizations focus on specific regions (the Northwest Atlantic, the Antarctic seas, etc.) or specific types of fishery (primarily tunas and tuna-like species). A majority of RFMOs oversee the creation of authoritative, hard-law rules, including quotas by country, and these rules are the focus of this discussion.[17] The creation of quotas for international fisheries has two steps: (1) the specification of an overall quota and (2) the division of that quota among member states. Nonmember states are not subject to quotas and cannot be required to join. This has traditionally been a key weakness of international fisheries regulation, because free riders can undermine the benefit of cooperation over common pool resources.[18] But member states have increasingly been addressing this problem by prohibiting imports of fish not caught under RFMO quotas.[19]

At first glance, state behavior in international fisheries politics seems to conform with rationalist assumptions. A common pool resource issue structure should encourage competitive overexploitation of the resource and should undermine efforts at cooperation,[20] and this is what we see in practice. But this first glance takes for granted a variety of assumed givens in international fisheries politics, givens that states, as represented by fisheries negotiators, use to define the interests they pursue in these negotiations. Identifying the expected outcomes of rational negotiations can help us to identify these givens and thereby to interrogate the norms that underpin international fisheries cooperation and its failures. One way of identifying these outcomes is to model them formally.

A Model of International Common Pool Resource Negotiations

The model developed here addresses two issues that make models in what is often called the rational cooperation literature problematic for the study of international environmental cooperation.[21] The first issue is the relationship between collective action and public goods, and the second is the role of shadows of the future in international negotiations. The interplay of these two issues can help to illuminate the power dynamics of negotiations over the creation of mechanisms for international fisheries cooperation. that the existing literature does not capture adequately. Traditional rational choice models of international cooperation tend to assume that the object of cooperation is the management of international public goods and that while different countries may care more or less about these particular goods, these differences are in current utility, rather than temporal. Both of these assumptions are problematic when applied to cooperation to manage the global commons, of which international fisheries are a classic example.

From the perspective of the rational cooperation literature, the goal of international cooperation is to overcome collective action problems, and collective action is often seen as a model of public goods provision.[22] However, the global commons and its related goods, the subject of most international environmental politics, are common pool resources. These are similar to public goods in that they are nonexcludable, but they differ from public goods in being rival.[23] As such, a variable worth exploring in applying the international cooperation literature to international environmental politics is rivalness.

Meanwhile, the "shadow of the future" is the extent to which agents value future gains compared with current gains. It is the flip side of the discount rate, an accounting mechanism that economists use to discount future gains in calculating present utility. A long shadow of the future can be operationalized as a low discount rate, a short shadow as a high discount rate. The rational cooperation literature has discussed the valuation of future gains, at some length. But most of the discussion has assumed similar valuations for all parties to a negotiation and has looked at the effect of higher or lower valuations overall on the chances of achieving a cooperative outcome in negotiation or on the robustness of that outcome.[24] The effects that differential valuations of the future compared with the present have across actors within given negotiations has been less well explored. Such differential valuation is notably salient in international environmental negotiations. For example, developing countries often argue that because of an imperative to develop in the near future, they cannot afford measures to improve the environment in the far future.[25]

The model addresses these issues by asking what the effect on negotiating power would be if we took into account different levels of rivalness of goods and differential shadows of the future that exist among negotiators, operationalized as differential discount rates. We begin with a game involving two players, A and B. The game has a policy space (S) equal to [0, 1], where A's utility per time unit is z, and B's utility per time unit is $(1 - z)$. In other words, A prefers outcomes closer to 1, and B prefers outcomes closer to 0. Assume that there are two possible deals in S that can be implemented, x and y, where $x > y$. This means that player A prefers x and that player B prefers y.

Players A and B also have permanent, fixed discount rates, d_A and d_B, where $0 \leq d \leq 1$. This means that the present value to each player of a particular outcome iterated in perpetuity is that outcome divided by its discount rate. Finally, both players have costs of noncooperation, C_A and C_B. These costs are the costs of delaying the beginning of an agreement. With nonrival goods, the cost includes forgoing the benefit of having an agreement in that round, plus perhaps the risk that negotiations will break off after the round. With rival goods, there is an additional cost, that of the depletion over time of the good in question. The more the good is depleted as a result of the additional turn of noncooperation (i.e., the less available it is in future rounds), the higher the cost of noncooperation is. The cost is higher as a country's discount rate is lower. Depletion of the good decreases potential future benefits per turn by a set amount per turn, amount q. The present value of future cooperation yielding any particular outcome is that outcome divided by the discount rate. The present value of a decrease in returns of q per turn is thus $-q/d$. Therefore, the bigger the discount rate, the smaller the loss in present value of a given level of depletion of the rival good. In other words, with rival goods, C will increase with faster depletion of the good and a smaller discount rate for the country in question.[26]

The game is a discrete-time game with simultaneous moves and is iterated.[27] In each round, each player can either concede to the other player's preferred outcome or hold out for its own preferred outcome. Assume that

		Player A	
		Concede	Hold Out
	Concede	$x+y/2$ $2-x-y/2$	x $1-x$
Player B			
	Hold Out	y 1-y	$-C_A$ $-C_B$

Fig. 8.1. Game matrix

once an outcome is decided on (i.e., once at least one player has conceded), the players continue to receive the benefits of that outcome in perpetuity. For example, if player *B* concedes to outcome *x*, each player receives its payoff for *x* (which is *x* for *A* and 1 – *x* for *B*) at each turn in perpetuity. For convenience, assume as well that if both players concede at the same time, the outcome is chosen randomly (i.e., there is a 50 percent chance of either cooperative outcome). Therefore, the payoff received in the "concede/concede" box is the mean of the other two cooperative outcomes.

The game matrix is depicted in figure 8.1. Player *A* should opt to hold out in any given round of play when the expected benefit of holding out is greater than the expected cost (when the two figures are equal, player *A* should be indifferent between strategies). The expected benefit of holding out is the value to player *A* of the "prize"—the added benefit of the preferred cooperative outcome—multiplied by the likelihood that she will get the prize. This is equal to the discounted difference between *x* and *y* times the probability (P) that player *B* will concede if player *A* holds out. This can be written as follows:

$P(B)(x - y)/d_A$. The expected cost is C_A. So *A* should hold out when

$$P(B)(x - y)/d_A > C_A.$$

As C_A goes up, *A* is less likely to hold out (more likely to concede), other things being equal. As d_A increases, the total value of the left part of the inequality decreases, and *A* is once again less likely to hold out (more likely to concede). The same logic holds for *B*.

In other words, if a good is non-rival, a low discount rate should have an effect similar to lower costs of holding out in negotiations. The cost of losing current gains because cooperation has been postponed should be perceived as low relative to the future gains promised by cooperation on the state's preferred terms. Thus, other things being equal, in the process of holding out for a preferred outcome, the actor with the lower discount rate would place a higher value on the future gains to be had from a more preferable deal, whereas the actor with the higher rate would place a relatively higher value on the current losses caused by holding out. With a non-rival good, therefore, the effect of a relatively higher discount rate is similar to the effect of higher current costs to holding out in a negotiating war of attrition,[28] and the actor with the lower discount rate can therefore be expected to have greater bargaining power. To stay with the example of trade negotiations used above, the country that felt that it needed to boost its trade in the short term (for whatever reason, be it a need for rapid development or for access to resources) could be expected to be at a bargaining disadvantage relative to a country that cared more about the long-term shape of the trade regime than about boosting trade in the short term.

The situation is different, however, when the good in question is rival. With non-rival goods, the actor with the lower discount rate can reasonably assume that the good will be as useful in the future, after a bargaining war of attrition, as it is now. To use the trade negotiation example again, even a negotiator's use of selective tariffs or sanctions as a negotiating tool, which has the effect of making the situation during a negotiating war of attrition worse than the status quo ante (i.e., of increasing the costs of holding out), need not decrease the value to that negotiator of the deal finally reached. However, when a good is rival, when it can be used up, the dynamic changes radically. The costs of holding out in an agreement are no longer just the present value of forgone cooperation. Added to these costs is the value of future gains lost due to mismanagement or overconsumption of the good while negotiations are ongoing.

Compare, for example, negotiations about the international trade regime with negotiations over the creation of a regime to manage a fishery on the high seas. Negotiators' use of, say, selective overfishing as a negotiating tool analogous to selective tariffs can have the effect of decreasing the total future value of the good in question—in this case, the fishery. Excessive use of such a tool or even continuation of a status quo ante that is unsustainable if negotiations drag on too long can even have the effect of completely eliminating the future value of the fishery, if it is overfished to the point where it is no longer commercially viable. Significant depletion of a good while negotiations are ongoing is common in international agreements relating to resources such as fisheries, forestry, and biodiversity. Failed bargaining rounds in international negotiations often mean that a new round is not likely to begin for a year and sometimes for several years. This means that there is enough time for considerable resource depletion before the next round takes place.

That rival goods can be depleted during the process of negotiation, diminishing their total future value, can reverse the pattern of negotiating power seen with non-rival goods. Depleting a rival good has an effect on bargaining power equivalent to that of increasing the current costs of noncooperation. Because the actor with the lower discount rate places a higher value on the benefit to be gained from the good in the future and because the total future benefit can be diminished the longer negotiations last, the actor with the lower discount rate has an incentive to come to an agreement as quickly as possible, to preserve as much of the value as possible for future benefit. Because the actor with the higher discount rate values this future benefit less, that actor can credibly hold out longer in negotiations, knowing that the cost in forgone future value is greater for the actor with the lower rate. To return to the fisheries example, the actor with the lower rate, knowing that the reproductive stock of the fishery will be increasingly depleted the longer negotiations last and valuing the health of the fishery in the future relatively more than the actor with the higher rate, will want to come to agreement on a management regime as soon as possible. Other things being equal, the actor with the lower rate should be willing to settle on the other actor's terms, as long as these terms preserve some of the future value of the fishery.[29]

Thus, when states that value the future differently are negotiating to secure a good that is purely non-rival, a lower discount rate should create greater bargaining power. However, when they are negotiating to secure a good that is purely rival over time (i.e., where each unit consumed in the present subtracts at least a full unit from the total future consumption available), a higher discount rate should convey greater bargaining power. The more quickly the rival good is being depleted, the more pronounced this advantage in bargaining power should be. We should expect the state with the greater bargaining power in either case to be able to get cooperation nearer to its preferred terms than to those of other states, other things being equal.[30] The greater the difference in discount rates is, with other things being equal, the greater the difference in bargaining power is. But not all goods are either purely rival or purely non-rival—the characteristic of rivalness is realistically best understood as a range, not a dichotomy.[31] This is true both of rivalness at any given point in time and of rivalness over time, but the temporal aspect of rivalness is key here. As we move along this range from the non-rival end toward greater rivalness, the cost of holding out increases for both players, but it increases more quickly for the player with the lower discount rate. The farther we move along this range, the more likely it becomes that the player with the lower discount rate will be willing to concede to the other player's preferred negotiated outcome.

The effects on player *A*'s costs of holding out in negotiations of both differing degrees of rivalness and differing levels of consumption of a good during negotiations can be expressed mathematically as follows:

$$\Delta C_A = Rq/d_{A.}$$

In this equation, ΔC_A is the change in player *A*'s costs; *R* is the rivalness of the good, expressed as a range between 0 (perfectly non-rival) and 1 (perfectly rival); and *q* is the quantity of the good used up in the period of time in question. As the rivalness of the good and the quantity of the good used increase, costs increase arithmetically. As player *A*'s discount rate falls toward 0, costs increase asymptotically toward infinity. The same logic applies to player *B*.

Modeling International Fisheries Politics

At first glance, the formal model presented above fits well with observed patterns of state behavior in international fisheries management. A result of the model is that in negotiations over common pool resources, actors with shorter shadows of the future will be empowered. The less excludable the good in question is, the greater the differential empowerment will be. High seas fisheries, being classic common pool resources, can be assumed to be toward the far nonexcludable end of the spectrum (although this assumption will be problematized below). This outcome can be found in the general patterns of RFMO structure and process, both among member states and between member and nonmember states.[32]

State behavior in international fisheries politics suggests that there are two general axes on which shadows of the future for fisheries management vary. The first, mirroring a more general pattern in cooperation in the international political economy, is overall level of development. Richer states, other things being equal, are relatively more concerned about the more distant future, while poorer states are relatively more concerned about development in the shorter term.[33] This distinction expresses itself in practice as less developed countries being significantly less likely to join

RFMOs in the first place. In practice, this observation is relevant to developed states on the one hand and to those middle-income states with distance fleets on the other. Low-income states generally do not support international fisheries.

The other axis is that of substitutability. The more a fishing fleet depends on a particular fishery, the longer the shadow of the future of the home state of the fleet is in negotiations over that fishery. Home states of fleets that have global range are generally much less concerned about the health of particular fisheries, because they can substitute new fishing grounds for overexploited ones.[34] In any case, regardless of the source of differential shadows of the future within member states of an RFMO, the logic of the model leads one to expect that states with shorter shadows in negotiations toward hard rules such as quotas would be able to structure the process to maximize their flexibility in avoiding rules, whereas states with longer shadows would be forced to acquiesce.

This is, in fact, what we see. All RFMOs that generate hard rules either require unanimity in agreeing with those rules or, more frequently, allow individual states to declare themselves not bound by specific rules even after those rules have been adopted by the organization as a whole.[35] This latter rule-making structure allows states to become free riders even while staying within the formal rules of the organization. Since the absence of an agreement within a given negotiating round means no quota, rather than last year's quota, states with longer shadows of the future are faced with a choice between free riders on a quota or no quota at all. Even when states with shorter shadows do not exercise their right to not be bound by specific rules, their ability to do so likely has a chilling effect on negotiations.[36]

In the first approximation, states act in and structure the politics of international fisheries regulation much as the rational choice model would lead one to expect that they would. But this first approximation draws on some assumptions about the interests and identities of those states and about the international normative structure within which they operate. Three of these assumptions are that states define their interests as maximizing the amount of fish caught over time (discounted at different rates for different country and fishery combinations), that developing states have a principled right to use international fisheries as a mechanism for economic development, and that the nonexcludability of international fisheries is a fixed background condition of negotiations. Looking in more detail at these three assumptions and at the extent to which they structure international fisheries politics helps to identify some of the interesting social constructions that constitute those politics.

At first glance, the first assumption—that states (or their negotiators) define their interests as maximizing the number of fish caught—seems a straightforward rationalist one. However, it seems straightforward because it implies an economic calculation (maximizing economic return from a fishery), whereas the calculation is, in fact, biological. The basis used for determining quotas in most RFMOs is a calculation called *maximum sustainable yield* (MSY). This calculation of the amount of a species that can be fished maximizes the amount that can be fished in the future. It does not speak at all to the question of whether it is profitable to fish that amount.[37] An equivalent economic calculation does exist, the *maximum economic yield* (MEY), which can be either more or less than MSY. While MEY is often discussed by economists and fisheries policy analysts, however, it is rarely mentioned in actual negotiations and plays no official role in the calculation of quotas.[38]

In those cases when MEY is higher than MSY, there is an environmental logic to not exceeding MSY, suggesting an ecological as well as economic logic to the interests embedded in the social structure of international environmental politics. But when MSY is higher than MEY, states are negotiating for the right to catch fish at an economic loss. Partly as a result, international fisheries often require massive subsidies to continue operating. In other words, states are negotiating for the right to subsidize overfishing.[39] Not all states choose to do so, but because of the dynamics of common pool resources, those states that do dominate international fisheries politics.

The focus on MSY can be explained partly by domestic politics and the regulatory capture of the fisheries bureaucracies that do the negotiating by the industry that gets the subsidies.[40] But it is reinforced by an institutional structure in which MSY is embedded and is constantly re-created through practice. Many participants know the problems with MSY, yet because it is embedded both in the rules and in the day-to-day practice of RFMOs, it continues to be the default mode of interest definition and self-definition in international fisheries politics.

The second assumption—that states have a principled right to use fisheries subsidies as a mechanism of economic development—fits in with a broader discourse of "common but differentiated responsibilities" for developing countries in international environmental politics.[41] This idea fits in neatly with the model, in that the development imperative can be seen as a measure of the length of a country's shadow of the future, wherein poorer countries' concern with development in the short term displaces a concern for the environment in the long term. This logic, however, suggests a continuum from poorer to richer states, with the shadow of the future gradually lengthening as one goes along it, rather than a simple dichotomy between developed and developing states.

In international fisheries politics, we often see this dichotomy. Furthermore, it is by no means clear that the fishing industry is a particularly effective mechanism for promoting economic development.[42] The World Bank, for example, argues that the cost of subsidizing the industry generally outweighs any gains in economic development.[43] Seen in this light, insistence generally on common but differentiated responsibilities in international fisheries governance and particularly on economic development rights looks less like a rational response to a given negotiating structure. Rather, it seems to result from two factors. The first is the identity of countries as "developing," a category that is itself a social construct rather than an objective measure. The second is a commitment to the rights of developing countries in international environmental politics broadly speaking, rather than fisheries politics specifically.[44] An insistence on rights of development in fisheries politics, then, is as much about identity politics as it is about fisheries politics.

The third assumption that the rationalist model draws on is that the nonexcludability of international fisheries is a fixed background condition of negotiations. Excludability in this context is partly a physical property of a good (sandwiches are easier to exclude than radio waves) but is also, importantly, a legal construct. Goods are excludable if owners have the legal right to exclude others from their benefits. Private gardens are excludable, for example, even if they are physically identical to nonexcludable public parks, because the former is owned privately and the latter publicly.

From an international perspective, fish in natural waters or EEZs are excludable, but those in the high seas are not. Of course, what counts as national waters changes over time, and EEZs are a relatively recent invention. In other words, states can decide among themselves how much of the global commons to privatize. Over the course of the past two decades, the norms governing the use of the ocean commons itself have been evolving. Until the early 1990s, high seas fisheries were truly nonexcludable, in the sense that fishers of any flag had the right to fish where and as much as they wanted, unless their flag state chose to join the relevant RFMO and accept binding limits. Beginning with the so-called Straddling Stocks Agreement of 1995,[45] however, the norm of open access has gradually been replaced by norms of precautionary and cooperative management.

These new norms have increasingly problematized participation in international fisheries outside of RFMO management. They are part of a broader evolution of the normative structure of international environmental politics toward collective management of the global commons rather than open access to it.[46] In a way, this represents a form of exclusion without privatization. This normative development legitimates a set of strategies by states with longer shadows of the future with respect to specific fisheries, to encourage nonmembers to cooperate with RFMO management, such as market restrictions, that would have faced more political opposition under open-access norms.[47] At the same time, fixing the new norms in place requires that these states reinforce them through both discourse and policy. In this sense, some of the negotiating positions of RFMO members can be understood as reinforcing the broader principle of collective management rather than making claims on specific fisheries resources.

None of these three assumptions, with the complications we find when we unpack them, fits neatly into either a consequential/appropriate dichotomy or Wendt and Fearon's two-step analytical process. Agents act both strategically and habitually with respect to existing norms and practices, and they participate both habitually in re-creating social structures and strategically in changing them. The two-step model is too limiting for two reasons. First, interests cannot neatly be exogenized from the rational to the normative realm, because agents participate strategically in the re-creation and change of that normative realm. Second, the category of interest is broad enough to be methodologically problematic; it covers everything from material preferences (more fish is better than fewer) to embedded discourses that frame action (the language of MSY rather than the language of MEY or of the precautionary principle).

In this case, the utility of juxtaposing rational choice modeling and constructivism is neither to adjudicate between two ultimately tautological logics of behavior nor to create a methodologically neat division of labor. Rather, the role of the model in constructivist analysis in the methodology used here is to illustrate the interconnections of strategic agency and social structure. In the context of international negotiations, it is reasonable to assume a certain level of strategic agency and that such strategic agency is informed by economically rational analysis. After all, this is (at least in part) what states pay their negotiators for—to maximize the national interest in a given structured bargaining setting. The model tells us what such rational action might look like and, in telling us this, helps to point out both the limits of such action and the social context in which it happens.

Conclusions

In many settings, including international fisheries negotiations, we often implicitly assume that agents act rationally. Why else would parties negotiate? Given that negotiations are designed as exercises in strategic interaction, what other assumptions can we use as starting points for understanding the actions of agents in such settings? This issue arises with any use of the concept of interests in constructivism. Discussion of interests really only makes sense in the context of strategic action. When Wendt, for example, talks of the social construction of interest and identity,[48] he is implying that once those interests are socially constructed, they motivate agentive behavior. Identities may well generate reactive or habitual behavior, but interest implies calculation.

In this way, rational calculation is built into constructivisms that speak of interests. How should we deal with this built-in calculation? Implicit assumptions of rationality are tricky. Without explicitly thinking through what rational behavior looks like in a given situation, there is no way to tell if we are assuming a rationality logic that actually works. Are we, for example, making a prior assumption about agent preferences and generating from that a rationalist logic, or are we inducing preferences backward from observed behavior? It can be difficult to tell when we are using rationality assumptions implicitly rather than explicitly.

In this context, the utility of a formal model is its clarity and specificity. Its role is not to predict how agents will act. Rather, its role is to anchor the analyst's assumption of rational action in a model that is internally coherent and explicit in its interpretation of interests and of the structure of interaction. As methodology, this is far removed from King, Keohane, and Verba's view of social science as hypothesis-testing; the role of the model is not to predict what will happen but to highlight both the utility and the limits of rationalist analysis in a broader constructivist setting. The role of the formal model as a heuristic is to discipline and clarify—both in the analyst's thinking and in the communication of that thinking—the role of rationality in social institutions that involve calculations of interest. In this sense, the limits of the model's predictive ability are part of its heuristic value, rather than an indicator of analytical weakness.

The use of formal rational choice models as heuristic devices in constructivist analysis can, however, be methodologically fraught. It asks us to use two completely different evaluative standards at the same time. Within the model, the standard is mathematic precision. The model must work and be internally consistent in its own terms. The rules for this kind of evaluation are both clear and dichotomous—the math either is correct or is not. In the relationship between the model and the constructivist analysis, the standard is one of usefulness. The model must help us to see things in the social structure of the relevant politics that we otherwise would not have seen or would have seen differently. The rules for this kind of evaluation are neither clear nor dichotomous. In this sense, usefulness can be perceived subjectively and argued intersubjectively but cannot be proven.

Yet it is partly precisely because of the tension between the two standards of evaluation that rational choice models can be a productive part of constructivist analysis. The formality of the model provides a precise and disciplined foil to the sociological analysis, while the latter embeds the model in an epistemologically sociological world. In the world of international fisheries politics, this tension points us to a more detailed analysis of MSY, development discourses, and the politics of exclusion from the high seas. We may have looked at these three features without the model, but even then, we would likely have arrived at them through the implicit application of rationalist assumptions. If one is going to use such assumptions to identify social structures to study, one may as well do so explicitly.

Notes

1. See, e.g., Paul MacDonald, "Useful Fiction or Miracle Maker: The Competing Epistemological Foundations of Rational Choice Theory," *American Political Science Review* 97, no. 4 (2003): 551–66.

2. For an extreme example of this sort of thing, see Steven Brams, *Biblical Games: Game Theory and the Hebrew Bible* (Cambridge, MA: MIT Press, 1980).

3. See MacDonald, "Useful Fiction."

4. The original source of the "as if" description seems to be Milton Friedman, *Essays in Positive Economics* (Chicago: University of Chicago Press, 1953).

5. Patrick Thaddeus Jackson, *The Conduct of Inquiry in International Relations: Philosophy of Science and Its Implications for the Study of World Politics* (New York: Routledge, 2010).

6. See Francis M. Bator, "The Anatomy of Market Failure," *Quarterly Journal of Economics* 72, no. 3 (1958): 351–79.

7. See J. Samuel Barkin, "On the Heuristic Use of Formal Models in International Relations Theory," *International Studies Review* 17, no. 4 (2015): 617–34.

8. See Jackson, *Conduct of Inquiry*, for a discussion of ideal types in this context.

9. With reference to IR specifically, see, e.g., Stephen Walt, "Rigor or Rigor Mortis? Rational Choice and Security Studies," *International Security* 23, no. 4 (1999): 5–48. More broadly, see Thomas Mayer, *Truth versus Precision in Economics* (Aldershot: Edward Elgar, 1993); Donald McCloskey, *The Rhetoric of Economics* (Madison: University of Wisconsin Press, 1985).

10. The distinction between thin/neoclassical and thick/postmodern constructivism is discussed in the introductory chapter to this volume.

11. James G. March and Johan P. Olsen, "The Institutional Dynamics of International Political Orders," *International Organization* 52, no. 4 (1998): 943–69.

12. James Fearon and Alexander Wendt, "Rationalism versus Constructivism: A Skeptical View," in *Handbook of International Relations*, ed. Walter Carlesnaes, Thomas Risse-Kappen, and Beth Simmons (London: Sage, 2002), 52–72.

13. For a more fully developed version of this argument, see J. Samuel Barkin, *Realist Constructivism: Rethinking International Relations Theory* (Cambridge: Cambridge University Press, 2010), 50–65.

14. See, e.g., Ronald Krebs and Patrick Thaddeus Jackson, "Twisting Tongues and Twisting Arms: The Power of Political Rhetoric," *European Journal of International Relations* 13, no. 1 (2007): 35–66; Janice Bially Mattern, "Why Soft Power Isn't So Soft: Representational Force and the Sociolinguistic Construction of Attraction in World Politics," *Millennium* 33, no. 3 (2005): 583–612.

15. This assertion will be complicated below.

16. For a full overview of this issue, see J. Samuel Barkin and Elizabeth R. DeSombre, *Saving Global Fisheries: Reducing Fishing Capacity to Promote Sustainability* (Cambridge, MA: MIT Press, 2013).

17. See Food and Agriculture Organization, *State of the World Fisheries and Aquaculture* (Rome: Food and Agriculture Organization of the United Nations, 2008).

18. See J. Samuel Barkin and George E. Shambaugh, *Anarchy and the Environment: The International Relations of Common Pool Resources* (Albany: State University of New York Press, 1999).

19. See Elizabeth R. DeSombre, "Fishing under Flags of Convenience: Using Market Power to Increase Participation in International Regulation," *Global Environmental Politics* 5, no. 4 (2005):73–94.

20. Exceptions to this generalization can happen, primarily at the local scale, when circumstances favorable to mutual coercion across the community of resource users allow for enforced cooperation. See Elinor Ostrom, *Governing the Commons: The Evolution of Institutions for Collective Action* (New York: Cambridge University Press, 1990).

21. This model appears originally in J. Samuel Barkin, "Time Horizons and Multilateral Enforcement in International Cooperation," *International Studies Quarterly* 48, no. 2 (2004): 363–82.

22. See, e.g., Mancur Olson, *The Logic of Collective Action: Public Goods and the Theory of Groups* (Cambridge, MA: Harvard University Press, 1965).

23. See Robert O. Keohane and Elinor Ostrom, eds., *Local Commons and Global Interdependence: Heterogeneity and Cooperation in Two Domains* (London: Sage, 1995).

24. See, e.g., Kenneth A. Oye, "Explaining Cooperation under Anarchy: Hypotheses and Strategies," *World Politics* 38, no. 1 (1985): 1–24; James Fearon, "Bargaining, Enforcement, and International Cooperation," *International Organization* 52, no. 2 (1998): 269–306.

25. See, e.g,, Duncan French, "Developing States and International Environmental Law: The Importance of Differentiated Responsibilities," *International and Comparative Law Quarterly* 49, no. 1 (2000): 35–60.

26. The effect of the discount rate in the cost term is discrete from its effect on the present value of cooperation once a cooperative agreement is reached.

27. This model bears significant similarities to that in Fearon, "Bargaining."

The major difference is that this is a discrete-time model, whereas Fearon used the continuous-time model of war of attrition. The latter assumes a fixed and known end point, whereas international negotiations are often ongoing processes without fixed end points.

28. See Fearon, "Bargaining," 277–79.

29. See Elizabeth R. DeSombre, "Tuna Fishing and Common Pool Resources," in Barkin and Shambaugh, *Anarchy and the Environment*, 51–69.

30. See Fearon, "Bargaining," 279. Among the other things held equal is the degree to which the actor that is disempowered in negotiations because of its discount rate is willing to access forms of international power that are outside the specific scope of the issue being negotiated. For a discussion of when this might happen in common pool resource situations, see J. Samuel Barkin and Elizabeth R. DeSombre, "Unilateralism and Multilateralism in International Fisheries Governance," *Global Governance* 6, no. 3 (2000): 339–60.

31. See Ronald B. Mitchell, "International Environmental Common Pool Resources: More Common than Domestic, but More Difficult to Manage," in Barkin and Shambaugh, *Anarchy and the Environment*, 26–50.

32. See Barkin and DeSombre, *Saving Global Fisheries*, chap. 3.

33. See, e.g. Robert Brent, "Country Estimates of Social Discount Rates Based on Changes in Life Expectancies," *Kyklos* 46 (1993): 399–409.

34. See Barkin and DeSombre, "Unilateralism and Multilateralism."

35. See Elizabeth R. DeSombre, *Global Environmental Institutions* (New York: Routledge, 2008), 84–93.

36. See Barkin and DeSombre, *Saving Global Fisheries*, 72.

37. See, e.g., Ray Hilborn, "Defining Success in Fisheries and Conflicts in Objectives," *Marine Policy* 31 (2007): 153–58.

38. See Colin W. Clark, *The Worldwide Crisis in Fisheries* (Cambridge: Cambridge University Press, 2006).

39. See Matteo Milazzo, *Subsidies in World Fisheries: A Reexamination*, World Bank Technical Paper 406 (Washington, DC: World Bank, 1998); World Wildlife Fund, *Hard Facts, Hidden Problems: A Review of Current Data on Fisheries Subsidies* (Washington, DC: World Wildlife Fund, 2001).

40. See Barkin and DeSombre, *Saving Global Fisheries*, chap. 4.

41. See Christopher D. Stone, "Common but Differentiated Responsibilities in International Law," *American Journal of International Law* 98, no. 1 (2004): 276–301.

42. See S. M. Garcia, K. Cochrane, G. Van Santen, and Francis Christy, "Towards Sustainable Fisheries: A Strategy for FAO and the World Bank," *Ocean and Coastal Management* 42, no. 5 (1999): 369–98.

43. World Bank, Agricultural and Rural Development Department, *Saving Fish and Fishers: Toward Sustainable and Equitable Governance of the Global Fishing Sector*, Report 29090-GLB (Washington, DC: World Bank, 2004).

44. See French, "Developing States."

45. The agreement is so called because of its unwieldy official name, "The United Nations Agreement for the Implementation of the Provisions of the United Nations Convention on the Law of the Sea of 10 December 1982 relating to the Conservation and Management of Straddling Fish Stocks and Highly Migratory Fish Stocks."

46. See Peter H. Sand, "Sovereignty Bounded: Public Trusteeship for Common Pool Resources?," *Global Environmental Politics* 4, no. 1 (2004): 47–71.
47. See DeSombre, "Fishing under Flags of Convenience."
48. Alexander Wendt, *Social Theory of International Politics* (Cambridge: Cambridge University Press, 1999).

CHAPTER 9

Theoretical Geometry, Critical Theory, and Concept Spaces in IR

LAURA SJOBERG AND KEVIN KNUDSON

As discussed in the introduction to this book, the "quantitative" methods traditionally used in the social sciences represent a limited subset of available methods in mathematics, statistics, and computational analysis, and the positivist ends for which they are usually deployed in the social science community represent a limited subset of the purposes for which they are intended and deployed in the philosophy of mathematics. The overwhelming majority of quantitative methods that are used in International Relations (IR) are statistical in nature. When the tools of theoretical mathematics are used, they are most often deployed in predictive, descriptive, or heuristic uses of game theory; that is, the tools of mathematics are used to try to gain leverage on the causal empirical realities in global politics that neopositivist IR scholars see as substantively important to know and understand. In this chapter, we argue not only that the tools of theoretical mathematics can be utilized for post-positivist ends but that such use is where many of those tools would be most at home in IR.

Particularly, we look to make an initial case for the argument that the tools of computational topology can be effectively utilized to explore questions of constitution, textuality, and performativity for critical IR. To that end, the first section of this chapter lays out an argument about the possible utility of thinking geometrically about concept formation and reification for post-structuralist IR, as well as possible ways to do that work. The second section introduces the concept of democracy in IR and argues that it might be possible to gain leverage on the dimensions of the concept by using computational topology to evaluate existing data. The third section shows the method in action and sketches out some of the possible ramifications for studying democracy from a critical perspective. The concluding section makes a case for the *value that methodological explorations like this have* for both political methodology and critical theory.

Critical IR and Geometric Topology

In Mark Hoffman's words, post-structuralist IR asks "how" questions, rather than "what" or "why" questions.[1] It asks, for example, "How are structures and practices replicated? How is meaning fixed, questioned, reinterpreted, and refixed?"[2] To answer these questions, post-structuralist IR rejects "the modernist belief in our ability to rationally perceive and theorize the world," in favor of "dis-belief in unproblematic notions of modernity, enlightenment, truth, science, and reason."[3] This move leads post-structuralists, methodologically, to a sort of scholarship that pays attention to discontinuity and disjuncture, assumes no beginning and no end, and therefore pays attention to complexity, contingency, and context.[4] This scholarship pays particular attention to discourses in global politics, where (actual and conceptual) "boundaries are constantly being redrawn and transgressed."[5]

We argue here that this *methodological* approach can be matched fairly easily with the capacities of the *methods* of geometric and computational topology. If critical IR rejects the objective and the linear—and, with them, their dichotomized frame of reference—topological analysis can accommodate significantly more complexity. If critical IR tries to unmask and deconstruct hidden meanings, there could be some power in representing those meanings geometrically. If critical IR embraces undecidability, is at home with liminality, is wary of metanarratives, and is attached to the "how" questions discussed above, the instability, creativity, and formalism of theoretical geometry may be a good fit.

If it were to be oversimplified for explanatory purposes, math is the study of patterns. Discrete ones (if such things exist) are arithmetic.[6] Continuous ones are geometry.[7] Immeasurable ones are symbolic logic.[8] Patterns not dependent on the empirical existence of their component parts are formalist.[9] In the sense of the philosophy of math, this chapter takes a formalist approach to mathematical symbolism.[10]

For the purpose of this analysis, that means that we argue that mathematical work is axioms with rules of inference that facilitate thought experiments and string manipulation games of almost infinite complexity. There is no "true meaning" underlying mathematical symbols. Instead, equations, formalizations, and quantifications are representations from which we learn about relationships—homologies, homeomorphisms, maps, dimensionality, commutativity, factorization.[11] In this view, the rules, laws, and procedures of mathematics are socially constructed, interested not only in quantity but also in structure, space, change, stochasticity, relationality, and formalization for its own sake. There are, for sure, many practitioners of math who think of it as science, discovery, and progress; but there are also many practitioners of math who see it as art, creation, signification, and representation.[12]

We argue that critical theory and geometric topology in the latter sense are not only compatible but kindred outlooks for the study of global politics generally and for concept analysis specifically. This is not the first time a critical theorist has suggested that there might be some benefit to thinking geometrically about the concepts being explored and critiqued.[13] Deleuze and Guattari see concepts as rhizomes, biological entities endowed with unique properties.[14] They see concepts as spatially representable, where the representation contains "principles of connection and heterogeneity: any point of a rhizome must be connected to any other."[15] They list the possible benefits of spatial representation of concepts, including the ability to represent complex multiplicity, the potential to free a concept from foundationalism, and the ability to show both breadth and depth.[16] In their view, geometric interpretations move away from the insidious understanding of the world in terms of dualisms, dichotomies, and lines, to understand conceptual relations in terms of space and shapes. The *ontology* of concepts is thus, in their view, appropriately geometric—a multiplicity "defined not by its elements, nor by a center of unification and comprehension" and instead measured by its dimensionality and its heterogeneity.[17] The conceptual multiplicity "is already composed of heterogeneous terms in symbiosis" and "is continually transforming itself" such that it is possible to follow and map not only the relationships between ideas but how they change over time.[18]

The French word that Deleuze and Guattari use for "multiplicities" can also be translated to the topological term "manifold."[19] A manifold is a topological space that is locally Euclidean (meaning that each point of an n-dimensional manifold has a neighborhood homeomorphic to the Euclidean space of dimension n).[20] We propose looking at concepts this way, as manifolds. With such a dimensional understanding of concept formation, it is possible to deal with complex interactions of like entities and interactions of unlike entities. Critical theorists have emphasized the importance of such complexity in representation a number of times, speaking about it in terms compatible with mathematical methods, if not mathematically. For example, Michel Foucault's declaration that "practicing criticism is a matter of making facile gestures difficult" both reflects and is reflected in many critical theorists' projects of revealing the complexity in (apparently simple) concepts deployed both in global politics and IR scholarship.[21] David Campbell's reading of the state in *Writing Security* is a good example of this: Campbell makes the argument that the notion of the state appears to be both simple and a priori; it is really danger built over other danger, where "the constant articulation of danger through foreign policy is thus not a threat to a state's identity or existence: it is its condition of possibility."[22] This leads to a shift in the concept of danger as well, where "danger is not an objective condition" but "an effect of interpretation."[23] Critical thinking about "how possible" questions reveals a complexity to the concept of the state, a complexity that is often overlooked in traditional analyses and that sends a wave of added complexity through other concepts as well. This work of *seeking complexity* serves one of the major underlying functions of critical theorizing: finding invisible injustices in (modernist, linear, structuralist) givens in the operation and analysis of global politics.

In a geometric sense, this complexity could be thought about as multidimensional mapping. In theoretical geometry, the process of mapping conceptual spaces is "not primarily empirical"[24] but is for the purpose of representing and reading the relationships between pieces of information, including identification, similarity, differentiation, and distance.[25] The reason for defining topological spaces in math, the essence of the definition, is that there is no absolute scale for describing the distance or relation between certain points. It makes sense to say that an (infinite) sequence of points approaches some other, but there is no way to describe "how quickly" or "from what direction" a point might be approaching. This relationship that is defined purely "locally"—that is, in a small locale around each point—seems weak but is often surprisingly powerful: using only the relationship of "approaching parts," one can distinguish between, say, a balloon, a sheet of paper, a circle, and a dot.

To each delineated concept, one should distinguish and associate a topological space, in a (necessarily) nonexplicit yet definite manner. Whenever we have a relationship between concepts (here we think of the primary relationship as being that of constitution, but not restrictively), we "specify" a function (or inclusion or relation) between the topological spaces associated to the concepts. In these terms, "a conceptual space is in essence a multidimensional space in which the dimensions represent qualities or features of that which is being represented."[26] Such an approach can be leveraged for thinking about conceptual components, dimensionality, and structure.[27] In these terms, dimensions can be thought of as properties or qualities, each with their own (often multidimensional) properties or qualities.[28] In this way, it is a multiplicity that is more than a sum of its parts—representing both ideas and their relationships in a matrix of complicated interactions of meanings.

A key (mathematical and theoretical) goal of mapping conceptual space is "associationism, where associations between different kinds of information elements carry the main burden of representation."[29] To this end, "objects in conceptual space are represented by points, in each domain, that characterize their dimensional values."[30] These dimensional values can be arranged in relation to each other: as Gardenfors explains, because "distances represent degrees of similarity between objects represented in space," conceptual spaces are "suitable for representing different kinds of similarity relation."[31] These similarity relationships can be explored not only across ideas of a concept and across contexts but also over time: as Mormann explains, "with the aid of a topological structure, we can speak about continuity, e.g., a *continuous change*"—a possibility that can be found *only* in treating concepts as topological structures and not in linguistic descriptions or set theoretic representations.[32] Such an approach is both complex and *anexact*—suiting it well to the contingent explorations of critical IR.

A Formalization of Concept Relationships

The first step in the formalization of concept relationships might be to gain information about the (actual, representational, or potential) relationship between a concept being examined and another concept that contributes something to the essence of how it is understood. Assume a complex concept K composed of (but not necessarily limited to) component parts $v_{0,}$ $v_{1,} \ldots v_{p}$. The concept can be explored as a simplicial homology, where an *abstract simplicial complex* K is specified by the following data:

- A vertex set V.
- A rule specifying when a p-simplex $\sigma = [v_0 v_1 \ldots v_p]$ belongs to K. Here, the vertices $v_0, v_1, \ldots, v_p$ are distinct elements of V.
- Each p-simplex σ has $p + 1$ faces that are the $(p - 1)$-simplices ob-

tained by deleting one of the vertices of σ. The membership rule has the property that if σ belongs to K, then all of its faces belong to K.

Given a simplicial complex K, we wish to define a collection of vector spaces that tell us the number of holes of various dimensions in K[33]—in other words, where and how concepts intersect and where they miss intersections.

The formal definition is as follows: Let k be the field of two elements. The i-th homology group, $H_i(K;k)$, will measure the number of $(i + 1)$-dimensional voids and is constructed as follows: Let $C_i(K;k)$ be the k-vector space with basis the set of i-simplices in K. If $\sigma = [v_0 v_1 \cdots v_i]$ is such a simplex, where $\partial\sigma$ is the element of $C_{i-1}(K;k)$ given by the formula

$$\partial\sigma = \sum_{j=0}^{i} (-1)^j [v_0 v_1 \cdots \hat{v}_j \cdots v_i],$$

where $[v_0 v_1 \cdots \hat{v}_j \cdots v_i]$ is the $(i - 1)$-simplex with vertices $\{v_0, \ldots, v_i\} - \{v_j\}$. In the field of two elements, we have $-1 = 1$, but we present the definition this way because it works over any field (e.g., the real numbers). We may extend this linearly to $C_i(K;k)$ to obtain a linear transformation:

$$\partial^i : C_i(K;k) \rightarrow C_{i-1}(K;k).$$

It is a straightforward exercise to show that $\partial^i \circ \partial^{i+1} = 0$ and hence that $im(\partial^{i+1}) \subseteq null(\partial^i)$ ($null(\partial^i)$ denotes the null space of the map ∂^i). It is then possible to define the i-th homology group as

$$H_i(K;k) = null(\partial^i)/im(\partial^{i+1}).$$

Elements of $null(\partial^i)$ are called *cycles*; the set of all such is denoted by Z_i. Elements of $im(\partial^{i+1})$ are called *boundaries*, denoted by B_i. Homology measures how many cycles are inequivalent and essential in the sense that they do not bound an object of higher dimension. Note that the group H_0 measures how many connected components the space K has.

For computational purposes, the goal is to pay attention to the *Betti numbers*, β_i, defined as $\beta_i = dim_k H_i(K;k)$. These numbers are indicators that distinguish topological spaces based on the connectivity of n-dimensional simplicial complexes—or how the data within them relate to each other. Along these lines, we have the simple equation

$$\beta_i = dim_k Z_i - dim_k B_{i+1}$$

$$= dim_k C_i - rank\partial^i - rank\partial^{i+1}.$$

This therefore reduces the calculation of Betti numbers to computing ranks of matrices over the field k.

As a simple example, consider the tetrahedron T. There are four vertices: v_0, v_1, v_2, v_3; six edges: $[v_0v_1]$, $[v_0v_2]$, $[v_0v_3]$, $[v_1v_2]$, $[v_1v_3]$, $[v_2v_3]$; and four faces: $[v_0v_1v_2]$, $[v_0v_1v_3]$, $[v_0v_2v_3]$, $[v_1v_2v_3]$. The groups $C_i(T;k)$ are then

$$C_0(T;k) = k^4 \qquad C_1(T;k) = k^6 \qquad C_2(T;k) = k^4$$

and the maps ∂^i are given by $\partial^0 = 0$, $\partial^i = 0$, $i \geq 3$, and

$$\partial^1 = \begin{bmatrix} -1 & -1 & -1 & 0 & 0 & 0 \\ 1 & 0 & 0 & -1 & -1 & 0 \\ 0 & 1 & 0 & 1 & 0 & -1 \\ 0 & 0 & 1 & 0 & 1 & 1 \end{bmatrix}$$

$$\partial^2 = \begin{bmatrix} 1 & 1 & 0 & 0 \\ -1 & 0 & 1 & 0 \\ 0 & -1 & -1 & 0 \\ 1 & 0 & 0 & 1 \\ 0 & 1 & 0 & -1 \\ 0 & 0 & 1 & 1 \end{bmatrix}$$

An easy calculation shows that $rank\partial^1 = 3$, that $rank\partial^2 = 3$, and therefore that

$$H_0(T;k) = k \quad \Rightarrow \quad \beta_0 = 1$$

$$H_1(T;k) = 0 \quad \Rightarrow \quad \beta_1 = 0$$

$$H_2(T;k) = k \quad \Rightarrow \quad \beta_2 = 1.$$

A basis for $H_0(T;k)$ is $[v_0]$, and a basis for $H_2(T;k)$ is $[v_0v_1v_2] - [v_0v_1v_3] - [v_0v_2v_3] - [v_1v_2v_3]$. There are three linearly independent 1-cycles—the boundaries of the four triangles form a linearly dependent set of dimension 3—but each is also a boundary, filled in by the interior of the triangle. Geometrically, that $\beta_0 = 1$ means that T is connected; that $\beta_1 = 0$ means that every loop in T bounds a disc; that $\beta_2 = 1$ means that T contains a closed surface—namely, T itself—that is not filled in by a three-dimensional object.

Homology groups are topological invariants; that is, if spaces X and Y are homotopically equivalent (one may be deformed to the other), then $H_\bullet(X;k) \cong H_\bullet(Y;k)$. They therefore provide a means to distinguish spaces, although it is possible for topologically distinct spaces to have the same homology groups. Tools for analyzing homology groups can be used for similarity and difference analysis in these concept spaces.

An increasingly popular technique for analyzing datasets topologically is the *persistent homology* of Edelsbrunner, Letscher, and Zomorodian.[34] The idea is as follows: When there is a finite nested sequence of finite simplicial complexes

$$K_{R_1} \subset K_{R_2} \subset K_{R_p},$$

where the R_i are real numbers $R_1 < R_2 < \cdots < R_p$. For each homological degree $\ell \geq 0$, we then obtain a sequence of homology groups and induced linear transformations

$$H_\ell(K_{R_1}) \to H_\ell(K_{R_2}) \to \cdots \to H_\ell(K_{R_p}).$$

Since the complexes are finite, each $H_\ell(K_{R_i})$ is a finite-dimensional vector space. Thus, there are only finitely many distinct homology classes. A particular class z may come into existence in $H_\ell(K_{R_S})$, and then one of two things happens. Either z maps to 0 (i.e., the cycle representing z gets filled in) in some $H_\ell(K_{R_t})$, $R_S < R_t$, or z maps to a nontrivial element in $H_\ell(K_{R_p})$. This yields a *barcode*, a collection of interval graphs lying above an axis parametrized by R. An interval of the form $[R_S, R_t]$ corresponds to a class that appears at R_S and dies at R_t. Classes that live to K_{R_p} are usually represented by the infinite interval $[R_S, \infty]$, to indicate that such classes are real features of the full complex K_{R_p}.

As an example, consider the tetrahedron T with filtration

$$T_0 \subset T_1 \subset T_2 \subset T_3 \subset T_4 \subset T_5 = T,$$

defined by $T_0 = \{v_0, v_1, v_2, v_3\}$, $T_1 = T_0 \cup \{\textit{all edges}\}$, $T_2 = T_1 \cup [v_0v_1v_2]$, $T_3 = T_2 \cup [v_0v_1v_3]$, $T_4 = T_3 \cup [v_0v_2v_3]$, and $T_5 = T$. In this sequence, components are initially born and then either "die out" or "live forever"—they either endure across data maps or do not. The ones that "live forever" produce the Betti numbers discussed above.

This approach can be used to sketch out relationships among concepts without data about how they are traditionally considered or to analyze the constitution of concepts for which point cloud data is collected. For analyzing point cloud data, one needs a simplicial complex modeling the underlying space. Since it is impossible to know *a priori* if a complex is "correct," one builds a nested family of complexes approximating the data cloud, computes the persistent homology of the resulting filtration, and looks for homology classes that exist in long sections of the filtration. A popular technique for this is the *witness complex* construction of de Silva and Carlsson.[35]

Suppose there is a dataset Z. Choose a subset $L \subseteq Z$; we call the elements of L *landmarks*. Say Z has N elements and L has n elements, and denote by D the $n \times N$ matrix of distances between the elements of L and the elements of Z. Fix a real number $R > 0$. The *witness complex*—or map of ideas—$W(D, R)$ is defined as follows:

1. The vertex set of $W(D, R)$ is $\{1, 2, \dots, n\}$.
2. The edge $\sigma = [ab]$ belongs to $W(D, R)$ if and only if there exists a data point $1 \le i \le N$ such that

$$\max(D(a, i), D(b, i)) \le R.$$

In this case, the point i is called a *witness* for σ.
3. The p-simplex $\sigma = [a_0 a_1 \dots a_p]$ belongs to $W(D, R)$ if and only if all its edges belong to $W(D)$; equivalently, there exists a witness $1 \le i \le N$ such that

$$\max(D(a_0,i),D(a_1,i),\dots,D(a_p,i)) \le R.$$

This definition may seem a bit opaque but can be described geometrically as follows: Imagine that dataset Z lies in some Euclidean space. The collection L of landmarks can be used to build a simplicial complex with vertex set L by looking for points in the dataset near the landmarks. Two landmarks are joined by an edge precisely when there is a data point in Z within R of both of them. In fact, if $L = Z$, this process yields the *Rips complex* on Z (with parameter $R/2$), in which two data points are joined when their distance apart is at most $R/2$. A good image to keep in mind for the Rips complex is that we place small balls of radius $r > 0$ around each data point. It is possible to join two data points if the balls meet. That this is a good thing to do from a topological point of view is well-established.[36] In the examples we analyze in this chapter, we take $L = Z$ and therefore compute the Rips complex on the underlying dataset.[37] This helps us see conceptual relationships through relationships between *groups* of data points.

Note that the construction of $W(D, R)$ takes as part of its input the parameter R. This allows us to construct a filtered collection of complexes by letting R increase from 0 to some large upper bound. Note that if R is sufficiently large, the complex $W(D, R)$ contains all possible simplices on the landmark set and is therefore a contractible $(n - 1)$-simplex. However, each simplex σ comes into existence at some particular value R_σ, called its *time of appearance*. Since there are only finitely many simplices possible on any landmark set, there is a discrete collection of parameter values $0 < R_1 < R_2 < \cdots < R_r$ for which we get distinct witness complexes

$$L = W(D,0) \subset W(D,R_1) \subset \cdots \subset W(D,R_r).$$

We may then compute the persistent homology of this filtration, searching for homology classes that persist for long intervals $[R_S, R_t]$.

In this way, analysis of persistent homologies can be used to show both similarities among concepts *and* similarities across components of concepts in particular cases to which those concepts and their components are applied. In other words, complex geometric mapping techniques can provide a number of different and complicated pictures of how concepts relate and of the implications of changing their relationships. For critical IR, mapping conceptual spaces like this can provide a "framework for representation" that demonstrates relationships among concepts without reaching necessary or essential conclusions about their genesis or origin.[38] Analyzing the geometric complexity of concepts could lead to the ability to gain leverage on how understanding signification in conceptual dimensionality could make current research better, more interesting, or deeper, either on its own terms or in terms of understanding complexity, hybridity, marginalization, social disadvantages, or other areas of global politics of interest to critical theory.

Thinking Critically about Democracy

Scholars in comparative politics and IR have long been interested in the nature and existence of democracy in the global political arena. Scholars of comparative politics investigate the structure and function of democratic institutions in states that they see as transitioning to democracy or as developing or mature democracies. Scholars of IR look to understand the ways in which states' regime types may affect their foreign policy propensities, including, but not limited to, trade patterns, likelihood to be involved in conflict, and conflict opponents.

A number of common assumptions that scholars in comparative politics and IR make about democracy permeate a significant amount of the research that is read, cited, and engaged in their respective fields. Each group of scholars assumes that democracy is an extant and practiced form of government. Each assumes that such a form of government is *measurably* different than other forms of government, which may vary but share the label "nondemocratic." Though not all scholars make the assumption that democracy is a more desirable form of government than autocracy, oligarchy, theocracy, or other possible forms of government, many of them, if not most, do.

That said, while scholars interested in either the internal or external politics of either democracies or democratizing states agree on the existence and distinguishability of democracy, many of them disagree on the components of democracy that are distinguishable or on the specific places and times in which democracy exists. In other words, while the idea of democracy is common among scholars interested in comparative or international politics, many of them disagree on what makes a democracy, which countries are democracies, which components of democracy are measurable, and which measurable components of democracy are most central to the concept of democracy. Here, we are interested in this concept from a critical perspective, in terms of both disciplinary scholarly norms and global political structures.

Critical theorists have been interested in the concept of democracy in the international arena in a number of different ways for an extended period of time. Of course, neither the breadth nor the theoretical depth of critical analyses of democracy (even in IR) can be done justice in this small section of a chapter. Some of the common critiques (and resultant "how possible" questions) can be explored briefly to give a sense of what the stake(s) in the concept of democracy may be for (different) critical IR researchers. Critical theorists have been concerned with the meaning of the concept of democracy, about the structure and normative value of the signification of the concept, and about the potential to revise and reappropriate the concept in search of a more just global political arena.

Some critical theorists have been interested in the way that democracy as a concept signifies the success of "the West" and distinguishes that locale from the rest of the world. As Amitav Acharya and Barry Buzan note, "the contemporary equivalent of 'good life' in international relations—democratic peace, interdependence and integration, and institutionalized orderliness, as well as the 'normal relationships and calculable results'—is mostly found in the West, while the non-West remains the realm of survival."[39] Accordingly Acharya and Buzan characterize democracy as a "Western idea."[40] As Fabrizio Eva notes, these origins hold in contemporary global politics: "The model for democracy nevertheless remains the Western version, which is tied in with capitalist economics. There is an acceptance, therefore, of the central ideology of liberal democracy."[41] Many critical theorists' concern with the Western-centric nature of deployed concepts of democracy in the international arena causes them (especially those interested in the question from a postcolonial perspective) to be critical of the use of the idea of democracy *writ large* in global politics or the analysis thereof. For example, Inayatullah and Blaney argue that "democracy is less a form of governance than a value that must be moderated, a set of practices to be disciplined by some prior claim to authority."[42] Another reading of this analysis might suggest that democracy is not *a thing* out there to be analyzed, achieved, or deconstructed but, instead, *a signifier* by which participants in the global political arena are organized hierarchically.

Roxanne Doty sees this both in the policy arena and in the academic study of democracy.[43] She explains that IR work interested in democracy often presumes that "some subjects were definers, delimiters, and boundary setters of importance . . . and that others not capable themselves of making such definitions, would have things bestowed upon them and would be permitted to enjoy them only under the circumstances deemed suitable by the United States."[44] This is why Tanji and Lawson argue that "the 'answer' to the question of what constitutes 'true democracy' is implicit in the model of democracy assumed by the thesis . . . , [which is] authoritatively assumed in advance, posited as an unassailable universal, and deployed as the foundation of the moral high ground in the global sphere."[45] These readings suggest a critical stance not only toward current concepts of and wieldings of democracy but also toward the use of the word and idea in general. This work in critical IR, then, is less concerned with reviving and rehabilitating the notion of democracy in global politics and more concerned with remedying the exclusions and silences produced by its current significations.

Still, even the most skeptical of critical theorists pay attention to the multiple significations of the term and idea of democracy in global politics. Doty draws on Laclau's use of the signifier of democracy, explaining that it "acquires particular meanings when it is associated with other signifiers," that is, that anticommunist democracy and antifascist democracy are signified differently, even if each is "an attempt to constitute a hegemonic formation."[46] Internally linked significations include democracy's perceived opponents and its perceived components and benefits. For example, Doty suggests that American masculinity is a key component and tie-in to nineteenth-century notions of democracy in global politics, where "American manhood was also linked to democracy" and where "this link served to construct a distinctly American version of masculinity that was part and parcel of American exceptionalism."[47] In other words, democracy and masculinity were co-constituted in a particular instantiation of democracy in global politics. More recently, Zalewski and Runyan suggest that the signification of democracy has come to be tied to how states treat their women, where gender quotas have been "enacted by a range of states as a sign of democracy and a method for reducing government corruption."[48] Richard Ashley suggests that democracy can also be conceptually linked with its goals, using the democratic peace as an example.[49] He explains that the "academically certified version of the democratic peace has led to a securitization of democracy" that is deeply problematic.[50] Andrew Linklater, who suggests that the tie to Western liberalism can be most insidious for the concept of democracy, advocates for theorizing democracy "without assuming that Western liberal democracy is the model of government which should apply universally."[51]

While many critical theorists agree that, in a variety of ways, the notion of democracy that is deployed in contemporary global politics *and* in contemporary IR research is both empirically and normatively problematic, they disagree strongly on how to handle the problem. Some suggest that the concept of democracy is now itself part of the problem (perhaps what Baudrillard, in *The Mirror of Production,* would call a "repressive simulation"), but others are interested in reviving a different understanding of democracy.[52] For example, Bieler and Morton suggest that the problem is not the concept of democracy itself but the hollowing of that concept.[53] They argue that a politics of supremacy that has come to replace democracy "involves a hollowing out of democracy and the affirmation, in matters of political economy, of a set of macro-economic policies such as market efficiency, discipline and confidence, policy credibility and competitiveness."[54] Some critical IR theorists, then, look to rescue the concept of democracy from that hollowness.

For example, Ken Booth, who suggests that what unifies critical theory in IR, "in addition to its post-Marxist sensibility," is democracy, contends, "Craig Murphy got it exactly right when he saw this emerging critical theory project being 'today's manifestation of a long-standing democratic impulse in the academic study of international affairs.' In other words, it was academe's contribution to 'egalitarian practice.'"[55] To follow up, Booth goes over a number of different types of possible democracy, arguing that finding a good notion of democracy is key to the emancipatory mission he attributes to critical IR. Booth explains that "there will be no emancipatory community without dialogue, no dialogue without democracy."[56] In emancipatory critical theorists' terms, though, this is a different type of democracy, one that, as Alison Brysk states, "begins with greater recognition, representation, and access within existing institutions and demands new mechanisms for popular control of local, global, and security issues."[57] Following William Connolly, Richard Shapcott describes the democracy favored by critical IR as "a democratic ethos" that is "an ethos of pluralisation" focused on creating room for difference.[58] This leads Shapcott to express interest in "an attempt to provide an account of democracy that does not privilege the 'abstract' other and a universal subjectivity or the territorial restrictions of the nation-state."[59]

While the dividing line is not perfect, it might be worth thinking about these differences in terms of poststructuralist and emancipatory critical theory. Both argue that there are problematic significations of current deployments of the notion of democracy in global politics. The latter is interested in reviving a more just concept of democracy, whereas the former is more interested in mapping the injustice that may well be inherent in the utterance and reification of the concept. What both share, in addition to critiquing current instantiations of the concept, is an interest in how democracy is being constituted, read, reproduced, and reified as a concept, both among states in global politics and among scholars of global politics interested in understanding state (and nonstate) interaction. It is possible, then, to find a number of "how possible" questions in critical IR analyses of democracy. What are the conditions of possibility of current understandings of what constitutes democracy? How are the indicators of democracy that are recognized by various scholars and policy makers chosen to the exclusion of those that are not recognized? What are the relationships between various (recognized and unrecognized) indicators of democracy? How is the concept of democracy deployed (and deployable) for (and against) certain political interests? What, if anything, about the idea of democracy allows for hollowing, encroachment, supremacy, and/or Western dominance, if such moves happen? How are relationships between the concept of democracy and its antagonists, its component parts, and/or its results formed and cemented? What possibilities (or impossibilities) with particular conceptions of what democracy is could change with the change (or even elimination) of the idea?

Certainly, answers to these "how possible" questions cannot be supplied easily with extant research, much less in the scope of this chapter. These questions share an interest in *how democracy is being read* across a variety of audiences in a variety of different ways. The remainder of this chapter suggests the plausibility and particular advantages of the formalization of concept relationships for gaining leverage on different questions about how democracy is being read.

Mapping Interpretations of Democracy

We collected more than one hundred indicators used to measure democracy over eight datasets, to gain interpretive leverage over what political scientists tend to think democracy is, how they tend to measure it, and how countries come to be classified as democracies and nondemocracies.[60] For the purposes of our pilot analysis, we used fourteen of the variables for a particular year to map country data points and look for commonalities. The variables that we used were from the Polity IV and Miller-Boix-Rosato datasets. From the Polity IV dataset, we used chief executive recruitment regulation, competitiveness of executive recruitment, openness of executive recruitment, executive constraints, participation regulation, participation competitiveness, and concept indicators for executive recruitment, executive constraint, and political competition. We used these executive-specific, individual-level variables next to the Miller-Boix-Rosato macrolevel variables about democratic status and change over time, including a dichotomous measure of democracy, a measure of sovereignty, a measure of democratic transition, the previous number of democratic breakdowns, and the duration of democracy in the state (consecutive years of a particular regime type).

Geometrically, a number of countries represent the same configuration; that is, their values on all fourteen included indicators are the same.[61] For the purposes of differing *interpretations* of what democracy is and of the indicators of democracy, then, the countries that are the same on all fourteen indicators are flat: they represent the same configuration of indicators, definitions, variables, and conclusions for the purposes of understanding the dimensionality of the concept of democracy. Using the fourteen indicators that we selected in the test year of 2007, we found eighty-eight unique data points—that is, eighty-eight meaningfully different configurations of the fourteen variables.[62] We then looked to analyze the relationships between those configurations geometrically.

Using the javaPlex package in MATLAB, we computed the persistent homology of the Rips complex for the eighty-eight configurations. The topology of that Rips complex shows a number of distinct features. First, there are ten connected components, represented by the United States, Cuba, the Dominican Republic, Equatorial Guinea, Swaziland, Ivory Coast, Mauritania, Togo, Tanzania, and Guinea. A connected component is a maximal subset of a space that cannot be covered by the union of two disjoint open sets; in other words, it is a distinct and distinguishable group. Eight of the ten connected components are contractible, which means that they have stronger relationships than would noncontractible connected components.[63]

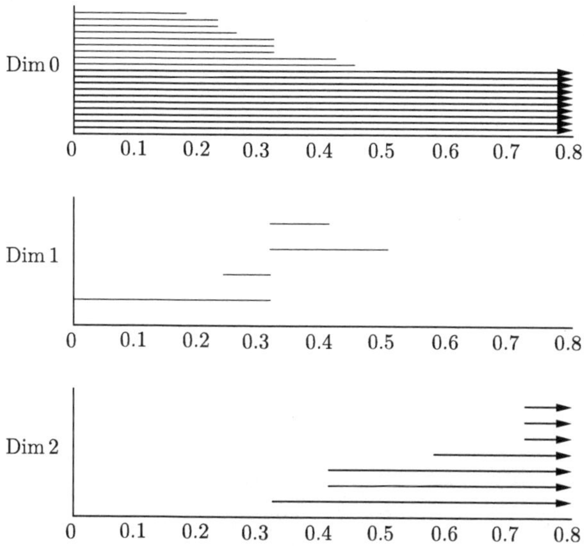

Fig. 9.1. Barcodes for fourteen-dimensional democracy data

The barcodes for the relationships between configurations can be seen in figure 9.1. These barcodes represent the durability of certain relationships over the addition of configurations in the construction of a multidimensional space descriptive of the concept of democracy *through* collected data about its indicators. Within the topology of the configurations that we analyzed are seven two-dimensional spheres. Six of them lie in the connected component represented by the Dominican Republic, and the seventh lies in the component represented by Swaziland. The representatives of components are the states that have the most in common with the most states within the geometric component, so they matter a little as signifiers. Here, the Dominican Republic is generally considered a durable, if imperfect, democracy, and Swaziland is generally considered autocratic.

Some of the shapes formed, then, have both clear relationships and clear implications about what ideas of democracy might be within the limitations of our truncated pilot study. Tetrahedrons formed by the Dominican Republic, Albania, Latvia, and Botswana and by the Dominican Republic, Latvia, Botswana, and Comoros are groupings of democracies with some durability and sustainability, but with (perceived) weakness on one or more indicators—here, largely, indicators that have to do either with the availability and health of political competition or with having had a democratic breakdown in the past. In this sense, these democracies are differentiable from the democracies that constitute a single point both in theory empirically (assuming that the measurements are accurate) and conceptually (that is, based on a difference on the indicators mentioned, there is a substantive difference about what *sort of* democracy a state is). Another tetrahedron is composed of Paraguay, Ukraine, Malawi, and East Timor. Using their Polity IV scores (not included in the geometric analysis), those countries are considered democracies, but they do not score as strongly as other countries on the democracy scale. Polity IV scores range from –10 (purely autocratic) to +10 (understood as a full democracy), but many studies that analyze democratic behavior require a score of +6 or higher to consider a country as a democracy. These four states often rank right around 6 (either a little above or a little below). These states differ from those ranked higher on the Polity IV scale on primarily three of the fourteen indicators used in this pilot study: competitiveness of participation in governance, regulation of participation in governance, and breakdowns in democratic governance. On the other indicators, their scores are the same or substantially the same as "full" democracies. Considering what the components of democracy are, this suggests that democratic breakdowns distinguish countries who have had them from countries that have not, even among democracies. It also suggests that different levels of struggle with competitiveness in participation have different significations for problems with democracy. A fourth tetrahedron is formed by Russia, Congo Kinshasa, Mozambique, and Namibia. This tetrahedron has similar Polity IV scores to the group just discussed but fares less well on a number of the indicators that we randomly selected. In the other data from the Polity dataset, there must be a counterbalance to these countries' negative scores not only on competitiveness and democratic breakdowns but also on openness and regulation of competition.

Three more complex shapes that emerge are depicted in figure 9.2. The first, to the left in figure 9.2, is an octahedron formed by the Dominican Republic, El Salvador, Colombia, Guyana, Georgia, and Sierra Leone. These countries match each other perfectly in regulation of participation in executive elections, competitiveness of executive elections, openness of executive elections, and competitiveness of executive recruitment. They exhibit small variations on competitiveness and regulation of participation in elections. These traits make them closely related but not collapsible into one configuration. The six states differ on the existence of democratic breakdowns in their recent history, which is one of the factors that creates space among them. What distinguishes this group as a group from other democracies is imperfect scores on participation competitiveness and regulation of executive recruitment—so it is a group generally understood to be democracies with particular weaknesses vis a vis certain indicators of democracy.

The second more complex shape, in the center of figure 9.2, is an unnamed irregular polyhedron with ten triangular faces, composed of the Dominican Republic, Colombia, Bolivia, Albania, Brazil, the Solomon Islands, and Sierra Leone. This shape shares a triangular face with the octahedron on the left, which means that the two are related, though not the same. The polyhedron includes three of the countries in the octahedron and four different ones. In the octahedron, those countries (which score 6 on both executive constraints indicators; that is, they are slightly more constrained than not) are paired with countries that score 5 (that is, in the middle of the scale); in the irregular polyhedron, they are grouped with countries that score 7 on those same indicators. The combination of these shape relationships suggests that both a middle ground and a threshold level for executive constraints may be meaningful in the constitution of a democracy.

The third more complex shape, on the right in figure 9.2, is unrelated to the first two. It is a triangular bipyramid of Swaziland, Morocco, Kuwait, Bahrain, and Oman. These states rank low on most of the indicators of democracy that were included in our pilot study. Their low scores vary and are substantially less low in the area of regulation of participation in executive selection. In other words, these countries, considered autocratic, lean more in the direction of democracy when it comes to the clarity of rules of executive selection. While that does not stop them from being classified as nondemocracies, it does place them in a group among those nondemocracies, distinguishable from states with mediocre scores on all of the indicators and from those with low scores on all of the indicators.

This is, of course, a very limited exploration of a few relationships between a few states on a few indicators over the course of one year. One might question the advantage of this sort of analysis over just looking at the state's Polity IV score or at some other aggregation of these individual indicators, rather than looking at indicators that are used to make composite measures. After all, are composite measures not their composers' full definitions of democracy, and are the (sometimes weighted) component parts not their understanding of the dimensionality? Would more information not be gained, then, by comparing composite measures? Certainly, such a comparison would be fruitful, and one is in our future plans.[64] The information such analysis would provide would be different and, no doubt, an addition, as would being able to use the other hundred indicators that we collected. The nature of this pilot study and, therefore, the information it can provide are

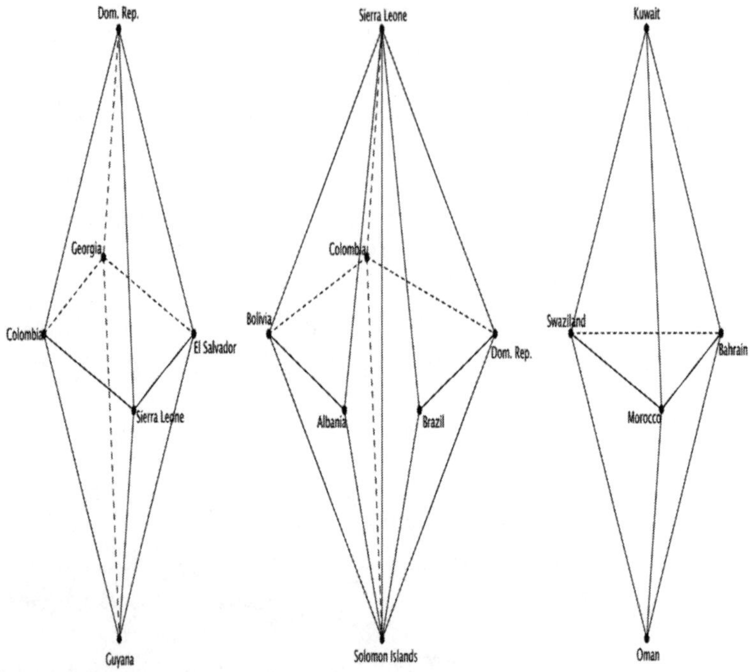

Fig. 9.2. Some 2-cycles in the fourteen-dimensional democracy data. These are representations of the figures in three-dimensional space; the actual cycles are embedded in R^{14}.

very limited. The study was able to show some contours of groups of states on the basis of some commonality about particular indicators of democracy that may serve as grouping or even tipping points. To know *a meaning* of democracy to IR scholars, much less *the* meaning, would require significantly more in-depth analysis.

Such a project is well within the methodological capacity of this approach. For example, if composite measures are, by definition, a combination of indicators *flattened* into one number, this sort of analysis can replicate those composite measures in geometric analysis so that a composite score means more than its statistical significance. It would then be possible to group states based not only on their composite scores but on the indicators on which they have the most similarity or even on indicators on which states with widely different composite numbers share common ground. Bending those models over time can show complex configurations that may be indicators of the change of form of a state. In other words, this sort of complex mapping is capable of expanding the possibilities for categorization of states among the multiple meanings of "democracy" and therefore of providing insight into multiple ways in which the concept is (and could be) thought about but that are not always explicit in quantitative or qualitative analysis in comparative politics and IR.

The biggest possible payoff in terms of looking at understandings of democracy, however, comes in the next four possible steps. First, looking at the data on democracy as abstract simplicial complexes and examining the filtrations and barcodes that come out of those constructions for the relationships *among states on indicators* can provide a basis for multidimensional mapping *of indicators in relation to each other*. How are these ideas related? What are the underlying conditions of possibility of their links? In other words, it would be possible to go beyond the positivist tendency to test collinearity, in order to look at the relationships among particular variables held to be indicators of democracy both definitionally and as operationalized and applied in the field. This might give insight into how certain indicators are chosen to the exclusion of others, that is, into what dominant understandings have in common and what they exclude. This sort of analysis could be done with existing data on democracy in the field of political science. A second step would be to compare the homological analysis of the indicators, measures, and definitions of democracy in political science to those used in the policy world, using critical discourse analysis[65] to collect data from state policy statements, press releases, and leader quotes in news publications. How is the concept of democracy deployed in political discourse? How is it deployed in political science? What do those deployments have in common? What differs across those deployments? Who benefits from particular constructions of the concept of democracy? Who suffers?

A third step could be comparing those results to survey data collected on the ground in a number of states around the world, where respondents were asked about what democracy is, how you can tell that a democracy exists, and whether neighboring states are democracies or not. These inquiries might provide evidence of how the concept of democracy can be or is deployed for political ends and of what about the overarching terminology of democracy allows for politicization, hollowing, and encroachment in the use of the term. A fourth step could compare these concept maps to concept maps for other, related but distinguishable concepts, like those discussed by Doty, Zalewski and Runyan, and Ashley.[66] This might shed light onto questions of how the concept of democracy comes to be constituted in certain ways and privileged over other ideas. What is possible (or impossible) by particular conceptions of what democracy is? How is the concept formed, related to its component parts, and cemented? What would change about IR scholarship or the world with the change or even elimination of the idea?

It is possible to be critical of these ideas for topological data analysis of democracy in IR by asking what is going on here. Is it not just a hyperactive process to critique (or even perfect) the positivist operationalization of democracy? Does this not open up a world of possibilities for mainstream analysis as well? Certainly, these methods could be used to such an end, making space for hypertechnical representations in regressions looking to figure out how regime type influences foreign policy or in predictions about the evolutions of forms of state government. But that is neither our intent nor, in our view, the primary benefit of this methodological innovation for constructivist and critical theorizing in IR.

Instead, we see the primary utility of an expansion of this sort of analysis in Shapcott's understanding that democracy "must forever be questioning itself and the boundaries that it invokes."[67] Mapping meanings of democracy, measurements of democracy, and comparisons on indicators of democracy in multidimensional space can help scholars understand the ways that various concepts are leveraged in favor of and related to certain notions of democracy, as well as maps and relationships of inclusion and exclusion. If it is possible to have some understanding of axes of rotation and points of engagement by just looking at a few configurations on a few indicators in one year, the analytical possibility of a full exploration of mapping understandings of democracy is almost unlimited. Such mappings could contribute to the analysis not only of some of the specific *"how possible"* questions above but also of other, yet unasked questions about relationships (tensions, similarities, and the simultaneous presence of both) between different ways in which democracy is read in global politics and in disciplinary IR.

The Potential Payoffs of Topological Analysis for Critical IR

If the above formalizations of concept vectors, concept spaces, concept topologies, and contexts are applicable to any concept in any theoretical context (in the informal sense), why deploy them for use in poststructuralist IR? In other words, even if these methods *could work for* poststructuralist analysis and provide some value added, why use them? Is the value added enough? After all, even if the ontological and epistemological positions of mathematical formalism and poststructuralist IR have commonalities, those commonalities do not dictate the fruitfulness of the two working together. While those commonalities (which we point out above) are the basis for our claim that the two are compatible despite the general association of quantitative work (of whatever flavor) with positivism and of poststructuralism with qualitative methods, our argument that this analysis is usefully employed in poststructuralist analysis is more based on the capacities that these sorts of representations have that the tools traditionally available to poststructuralist scholars do not easily replace and/or replicate.

Particularly, we argue that there are three principal potential benefits to the deployment of this methodology for poststructuralist IR. The first is that the complex concept modeling can be used to reveal dimensions of concepts (formally and informally) previously underexamined, in either mainstream or critical analysis. Thinking about the contours of concepts helps scholars to understand not just the ideas that go into concepts and/or their underlying assumptions. If topological concept mapping can capture the complexity of relations between features,[68] this provides a different way to think about the underlying assumptions, building blocks, inscriptions, and fixings of meanings in poststructuralist terms. Multidimensional concept modeling also provides a tool to think about the change of concepts over time, over place, and in the ways that they are thought about—either in the discipline or in the policy world.

Second, perhaps more interestingly, the tool of topological concept mapping can be based in empirical and representative studies but is not confined to them; a model built to represent the dimensionality of a concept and the relations between those dimensions can be studied with changes to that dimensionality to see about potential changes in the concept. This serves the purposes of emancipatory critical theorizing, that is, of asking if the world would be a better place if we thought about things differently It also serves the purposes of post-structuralist critical theorizing, that is, of asking how concept structures become sticky and reified, as well as what it would look like to unstick a particular dimension of a concept. If concept mapping can be manipulated temporally,[69] utilized to analyze transitional effects,[70] tessellated to unpack the relations between different compiled meanings,[71] morphologized to explore metaphorical relationships,[72] and translated to fuzzy geometry to understand liminality,[73] there is significant potential for developing critical analysis of what global politics is, how it is possible, and how it is constituted, reified, and performed. There is also significant potential to do work on one of the root inspirations for critical theory in IR, understanding how the world works in order to change it for the better. The potential to model how one change in the representation of a concept could affect and inspire changes in the other dimensions opens up nearly unlimited ground for looking for change for the better. While the math *identifies the good*, it can explore the effectiveness of intended changes and the unintended consequences of conceptual shifts.

This could be done in a way that emphasizes relative relationality, which, in our view, is the third major potential payoff for critical theorizing. While the descriptors for conceptual relationships are limited in terms of the sorts of relationships we can think about (in between, close to, far from, and so on), the topological descriptors are, in theory, both unlimited and more clearly specifiable (given the potential for multidimensionality). In fact, the complexity of both representation and exploration is theoretically unlimited. In practice, it is limited only by the possible accessibility of time and information and by the possible specification of configurations. Neither of these limits are concerning, though, given that even the least complex representations have potential exploratory value, both descriptively and relationally.

Notes

1. Mark Hoffman, "Critical Theory and the Interparadigm Debate," *Millennium: Journal of International Studies* 16, no. 2 (1987): 231–49.
2. Ibid.
3. Lene Hansen, "A Case for Seduction? Evaluating the Poststructuralist Conceptualization of Security," *Cooperation and Conflict: Journal of the Nordic International Studies Association* 32, no. 4 (1997): 369–97.
4. Ibid., 372.
5. Hoffman, "Critical Theory and the Interparadigm Debate."
6. See, e.g., Jonathan Lear, "Aristotle's Philosophy of Mathematics," *Philosophical Review* 91, no. 2 (1982): 161–92.
7. See, e.g., J. C. Fisher, "Geometry according to Euclid," *American Mathematical Monthly* 86, no. 4 (1979): 260–70.
8. See, e.g., Bertrand Russell, "Mathematical Logic Based on the Theory of Types," *American Journal of Mathematics* 30, no. 3 (1908): 222–62.
9. See, e.g., Carl B. Boyer, "Descartes and the Geometrization of Algebra," *American Mathematical Monthly* 66, no. 5 (1959): 390–93.
10. As noted by Alan Weir in "Formalism in the Philosophy of Mathematics" (2011), in the *Stanford Encyclopedia of Philosophy* (http://plato.stanford.edu/entries/formalism-mathematics/, accessed March 15, 2014), such an approach sees mathematics not as "a body of propositions representing an abstract sector of reality" but "much more akin to a game, bringing with it no . . . commitment to an ontology of objects or properties." In this sense, formalists "do not imply that these formulas are true statements" but, instead, see that "such intelligibility as mathematics possesses derives from the syntactical or metamathematical rules governing those marks" (Nelson Goodman and W. V. Quine, "Steps toward a Constructive Nominalism," *Journal of Symbolic Logic* 12 [1947]: 97–122, 122, 111).
11. To understand that assertion, it is important to distinguish, in discipline and

in substance, between statistics and mathematics. Statistics is the representation of quantity and correlation; mathematics is the spatial or equative representation of relationships, particularly as they become increasingly (and even impossibly) complex. We contend that critical theory wants what math can do, spatial concept maps of multidimensional, overlayered, folded, twisted manifolds of the stuff of politics. Math can represent the mess. It can even suggest tweaks, trades, changes, foldovers—alterations to the map. Imagine math like the Matrix (in the popular sci-fi film by the same name)—but used to understand transparently rather than to manipulate. It is possible to look at this theoretical discussion as abstract and impossible to materialize. That is an admitted weakness.

12. See, e.g., Nathalie Sinclair, "The Role of the Aesthetic in Mathematical Inquiry," *Mathematical Learning and Thinking* 6, no. 3 (2004): 261–84; Edward A. Silver and Wendy Metzger, "Aesthetic Influences of Expert Mathematical Problem Solving," in *Affect and Mathematical Problem Solving, ed. Douglas B. McLeod and Verna M. Adams* (New York: Springer, 1989), 59–74; Henri Poincare, "Mathematical Creation," *Monist* 20 (1910): 321–35; Gontran Ervynck, "Mathematical Creativity," *Advanced Mathematical Thinking* 11 (1991): 42–53; Loren Graham and Jean-Michael Kantor, *Naming Infinity: A True Story of Religious Mysticism and Mathematical Creativity* (Cambridge, MA: Harvard University Press, 2009); Gian-Carlo Rota, "The Phenomenology of Mathematical Beauty," *Synthese* 111, no. 2 (1997): 171–82; David Wells, "Which Is the Most Beautiful?" *Mathematical Intelligencer* 10, no. 4 (1988): 30–31.

13. A number of qualitative methodologists in IR have characterized concepts in geometric terms. E.g., in *Social Science Concepts: A User's Guide* (Princeton, NJ: Princeton University Press, 2012), 104, Gary Goertz discusses concepts as an amalgamation of dimensions weighted differently. In *Redesigning Social Inquiry: Fuzzy Sets and Beyond* (Chicago: University of Chicago Press, 2009), 80, Charles Ragin talks about dimensions of variation between entities. See also David Collier, Jody LaPorte, and Jason Seawright, "Putting Typologies to Work: Concept Formation, Measurement, and Analytic Rigor," *Political Research Quarterly* 65, no. 1 (2012): 217–32. While the methods herein could be deployed in service of the ends that those scholars discuss (components of variation and multifaceted causes), we are more interested in the critical potential—what these methods can do that geometric descriptions cannot and what critical theorizing can do that causal assumptions of knowledge cumulation cannot.

14. Gilles Deleuze and Felix Guattari, *A Thousand Plateaus: Capitalism and Schizophrenia*, trans. Brian Massumi (Minneapolis: University of Minnesota Press, 1987).

15. Ibid., 7. As the authors continue on to explain, "A rhizome ceaselessly establishes connections between semiotic chains, organizations of power, and circumstances relative to the arts, sciences, and social struggles. A semiotic chain is like a tuber agglomerating very diverse acts, not only linguistic, but also perceptive, mimetic, gestural, and cognitive: there is no language in itself, nor are there any linguistic universals, only a throng of dialects, patios, slangs, and specialized languages."

16. Ibid., 8.

17. Ibid., 267.

18. Ibid. In fact, the authors claim that geometric interpretations of concepts have further benefits that are unavailable in other frames of references. They outline the

unique contribution of geometric models to the understanding of contingent structure: "Principle of cartography and decalcomania: a rhizome is not amenable to any structural or generative model. It is a stranger to any idea of genetic axis or deep structure. A genetic axis is like an objective pivotal unity upon which successive stages are organized; deep structure is more like a base sequence that can be broken down into immediate constituents, while the unity of the product passes into another, transformational and subjective, dimension" (ibid., 12).

19. If we thought about their multiplicities *as manifolds,* there are a virtually unlimited number of things one could come to know, in geometric terms, about (and with) our "object of study," abstractly speaking. Among those unlimited things we could learn are properties of groups (homological, cohomological, and homeomorphic), complex directionality (maps, morphisms, isomorphisms, and orientability), dimensionality (codimensionality, structure, embeddedness), partiality (differentiation, commutativity, simultaneity), and shifting representation (factorization, ideal classes, reciprocity). *Each* of these functions allows for a different, creative, and potentially critical representation of global politics' concepts, events, groupings, and relationships.

20. For a relatively accessible explanation, see http://www.euclideanspace.com/maths/geometry/surfaces/manifold/.

21. Michel Foucault, *Politics, Philosophy, Culture* (New York: Routledge, 1988), 154.

22. David Campbell, *Writing Security: United States Foreign Policy and the Politics of Identity* (Minneapolis: University of Minnesota Press, 1992), 10.

23. Ibid., 1–2.

24. Peter Gardenfors, "Mental Representation, Conceptual Spaces, and Metaphors," *Synthese* 106, no. 1 (1996): 21–47.

25. See Janet Aisbett and Greg Gibbon, "A General Formulation of Conceptual Spaces as Meso-Level Representation," *Artificial Intelligence* 133 (2001): 189–232, 190.

26. Ibid., 192.

27. See Gardenfors, "Mental Representation," 33.

28. See Aisbett and Gibbon, "General Formulation of Conceptual Spaces," 192.

29. Peter Gardenfors, "Conceptual Spaces as a Framework for Knowledge Representation," *Mind and Matter* 2, no. 2 (2004): 9–27, 9.

30. John T. Rickard, "A Conceptual Geometry for Conceptual Space," *Fuzzy Optimum Decision Making* 5 (2006): 311–29 (original emphasis removed).

31. Peter Gardenfors, "Concept Learning: A Geometrical Model," *Proceedings of the Aristotelian Society* 101, no. 1 (2001): 169.

32. Thomas Mormann, "Natural Predicates and Topological Structures of Conceptual Spaces," *Synthese* 95, no. 2 (1993): 219–40, 220.

33. We here offer two simpler examples. First, let T be a hollow tetrahedron; topologically, this is a sphere. Observe that any simple closed loop on the surface of T bounds a disc. This means that there are no one-dimensional loops in T that cannot be filled in by a two-dimensional surface in T. There is a two-dimensional surface, though—namely, T itself—that cannot be filled in without leaving T. The corresponding homology vector spaces would then be zero-dimensional in degree 1 (every

loop bounds a disc) and one-dimensional in degree 2 (there is a two-dimensional surface in *T* that is not filled in by a three-dimensional object). Second, by contrast, consider the surface *S* of a donut. This has a three-dimensional void (the interior of *S*) and has some loops that do not bound discs on *S*—choose any meridian and any longitude. The degree 1 homology space would then have dimension 2.

34. See Herbert Edelsbrunner, David Letscher, and Afra Zomordian, "Topological Persistence and Simplification," *Discrete and Computational Geometry* 28 (2002): 511–33.

35. See V. de Silva and G. Carlsson, "Topological Estimation Using Witness Complexes," paper presented at the EG/IEEE *Symposium on Point-Based Graphics*, Zurich, Switzerland, June 2–4, 2004.

36. See, e.g., James Munkres, *Elements of Algebraic Topology* (Menlo Park, CA: Benjamin/Cummings, 1984).

37. For larger datasets, however, it is often impractical to build a simplicial complex on the entire set. One therefore turns to the witness complex construction on a much smaller subset of landmarks. We refer the reader to de Silva and Carlsson, "Topological Estimation Using Witness Complexes," for an analysis of the effectiveness of this process.

38. See Gardenfors, "Mental Representation."

39. Amitav Acharya and Barry Buzan, "Why Is There No Non-Western International Relations Theory? An Introduction," *International Relations of the Asia-Pacific* 7, no. 3 (2007): 287–312, 288, citing J. M. Goldgeier and M. McFaul, "A Tale of Two Worlds: Core and Periphery in the Post–Cold War Era," *International Organization* 46, no. 2 (1992): 467–91.

40. Acharya and Buzan, "Why Is There No Non-Western International Relations Theory?," 295.

41. Fabrizio Eva, "International Boundaries, Geopolitics, and the (Post)Modern Territorial Discourse: The Functional Fiction," *Geopolitics* 3, no. 1 (1998): 32–52, 49.

42. Naeem Inayatullah and David Blaney, *International Relations and the Problem of Difference* (New York: Routledge, 2004).

43. Roxanne Lynn Doty, *Imperial Encounters: The Politics of Representation in North-South Relations* (Minneapolis: University of Minnesota Press, 1996), 135.

44. Ibid.

45. Miyume Tanji and Stephanie Lawson, "'Democratic Peace' and 'Asian Democracy': A Universalist-Particularist Tension," *Alternatives* 22, no. 1 (1997): 135–55, 151. See discussion in Inayatullah and Blaney, *Problem of Difference.*

46. Doty, *Imperial Encounters*, 8–9.

47. Ibid., 31.

48. Marysia Zalewski and Anne Runyan, "Taking Feminist Violence Seriously in International Relations," *International Feminist Journal of Politics* 15, no. 3 (2013): 293–313, 299.

49. Richard K. Ashley, "Untying the Sovereign State: A Double Reading of the Anarchy Problematique," *Millennium: Journal of International Studies* 17, no. 2 (1988): 227–62.

50. Ibid.

51. Andrew Linklater, "The Achievements of Critical Theory," in *International Relations Theory: Positivism and Beyond,* ed. Ken Booth, Steve Smith, and Marysia Zalewski (Cambridge: Cambridge University Press, 1996), 279–300, 294.

52. Jean Baudrillard, *The Mirror of Production* (Candor, NY: Telos, 1975).

53. Andreas Bieler and Adam David Morton, "A Critical Theory Route to Hegemony, World Order, and Historical Change: Neo-Gramscian Perspectives in International Relations," *Capital and Class* 82 (2004): 85–113, 97.

54. Ibid.

55. Ken Booth, *Theory of World Security* (Cambridge: Cambridge University Press, 2007), 55, citing Craig N. Murphy, "Critical Theory and the Democratic Impulse: Understanding a Century-Old Tradition," in Richard Wyn Jones, *Critical Theory and World Politics* (Boulder, CO: Lynne Rienner, 2001), 61–76.

56. Booth, *Theory of World Security*, 272.

57. Alison Brysk, *From Tribal Village to Global Village: Indian Rights and International Relations in Latin America* (Stanford, CA: Stanford University Press, 2000), 293.

58. Richard Shapcott, *Justice, Community, and Dialogue in International Relations* (Cambridge: Cambridge University Press, 2001), 70.

59. Ibid., 69.

60. The datasets that we compiled include the Comparative Study of Electoral Systems (http://www.cses.org, accessed April 2, 2015); Coppedge's Democracy Diffusion data (used in Daniel Brinks and Michael Coppedge, "Diffusion is No Illusion: Neighbor Emulation in the Third Wave of Democracy," *Comparative Political Studies* 39, no. 4 [2006]: 463–89); the Democracy Barometer (http://democracybarometer.org, accessed April 2, 2015; Wolfgang Merkel and Daniel Bochsler [project leaders], Karima Bousbah, Marc Bühlmann, Heiko Giebler, Miriam Hahni, Lea Heyne, Lisa Müller, Saskia Ruth, and Bernhard Wessels, *Democracy Barometer: Codebook*, version 4.1 [Aarau: Zentrum für Demokratie, 2014]); Varieties of Democracy (https://v-dem.net, accessed April 2, 2015; Michael Coppedge, John Gerring, Staffan I. Lindberg, Jan Teorell, David Altman, Michael Bernhard, M. Steven Fish, Adam Glynn, Allen Hicken, Carl Henrik Knutsen, Matthew Kroenig, Kelly McMann, Daniel Pemstein, Megan Reif, Svend-Erik Skaaning, Jeffrey Staton, Eitan Tzelgov, and Yi-ting Wang, "Varieties of Democracy Codebook v4," Varieties of Democracy Project: Project Documentation Paper Series, Freedom House [https://v-dem.net/en/reference/version-4-mar-2015/, accessed April 2, 2015]); Miller-Boix-Rosato Dichotomous Codings of Democracy (Carles Boix, Michael K. Miller, and Sebastian Rosato, "A Complete Data Set of Political Regimes, 1800–2007," *Comparative Political Studies* 46, no. 12 [2013]: 1523–54); Pippa Norris' Democracy Time-Series Dataset (http://www.hks.harvard.edu/fs/pnorris/Data/Democracy%20TimeSeries%20Data/Codebook%20for%20Democracy%20Time-Series%20Dataset%20January%202009.pdf, accessed April 2, 2015), Polity IV (http://www.systemicpeace.org/polityproject.html, accessed April 2, 2015); Vanhanen's Polyarchy Dataset (https://www.prio.org/Data/Governance/Vanhanens-index-of-democracy/, accessed April 2, 2015); World Governance Indicators compiled by Daniel Kaufmann, Aart Kraay, and Massimo Mastruzzi (http://info.worldbank.org/governance/wgi/index.aspx#home, accessed April 2, 2015); and Unified Democracy Scores (Daniel Pemstein, Stephen A. Meserve, and James Melton,

"Democratic Compromise: A Latent Variable Analysis of Ten Measures of Regime Type," *Political Analysis* 18, no. 4 [2010]: 426–49).

61. Some of these indicators are dichotomous, and some are on a one-to-ten scale.

62. For the sake of the simplicity of this already-complicated example, we have weighted these indicators equally, where other choices could have been made, both geometrically and substantively.

63. Formally, the identity map between them is null-homotopic. As a result, in theory, a contractible space could be shrunk to a point.

64. We were able to use a very limited portion of this dataset here, partly because of incompatibilities across software about how to deal with missing data and partly because of the labor-intensive nature of the initial work plan. Currently, research assistants are working on cleaning up the dataset for future work across other indicators, on composite measures, and over time.

65. See Ruth Wodak and Michael Meyer, *Methods for Critical Discourse Analysis* (London: Sage, 2009).

66. See nn. 42–48.

67. Shapcott, *Justice, Community, and Dialogue*, 68.

68. See Aisbett and Gibbon, "General Formulation of Conceptual Spaces," 217.

69. See ibid., 218.

70. See ibid., 220.

71. See Rickard, "Conceptual Geometry for Conceptual Space," 315.

72. See Gardenfors, "Mental Representation," 40.

73. See Rickard, "Conceptual Geometry for Conceptual Space," 311.

PART 3

Reflections and Looking Forward

CHAPTER 10

Practicing (Social-)Scientific Pluralism

PATRICK THADDEUS JACKSON

According to Ian Hacking's famous definition, to say that something is "socially constructed" is to maintain that that thing is not the way it is because of inevitable natural necessity; things could have been and perhaps still could be different.[1] If a constructivist attitude or perspective involves precisely this kind of shift from natural necessity to conventionality, it is entirely appropriate to characterize this book, as a whole, as a broadly constructivist intervention. The authors of its various chapters treat the connections between formal and quantitative methods, on one hand, and hypothesis-testing exercises involving material attributes, on the other, less as inevitable and more as instrumental: good for some purposes and not for others. That expanded range of scholarly choice is, in turn, made possible by a rejection of the notion that the only thing that formal and quantitative methods are good for is the elaboration and evaluation of hypothetical generalizations about material factors. Here as elsewhere, practical agency (the agency of the scholar, in this case) goes hand in hand with a weakening of supposedly parametric constraints.

There is another sense in which this is a constructivist book, a more prosaic sense in which the term *construction* means simply that things are built. Part of a constructivist agenda involves the conceptual "underlaborer" work of dismantling supposed unities, showing that notions like "science" (or "social science") do not have univocal meanings or fixed and firm boundaries. This can be done in a variety of ways: historically, by teasing out the various streams that informed and continue to inform what we mistakenly think of as a single "scientific" way of knowing;[2] sociologically, by tracing out connections between the institutions[3] and technical practices[4] of scientific inquiry on one hand, and the content of the results achieved on the other; and philosophically, by showing the irreducible plurality and diversity of ways of being scientific.[5] But all of this underlaborer work, important though it is, merely sets the stage for the next task, which is the construction of actual, operational strategies of knowing that take advantage of this openness and build novel combinations of principles and conceptions and techniques. After demolition comes the building of new places to live and work and know, and this volume contains a number of impressive developments.

Really cashing in on this promise requires clarity about exactly what kind of space of possibility has been opened. As the editors of this book note in their introduction, our very terminology tends to obscure this, because we treat the relationships between ontology, epistemology, methodology, and method as an airtight progression from what there is in the world (ontology), to how we know about it (epistemology), to the research design (methodology) and research techniques (method) we ought to use. The editors want to loosen up these connections and make them not unidirectional (ontology → epistemology → methodology → method) but multiple (ontology ↔ epistemology ↔ methodology ↔ method), so that different connections between the categories are made literally thinkable, and so that novel combinations of these categories are made practically possible.

That I agree with the general thrust of the editors' argument and of this book project as a whole should come as no surprise to anyone familiar with arguments I have made elsewhere on this topic. Extracting methodology from its conventional position in the one-dimensional stream that connects ontology to method and arguing that methodology is more helpfully thought of as philosophical ontology—as concerned with the mind-world hookup—were central themes of my book *The Conduct of Inquiry in International Relations*, and the kind of epistemic diversity I advocated there is clearly on display in the present project too. Indeed, it would not be too much of a stretch to say that this project cashes in on the critical potential of separating methodology both from method and from theory and shows what is thereby made possible. My own thinking, though, would prefer not a four-part distinction between ontology, epistemology, methodology, and method, but a tripartite distinction between theory, methodology, and method. I do not think this is inconsistent with the editors' formulation, but I suggest that it might be a more useful framing of the broader conceptual issues—useful in the sense that it can prevent the accidental collapse of admirable epistemic diversity into a methodological monoculture.

As I have argued elsewhere, the very notion of "epistemology" as a separate thing carries with it a basically Cartesian, dualist apprehension of the mind-world hookup. If "how we know" is conceptually separated from "what there is to know," the knower and the known are existentially sundered from one another, producing a great gulf or gap that has to be properly crossed in order for knowledge to be something other than mere fancy.[6] Epistemology also takes a decidedly secondary role in such a worldview, because how we know is subordinate to what there is to know; scientific realists call this "putting ontology first" and maintain that only doing so allows us to avoid the "epistemic fallacy" of limiting what is by what we can know of it.[7] This notion of "epistemology" carries with it, then, a dualist conception whereby mind and world are separate from one another, and maintaining a separation between epistemology and ontology tacitly contributes to a dualist account of knowledge and knowing.

I am not in the business of disputing dualism or arguing that scientific realism is somehow illegitimate as a way of thinking about the production of knowledge. I have no idea on what basis one would even do so: to dispute dualism, it would have to be possible to either adduce evidence or marshal arguments against dualism that did not at least tacitly already presume that dualism was not true—and to reject scientific realism definitively, it would have to be possible to fall back on an incontestable definition of social science that did not accord with scientific realist notions. But these things do not exist. "Science" is internally diverse and philosophically contestable, and mind-world dualism—much like its ideal-typical opposite, mind-world monism—is not so much a contestable claim as a world-disclosing commitment or wager. The proper response to epistemic diversity is pluralism, not a subtle reassertion of one or another perspective in the putatively neutral guise of a conceptual architecture that privileges some accounts rather than others.

Scientific or epistemic pluralism, I argue, is better served by a change of vocabulary. If we follow Martin Heidegger's pathbreaking reformulation of the basic questions of traditional metaphysics,[8] we quickly realize that it is senseless to talk about "ontology"—accounts of what is, or, in Heidegger's formulation, accounts of the "Being of beings" and of the meaning of existence or Being—without talking about the (human) being that lets beings be and thus encounters them in their Being. In other words, to translate this insight from Heidegger's rather idiosyncratic formulation (which works better in German than in English), accounts of what *is* rely on logically prior, often implicit assumptions about *us*, not just as cognitive "knowers," but as worldly creatures involved with the world and the things in it. Epistemology—the very notion of which is inextricably entwined with mind-world dualism—is only one way of cashing out the character of that primordial worldly involvement. There are others, and they carry different assumptions about how we are connected to our objects of study and, thus, how we might come to produce knowledge of them. In this sense, ontology (necessarily!) comes first—ontology in the sense of a basic conception of how knowers and known are related, a *philosophical* ontology of mind-world relations. Strategies of knowing—how we might design our research projects so as to generate new and valid knowledge—supervene on philosophical ontology; the result is *methodology*, a sense of the rationale for and intent involved in conducting one's investigations in a particular way.

In the more conventional account I have been criticizing, ontology is understood as a bestiary, as a listing of what there is to be studied. Especially given that this catalog of existents is not a transhistorical constant—the chart of "fundamental constituents of the world" evolves and changes over time, as new things are invented or discovered, old things are reconceptualized and recategorized, and novel notions (e.g., "international society" or "human security") are proposed and debated—it is important that we have some way of referring to that aspect of a piece of scientific research distinct from its methodology. The conception of existing things that informs a piece of research, as distinct from the ways that the research and the researcher deals with producing valid knowledge about those things, might be called "scientific ontology"[9] or—to avoid confusion with philosophical ontology—*"theory."*[10] This formulation accords with common use in international studies, where one frequently encounters references to "state-centric theory" or "structural theory"; being picked out in these formulations are those parts of particular pieces of scientific research that both rest on and refine particular substantive conceptions of things in the world, and that ordinarily do so for explanatory purposes.

So some of what was picked up by the category of "ontology" in the conventional four-part research scheme falls into the category of "theory," and the rest of "ontology"—together with all of "epistemology" as a subcategory—falls into a philosophically reformulated category of "methodology." An advantage of formulating things in this way is that theory and methodology are obviously independent of one another. In international studies, for example, we have numerous examples of "realists" using similar theories—more precisely, theories bearing such strong family resemblances to one another that we are comfortable characterizing them as, in some sense, a theoretical aggregate, to which aggregate we usually inaccurately append a designator like "paradigm" or "research programme"[11]—with wildly divergent methodologies. The same is true of IR "liberals." IR "constructivists," by contrast, have sometimes argued and have been characterized as arguing that only certain methodologies fit with theories that embrace agent-structure co-constitution and a central role for social processes of meaning-making. Along the theory-methodology axis, this volume intervenes to suggest, to the contrary, that a scientific ontology that highlights and foregrounds agency and meaning-making necessitates neither a reflexive, critical methodology nor a hypothesis-testing, nomothetic-generalization-oriented one.

What of "method"? If we take seriously the notion that method refers to techniques of gathering and manipulating data, it should be clear that method is conceptually distinct from both theory and methodology. Therefore, the other central contention of this volume is more sharply formulated as involving not one but two axes: method-methodology and method-theory. Quantitative and formal methods—techniques for collecting and analyzing data—can be combined with any theory and with any methodology, and there is no reason that constructivist theories or critical methodologies cannot be productively cashed out in quantitative and formal terms. That probably comes as a surprise to scholars socialized to equate quantitative/formal methods with a neopositivist methodology of hypothesis-testing and with theories involving relatively stable material attributes. But in demonstrating that these novel combinations are possible, the chapters in this volume reveal the conventionality of that belief.

Rather than using a line to show the relationship between theory, methodology, and method, we need a triangle, as depicted in figure 10.1. Our "typical" way of proceeding in the field is to presume that there are only certain sensical combinations of values for the end points of this triangle—for instance, quantitative-neopositivist-liberal or textual/hermeneutic-critical-feminist. But a number of other combinations are on offer in this volume; this is the productive, constructive aspect of this project, in which the various authors seek to fill out the space of possibilities generated by giving up the seeming inevitability of those typical groupings.

Not all of the chapters in this volume feature clear commitments on all three points of the triangle. Thies and Lustick do not have explicit theoreti-

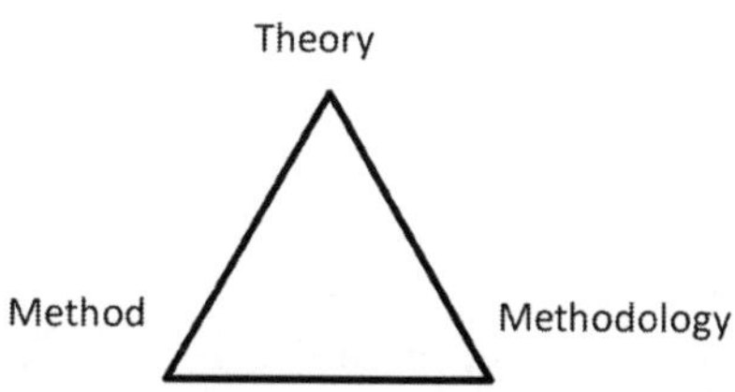

Fig. 10.1. Relationship between theory, methodology, and method

cal commitments in their chapters; they seek to provide what we might call *research plans*: theory-neutral combinations of research design parameters and techniques that might, in principle, be combined with any number of substantive theoretical notions to generate findings. Hoffmann, Kowert, Sylvan, and Sjoberg are more focused on how particular techniques can be used to produce theory-laden *descriptions* of phenomena; they offer a number of diverse illustrations of how one can use a generally constructivist theoretical commitment about the centrality of meaningful action to produce systematic accounts of concepts, arguments, and patterns of sensibility. The goal of their contributions is to use broadly constructivist theory to characterize things in ways that we might miss if we were to limit ourselves to the material aspects of situations. Finally, in the chapters by Ackerly and Barkin, we have sketches of full-blown *explanations* for why we observe the particular things we observe in the world, combining theory, methodology, and method in order to produce knowledge of observed outcomes.

These three groups of chapters point to the work that remains to be done in occupying all of the possible points of combination of theory, methodology, and method that a pluralist science of international affairs might encompass. The theory-independent research plans of Thies and Lustick are neopositivist in methodology; despite using different techniques, they are on the same basic page epistemically, and the resulting illustration of diversity is somewhat narrower than it might have been. The descriptive chapters of Hoffmann, Kowert, Sylvan, and Sjoberg combine "nonstandard" methods with broadly constructivist theory and thus provide a nice counterweight to the prevalence of "conventional constructivist" research using broadly "qualitative" methods in the field, but by avoiding the methodology question, they leave open the possibility that their innovative descriptions will be turned into coding schemes for neopositivist hypothesis-testing exercises, which would foreclose diversity that might otherwise have been. Ackerly and Barkin produce sketches of explanations featuring nonstandard combinations of theory, methodology, and method, but, of course, they can only illustrate two such combinations. The potential number of other such combinations is only limited by the number of theories, methodologies, and methods available to be combined, so even if we limited ourselves to three families of theory (the IR "isms"), four methodologies (neopositivism, critical realism, analyticism, and reflexivity), and three families of method (numerical, textual, and participant-observation), we would still be talking about thirty-six different combinations of theory, methodology, and method. Working through all of these potential combinations would take much more space than this or any other single essay or book could afford. I hope that the opening signaled by this volume inspires other researchers to develop and work with novel combinations in the future.

Research Plans

Neopositivism is a methodology defined by a pair of commitments in philosophical ontology: mind-world dualism and the limitation of knowledge to the sphere of the in-principle experienceable, which I have elsewhere called "phenomenalism." These combine to underpin the central features of any neopositivist research: the preference for systematic empirical associations and nomothetic generalizations; the emphasis on falsifiability and the testing of hypotheses as the route to the production of valid knowledge, through the progressive elimination of inaccurate or false conjectures; and the notion that an outcome is explained once we show that it was, in Carl Hempel's phrasing, "to be expected, that it was not a matter of chance."[12] It is perhaps not surprising that both of the contributors to this volume who offer theory-neutral research plans are firmly in the neopositivist methodological camp.

Neopositivism supports a focus on the form of a knowledge claim rather than its content, a tendency that stems from the roots of neopositivist thinking about knowledge in the effort to cleanly demarcate scientific from nonscientific or pseudoscientific claims; where the Vienna Circle's initial emphasis on verifiability fell short, the Popperian criterion of falsifiability appeared to many to do the trick. But the impetus is the same: we determine science by its form, by the procedures that scientists use to make and evaluate conjectural claims, and not by its content. Theory takes a backseat here, reconfigured as both a source of hypothetical conjectures and a cumulative record of those already-vetted conjectures for which we are sufficiently confident of validity. Knowledge grows through a process of evolution, as scientists make and evaluate conjectures and as the collective stock of human knowledge increases.

Both Thies and Lustick provide examples of neopositivism in action, albeit using different methods; therein lies their important contribution to the pluralism of this volume. Thies takes certain constructivist theoretical notions, such as the Wendtian typology of cultures of anarchy, and converts them into codable, operational variables that can be incorporated into statistical models, more or less seamlessly, alongside variables drawn from other theoretical traditions; this makes it possible to assess the relative importance of things like role structures in explanations—in the neopositivist sense of "explaining," meaning accounting for systematic cross-case covariation—for more peaceful inter-state outcomes. This is relatively orthodox neopositivism plus quantification, and the novelty here is in illustrating that there is no special barrier to incorporating ideational factors into such models. Lustick, despite his embrace of computer simulation techniques rather than conventional hypothesis-testing, is no less a neopositivist; his stated aim is "to do much better than any other method available in producing outputs closer to the complexity of the worlds inhabited by politicians and policy makers," through a procedure of, in effect, generating hundreds of hypothetical conjectures and then combining them to produce probabilistic depictions of the space of the future. The epistemic goals remain the same—to explain an actually occurring outcome by locating it within a general set of propositions and to predict likely outcomes by treating that set of general propositions as provisionally valid—and although Lustick also utilizes quantitative measures and techniques, his computer simulation techniques are significantly different from the estimation procedures utilized by Thies.[13]

The punchline here is that simply being a neopositivist methodologically does not dictate the kinds of methods one is constrained to use. This should not be a surprise; the "qualitative methods" movement in the field of U.S. political science and international relations has been harping on this for years, seeking to carve out a place for small-*n* "qualitative" case study research largely on the grounds that while the *methods* differ from those of large-*n* statistical-comparative work, the *methodology* remains the same. No matter the flavor, neopositivist work is invariably about a strategy of inference that aims to move from individual cases to empirically general relationships. In the case of the chapters here by Thies and Lustick, that strategy is intact whether it is implemented by estimating the values of coefficients from a dataset or by repeatedly running a model with statistical perturbations and combining the results.

There is no especially insurmountable problem involved in quantitatively operationalizing constructivist notions like a "culture of anarchy." A creative researcher can come up with operational indicators of any variable, no matter its theoretical source; this is a testimony to the creativity of the researcher and in no way a reflection on the inherently "quantifiable" or "unquantifiable" nature of the factor in question. Thies does this directly, proposing specific metrics for constructivist factors. Lustick is more ambiguous on this point, as the only specific mention of constructivism in his chapter comes in a discussion of methodology, not of theory: "Constructivism's angle of attack on this problem is to explore how different meanings or understandings of the same perceived 'events' can be a function of different frames of reference." Nevertheless, there is no a priori reason that one could not incorporate constructivist notions into Lustick's modeling procedure, which allows, in principle (as he states), for any variety of "substantive theoretical knowledge to be quickly and intuitively encoded"—just as Thies's equations do.[14]

It might be thought that only neopositivism lends itself to such elaborations of research plans without determinate theoretical content. While there are certainly more plans of this sort floating around, written into "methods" textbooks and taught in "methods" courses (especially across that part of international studies dominated by U.S. political science), there is no necessary reason for this. We are not completely devoid of examples of non-neopositivist research plans combining methodology and method with a relative downplaying of theory. Jennifer Milliken, Lene Hansen, Janice Bially Mattern, and Vincent Pouliot (to name just a few scholars) have produced such "technical" guidelines for doing non-neopositivist research.[15] Except for some theoretical/substantial notions that Jason Glynos and David Howarth build into their "fantasmic" logic, their book *Logics of Critical Inquiry* does likewise.[16] None of those contributions incorporates quantitative or formal techniques in any profound way, so we are still waiting for *that* combination to be clearly articulated. Thies and Lustick show us that there is room for method variation within neopositivism, but the reverse direction—combining formal and quantitative methods with non-neopositivist methodologies in a theory-neutral way—remains to be fleshed out.[17]

Description

Description gets a bad rap in the contemporary social sciences. Causation, explanation, and prediction rule the epistemic roost; description often shows up, disparagingly, as "mere description," to be contrasted with more noble epistemic goals. At its worst, this becomes the "senior partner"/"summer intern" distinction made (in)famous by Ted Hopf: description, including the "thick description" associated with participant-observation methods, becomes the source of raw data that the real scientists can take and incorporate into the real work of scientific inference.[18] As King, Keohane, and Verba (hereafter KKV) put it rather bluntly, "If we make no effort to extract the systematic features of a subject, the lessons of history will be lost, and we will learn nothing about what aspects of our subject are likely to persist or to be relevant to future events or studies."[19] Describing is thus insufficient, except as a temporary stopping point on the way to the real goal of identifying valid nomothetic generalizations.

This is a very problematic notion of description, as it presumes that there is such a thing as a more or less atheoretical way of describing phenomena of interest to international studies scholars. We see this presumption cropping up in the occasional declarations that the difference between social scientists and historians is that the latter just provide raw data that the former can use to evaluate their theoretical conjectures,[20] but it is not merely history that is mistakenly thought to be somehow atheoretical; rather, observation itself is often thought to provide some kind of immediate, unmediated set of facts against which theory can be compared. That this is philosophically ridiculous and completely unsustainable has been common knowledge at least since Immanuel Kant; Karl Popper used the theory-dependence of observation as part of his case for shifting away from verifiability toward falsifiability, and contemporary accounts of perception, to say nothing of phenomenological accounts of experience, agree that there is no such thing as description that does not involve theory. Any single object simply has too many potentially relevant features to be completely described; selecting some of those features to focus on and to incorporate into the description is therefore, at its base, a "theoretical" endeavor. Even often-repeated, widely circulated, quasi-naturalized notions like the "GDP" of a state or "number of casualties" in a conflict depend, albeit often implicitly, on theoretical notions that tell us to be interested in these factors as opposed to others.

All of this suggests that description is never just "mere." Instead, description enacts or performs theory. As I describe the things happening outside of my window as a "riot" or a "protest" or a "mass demonstration," I invoke and draw on theoretical notions, using them to organize my experience and communicate with other people. This is no different than describing the table in front of me as "brown"; the description only makes sense in the light of a whole color scheme that is less a naturally given part of the world and more a set of conventions that "we" use to make sense of the world, and if I were interested in using the table as a place to rest a heavy box and needed to know how much weight the table could support, that description (of its color) might be completely useless to me.[21] Descriptions are linked to theories and do not arise inevitably from the world or from the objects in it.

A scientific description differs from an everyday description only in being more systematic, more precise, more methodical, than many of the descriptions that pass in day-to-day social interactions. Theory plus method gives us a set of instructions for describing things precisely in accord with a particular scientific ontology. The resulting description is *methodologically* neutral, because neither theory nor method necessarily entail any particular methodology, and vice versa; I could take a set of scientific descriptions and combine them into values of a variable, but I could just as easily turn that set of descriptions into categories for classifying cases, evidence of a systematic bias in how "the facts" are presented, and so on. Neither the neopositivist strategy of turning descriptions into variables for the sake of testing hypotheses nor the neopositivist preference for cross-case descriptions that can be used for case comparison is any more or less scientific or precise than the careful ethnographic description of a form of life undertaken in order to make plain the hidden or tacit social rules operating in that particular situation or community.

It therefore follows that scientific descriptions, by instantiating particular theories, can show us what the world looks like when viewed through a particular set of conceptual lenses. The four descriptive chapters in this volume adopt a broadly "constructivist" theoretical sensibility, in that they all foreground meaning-making, language, culture, and the sorts of factors one generally expects to see in a constructivist account. But then they diverge in a way that leads them to produce very different descriptions.

Kowert looks at perception, although he calls this "phenomenology"; he is interested in the patterns into which people's perceptions of states fall and, in particular, whether there is an emergent order of such perceptions, a dimensionality to the perceptual space, revealed through a factor analysis of survey responses. His approach is both constructivist, inasmuch as it deals with intersubjectively meaningful components of social action, and descriptive, inasmuch as it aims to tell us about those perceptions and not about why we have them or what they do in the world. From Kowert's closing comments, it seems as though incorporating his five dimensions into a causal account of some sort lies in the future, but this is not *necessarily* entailed by his systematic description of those dimensions.

Hoffmann, by contrast, pulls on the thread in constructivist theory that emphasizes the relational character of identity, using the tools and methods of social network analysis to describe patterns of state action and interaction in terms of positional, rather than categorical, attributes; in this way, Hoffmann's "constructivism" is quite different from Kowert's "constructivist" emphasis on the perceived categorical attributes of states. But like Kowert's systematic description, Hoffmann's does not inevitably lend itself to any particular methodology; one could test hypotheses about state positionality using this data, but one could just as easily use the data to suggest that changes had occurred in the deep constitutive structure of the international system. From a similar theoretical orientation, Hoffmann and Kowert produce quite different "constructivist" descriptions of state identity, but those descriptions retain a family resemblance.

Sylvan and Sjoberg share a narrower construal of "constructivism," but their differences of method also produce appreciably distinct descriptions. Both authors are enmeshed in that part of constructivist theory that emphasizes language-in-use and that foregrounds the way that meaning emerges from such use, including from the implicit grammar that makes particular uses intelligible in the first place. Sylvan focuses on conversations, using particular bits of contentious diplomatic interaction to reveal broader ecologies of social convention; Sjoberg utilizes formal concept analysis to probe the complexity of how international studies scholars talk about "democracy." In both cases, the description in question "surfaces" what is often tacit in individual usages of terms and phrases, thus instantiating a theoretical conception of language that abandons simple notions of "mirroring" or "representation" in favor of a postrepresentational or "linguistic turn" approach (Sjoberg calls it post-structural, and Sylvan embeds it in relational sociology and discursive psychology, but these are merely differences in dialect). Neither author specifies just what the resulting description is for, which is as it should be for a description: theory informs the result, but that does not dictate any particular methodological purpose to which that result might be put.

This strength of descriptive exercises is also their potential weakness, especially in a field so dominated by an unreflective and often even unacknowledged neopositivist methodology. Cashing in on the promise of scientific pluralism requires not just that novel combinations be explored but that they be able to grow and develop without being assimilated to any one approach to the production of knowledge. Kowert's references into personality theory suggest that he would be just fine with his typology becoming the basis for a set of neopositivist hypothesis-testing exercises, and Hoffmann's cautionary note about social network analysis often being used in the field as part of such an exercise (despite the fact that it need not be) gives some cause for concern that these descriptive innovations might, in the end, simply amount to, as Steve Smith once put it, rearranging deck chairs on the Titanic[22]—or, more neutrally, a continuation of the dominant presumption that neopositivism has an exclusive lock on "scientific" methodology. Confronting this presumption head-on strikes me as absolutely necessary if a robust, vibrant pluralism is to persist in the field of international studies; otherwise, we will get a pluralism of theories and a pluralism of methods, but no pluralism where it matters most, in the methodological presumptions that structure our research designs and connect particular epistemic goals to concrete ways of producing knowledge. The four descriptive chapters here clearly illustrate how one might produce a variety of broadly constructivist descriptions of international phenomena, using formal and quantitative techniques. But the danger remains that they will be assimilated to a neo-positivist methodology. While this is not a problem for the authors, it is a challenge for the field, moving forward.

Explanations

The antidote to methodological assimilation is to produce alternative complete packages, combining theory, methodology, and method in ways that are not standard in the field. This volume offers two such complete packages: Barkin's explanation of international fisheries policy and Ackerly's account of rights enjoyment in Bangladesh. Each combines theory, methodology, and method in novel ways, demonstrating both the explanatory productivity of their combination and the fact that not all productive explanations fall into one of the two established camps of realism/liberalism-neopositivism-"quantitative" or constructivist-critical-"qualitative."

Barkin self-consciously grounds his account in constructivist theory, emphasizing human agency and the contribution it makes to sustaining social arrangements. The individualist rationalism he introduces is, so to speak, a particular variant of that emphasis: international institutions emerge because of things that people do, and rational choice theory is one way of making sense of what they do. (Contrast rational choice accounts that are interested not in what people do but in how input factors are "rationally" connected to outcomes; such accounts are more common in liberal and some realist IR scholarship.) But unlike most people in the field who are utilizing the tools of formal rational choice analysis, Barkin treats the rational model as a model in the analyticist sense, as an unrealistic construct not showing what is or what should be, but instead giving an instrumental baseline against which to evaluate the impact of factors that fall outside of the model. Those factors are the things more commonly associated with constructivism in the field: intersubjective meaning, symbolic value, social identities. The resulting explanation is not and does not aim to be generalizable, does not test general hypotheses about international behavior, and does not "validate" the model. Instead, it helps us understand why we have the arrangements we have in global fisheries policy.

In some ways, Ackerly's chapter goes even further. Drawing not only on some insights that might be thought of as "constructivist" (about the importance of meaning-making, but also, in no small measure, on feminist sensibilities and theory about the experiences of relative outsiders and those deliberately marginalized), Ackerly and her collaborators produce a critical/

reflexive account of rights enjoyment in Bangledesh that brings to the foreground the inequities in the distribution of such rights. But they use tools most often claimed by neopositivists, such as opinion polls, surveys, and demographic statistics. This is reminiscent, at least to my mind, of Pierre Bourdieu's statistical studies of the class origin of French scholars[23] and of C. Wright Mills's study of the "power elite."[24] In all of these cases, we have tools designed to reveal systematic patterns—that is built into the method—not being used to evaluate hypothetical generalizations about the causal impact (which would be methodology) of more or less quantifiable material factors (which would be the kind of theory most commonly utilized in "mainstream" Anglophone international studies scholarship). Instead, revealed systematic patterns are used for critical disruption, for a shaking of common presuppositions, for producing a solid indictment of what exists, in the hope of pressing it to become better. By placing oneself at the margins and seeking to elucidate the world from that perspective, critical scholarship aims to show us the world "from below" and to generate knowledge that is robustly and unapologetically perspectival. Ackerly demonstrates, quite unequivocally, that statistical tools can be a help in that endeavor.

The chapters by Barkin and Ackerly most concretely point the way forward for a robust scientific pluralism in international studies. Thies and Lustick showed the diversity of neopositivism in terms of method; Hoffmann, Kowert, Sylvan, and Sjoberg showed that constructivist theory and formal and quantitative methods were in no way incompatible; and Barkin and Ackerly proceeded to sketch novel explanations of a sort that would be ruled out by a more univocal international studies field that insisted on determinate links between particular theories, methodologies, and methods. These are, of course, only the first tentative steps, and the combination of constructivism, analyticism, and rational choice and that of feminism, critical/reflexive methodology, and statistical analysis are only two of the many possible combinations of theory, methodology, and method. Unless we are so arrogant as to believe that we can legislate the boundaries of social science in advance, unless we are so confident in our present stock of knowledge that we are comfortable ruling out alternative combinations before seeing what they can actually do in practice, we have a moral responsibility to nurture and cherish epistemic diversity in all three of those registers. This volume is an important contribution to that endeavor. In the end, there is no substitute for actually doing the work. Absolutists, gatekeepers, and disciplinary police should get out of the way and let that scholarly work get under way.

Notes

1. Ian Hacking, *The Social Construction of What?* (Cambridge, MA: Harvard University Press, 1999), 6.

2. See Sandra Harding, *Is Science Multicultural? Postcolonialisms, Feminisms, and Epistemologies* (Bloomington: Indiana University Press, 1998).

3. See Inanna Hamati-Ataya, "Transcending Objectivism, Subjectivism, and the Knowledge In-between: The Subject in/of 'Strong Reflexivity,'" *Review of International Studies* 40, no. 1 (2014): 153–75; Ido Oren, *Our Enemies and US: America's Rivalries and the Making of Political Science* (Ithaca: Cornell University Press, 2002); Steven Shapin and Simon Schaffer, *Leviathan and the Air-Pump* (Princeton, NJ: Princeton University Press, 1985).

4. See Andrew Pickering, *The Mangle of Practice: Time, Agency, and Science* (Chicago: University of Chicago Press, 1995); Bruno Latour and Steve Woolgar, *Laboratory Life: The Construction of Scientific Facts* (Princeton, NJ: Princeton University Press, 1986).

5. See Patrick Thaddeus Jackson, *The Conduct of Inquiry in International Relations* (London: Routledge, 2011); Stephen H. Kellert, Helen E. Longino, and C. Kenneth Waters, eds., *Scientific Pluralism* (Minneapolis: University of Minnesota Press, 2006); Nancy Cartwright, *The Dappled World: A Study of the Boundaries of Science* (Cambridge: Cambridge University Press, 1999).

6. For a broadly similar critique of "epistemology," see Frank Ankersmit, "The Dilemma of Contemporary Anglo-Saxon Philosophy of History," *History and Theory* 25, no. 4 (1986): 1–27.

7. See Heikki Patomäki and Colin Wight, "After Postpositivism? The Promises of Critical Realism," *International Studies Quarterly* 44, no. 2 (2000): 213–37; Roy Bhaskar, *The Possibility of Naturalism* (London: Routledge, 1998).

8. Martin Heidegger, *Being and Time* (San Francisco: HarperCollins, 1927).

9. See Patomäki and Wight, "After Postpositivism?"

10. See Patrick Thaddeus Jackson and Daniel H. Nexon, "International Theory in a Post-Paradigmatic Era: From Substantive Wagers to Scientific Ontologies," *European Journal of International Relations* 19, no. 3 (2013): 543–65.

11. See Patrick Thaddeus Jackson and Daniel H. Nexon, "Paradigmatic Faults in International-Relations Theory," *International Studies Quarterly* 53, no. 4 (2009): 907–30; Colin Wight, "Incommensurability and Cross-Paradigm Communication in International Relations Theory: 'What's the Frequency Kenneth?,'" *Millennium: Journal of International Studies* 25, no. 2 (1996): 291–319.

12. Carl G. Hempel, "The Function of General Laws in History," in *Aspects of Scientific Explanation, and Other Essays* (New York: Free Press, 1965), 231–44.

13. In Thies's flavor of neopositivism, the knowledge products are nomothetic generalizations connecting specific independent and dependent variables; in Lustick's flavor, the knowledge products are whole models and the state spaces that repeated simulation runs of those models produce. Both kinds of knowledge product have the epistemic character of a general statement connecting inputs and outputs, and the differences between "given *X*, *Y* follows with probability *p*" and "given initial parameters

$x_1 \ldots {}_{xn}$, outcome ${}_{yn}$ occurs with probability p" are merely cosmetic and semantic, not philosophical.

14. Of course, the "substantive theoretical knowledge" in question has to take the form of nomothetic generalizations in order to be coded in the way that Lustick's procedure requires. I argue that this is a function of Lustick's methodology and not his method, however, inasmuch as there are other ways to formally code knowledge and mathematically express insights. On this point, see Hayward R. Alker, "The Long Road to International Relations Theory: Problems of Statistical Nonadditivity," *World Politics* 18, no. 4 (1966): 623–55.

15. Jennifer Milliken, "The Study of Discourse in International Relations: A Critique of Research and Methods," *European Journal of International Relations* 5, no. 2 (1999): 225–54; Lene Hansen, *Security as Practice: Discourse Analysis and the Bosnian War* (London: Routledge, 2006); Janice Bially Mattern, "The Power Politics of Identity," *European Journal of International Relations* 7, no. 3 (2001): 349–97; Vincent Pouliot, "'Sobjectivism': Towards a Constructivist Methodology," *International Studies Quarterly* 51, no. 2 (2007): 359–84.

16. Jason Glynos and David R. Howarth, *Logics of Critical Explanation in Social and Political Theory* (New York: Routledge, 2007).

17. For intriguing openings in this direction, see Roberto Fransozi, *From Words to Numbers: Narrative, Data, and Social Science* (Cambridge: Cambridge University Press, 2004); Hayward R. Alker, *Rediscoveries and Reformulations: Humanistic Methodologies for International Studies* (Cambridge: Cambridge University Press, 1996).

18. Ted Hopf, "Ethnography and Rational Choice in David Laitin: From Equality to Subordination to Absence," *Qualitative Methods* 4, no. 1 (2006):18.

19. Gary King, Robert O. Keohane, and Sidney Verba, *Designing Social Inquiry: Scientific Inference in Qualitative Research* (Princeton, NJ: Princeton University Press, 1994), 63.

20. See Friedrich Kratochwil, "History, Action, and Identity: Revisiting the 'Second' Great Debate and Assessing Its Importance for Social Theory," *European Journal of International Relations* 12, no. 1 (2006): 5–29; Rodney Bruce Hall and Friedrich Kratochwil, "Medieval Tales: Neorealist 'Science' and the Abuse of History," *International Organization* 47, no. 3 (1993): 479–91.

21. See Ludwig Wittgenstein, *Philosophical Investigations* (Oxford: Blackwell, 1953).

22. Steve Smith, "Rearranging the Deckchairs on the Ship Called Modernity: Rosenberg, Epistemology, and Emancipation," *Millennium: Journal of International Studies* 23 (1994): 395–405.

23. See Pierre Bourdieu, *Science of Science and Reflexivity*, 1st ed. (Chicago: University of Chicago Press, 2004).

24. See C. Wright Mills, *The Power Elite* (New York: Oxford University Press, 1967).

CHAPTER 11

Conclusion

Prospects for Interpretive Quantification

J. SAMUEL BARKIN AND LAURA SJOBERG

As far as the laws of mathematics refer to reality, they are uncertain; as far as they are certain, they do not refer to reality.[1]

We see it as ironic that the fetishization of neopositivism in the social sciences can often be fairly attributed to physics envy, based on a false understanding of physics as a model of (neopositivist) rigorous scientific inquiry. The fantasy of physics that social scientists often envy is one attributed to its greats, such as Albert Einstein and others, who are seen to have significantly advanced what is known about the world "out there" by applying the principles of inquiry that (neo)positivist social scientists would like to model. This fantasy is ironic for two reasons. First, as Alexander Wendt shows, the contemporary physics of quantum theory and quantum mechanics is anything but certain and straightforward.[2] Second, as the epigraph above suggests, Einstein was anything but a neopositivist when it came to understanding the production of knowledge in his work.

In fact, our reading of his work suggests that Albert Einstein was a hell of a critical theorist at the end of the day. In Einstein's view, it was not that the laws of mathematics were representative of some empirical reality that exists outside of the production of the mathematical axioms that describe and measure it. Rather, the beauty of mathematics is in its axiomatic qualities.

> The progress achieved by axiomatics consists in its having neatly separated the logical-form from its objective or intuitive content; accord-

> ing to axiomatics the logical-formal alone forms the subject matter of mathematics, which is not concerned with the intuitive or other content associated with the logical-formal. . . . Geometry treats of objects, which are denoted by the words straight line, point, etc. No knowledge or intuition of these objects is presumed but only the validity of the axioms . . . which are to be taken in a purely formal sense, i.e., as void of all content of intuition of or experience. These axioms are free creations of the human mind.[3]

In other words, Einstein saw mathematics as the product of creative thinking, elegant because of the near-infinite possibility for *internal* exploration and consistency, without need for *external* validity. The lack of concern with empirical verifiability does not, in Einstein's view, *degrade* the value of mathematics in helping us to understand the world. Instead, it increases the potential utilities of formalization and establishes a relationship between mathematics and imagination. As Einstein details, "A geometric-physical theory as such is incapable of being directly pictured, being merely a system of concepts. But these concepts serve the purpose of bringing a multiplicity of real or sensory experiences into connection in the mind."[4]

Einstein is not suggesting that mathematics *cannot* be used in the traditional way of (neo)positivist social science and many of the "hard" sciences—as a way to represent and engage a perceived world "out there." He goes to significant lengths to suggest that accounting for relativity does not exclude the geometry and physics of the visible.[5] He is suggesting that there is another layer of the potential utility of mathematics—as creation, exploration, and signification.

That is the sort of thinking we would like to unlock for social science generally and IR specifically. Without rejecting the validity of the current ways in which social scientists use quantification, we are interested in demonstrating a number of other potential uses of mathematical (quantitative/computational/formal) methods, particularly those that transgress traditional disciplinary assumptions about the function of quantification and make quantification useful for the knowledge ends of critical/constructivist theorizing. To demonstrate these uses, we need to undermine the links between quantitative methods, the search for methodological certainty, and the assumption of an external, measurable reality that underlie neopositivist IR. These links, in turn, build on a perceived divide between quantitative work, seen as precise and therefore appropriate to neopositivism, and qualitative work, seen as more evocative but woolier, as the language of critical IR.

We are, of course, not the first to have critiqued the quantitative/qualitative divide in IR specifically or the social sciences more generally.[6] In fact, positivists like King, Keohane, and Verba (hereafter KKV), writing on inference in qualitative research, assert that the difference in quantitative and qualitative research is not in the theory behind the research but in the tools used to do the research.[7] Patrick Thaddeus Jackson similarly sees the difference as one of tools rather than methodology or ontology. As he notes in *The Conduct of Inquiry in International Relations*, he uses scare quotes for the terms *quantitative* and *qualitative* "largely to underscore the extent to which I think the 'quantitative'/'qualitative' divide to be a distinction without a difference—a distinction of *method* without a difference of *methodology*."[8] This distinction is foundational to our primary point here—that social scientists, too frequently and without justification, tether research tools and research strategies together, neglecting the powerful research potential that decoupling and recoupling those tethered tools and strategies might have.

It is perhaps that untapped potential that leads Jackson[9] to cite KKV's observation that "all good research can be understood—indeed, is best understood—to derive from the same underlying logic of inference."[10] Jackson agrees with their observation to the extent that, whether quantitative or qualitative, neopositivist research derives from the same logic. Looking at the current state of research in the field of IR, Jackson observes that "whether one uses numerical or non-numerical data, or whether one considers a small or large number of empirical cases. . . . *Large-n 'quantitative' and small-n 'qualitative' research in IR are fundamentally the same*, in that it is basically all neopositivist in approach."[11]

We agree that these various methods, among others, are tools that do not mandate specific theories or methodologies. Our goal here is to show that this is equally true in research contexts in IR and in social sciences more generally, other than neopositivist hypothesis-testing. In other words, this project is at least partly about taking seriously KKV's observation about the logic of inference transcending the methods used seriously enough to apply it to a spectrum of non-neopositivist logics of inference and to a range of methods in quantitative, formal, and computational toolboxes. Critical theory, for example, has its own methodological logic. In contradistinction to neopositivist precision, the logic of critical research is social, complex, deconstructive, argumentative, uncertain, interpretive, and/or counterhegemonic. We propose that this methodological logic is not only compatible with but can usefully be paired with many quantitative tools, from IR research and beyond. As is the case with neopositivist methodology, the logic of methods often categorized as qualitative and quantitative is compatible with the same underlying critical methodology. It is from this proposal that we get the foundational argument for this book: that quantitative methods are not only methodologically compatible with constructivist and critical theory but can be useful to the promotion and development of those approaches' research agendas.

Breaking the presumed tie between neopositivism and quantification reveals that there are existing quantifications and/or claims to quantification in current constructivist and/or critical work in IR. For example, when Cynthia Enloe asks where the women are, she is partly making a feminist claim on quantitative methods.[12] When Laura Sjoberg and Caron Gentry urge the recognition that women's political violence is not an anomaly, they are also making a feminist claim on quantitative methods.[13] Any question involving "how many" or "how often," as well as many questions involving "under what circumstances," might usefully draw on statistical analysis, for both theory construction and theory analysis. Such analysis can be applied to the sorts of things that neopositivists often look at, like money, but can also be applied to norms, expressed either as behaviors or as opinions, and to discourses, expressed either as measures of frequency or of pattern. In a number of situations, claims to quantification in constructivist or critical IR research can usefully be translated into actual quantification, leveraged for a variety of different knowledge ends. Statistics can tell us about relationships, degrees of correlation, and even co-constitution; data analysis is not tied to positivist epistemology or objectivist ontology. Simply removing the presumption that quantification is useless to critical inquiry is enough to show some of the potential of interpretive quantification.

Delving further into that potential shows that interpretive quantification has utility for constructivist/critical IR outside of measures of frequency or patterns. For example, behavioral modeling can be useful in identifying the ramifications of behavioral assumptions in both constructivist and critical theories, when these are used to construct explanatory models (and they must have behavioral assumptions, whether stated explicitly or not.) It can also be used as a means of communication between critical and rationalist theory. To the extent that critical theories discuss structural power, they often assume kinds of individual behavioral responses that are not, in themselves, incompatible with the assumptions made by soft rational choice theorists. Gaming a critical argument, in other words, can be an effective way of explaining to formal theorists how structural power matters.[14] More broadly, behavioral modeling, whether based on rational choice assumptions or computational gaming, is a useful mechanism for thought experiments, which can be applied to any explanatory theory of international politics.

Moving even farther afield, one can envision using Einstein's creative, internal formalizations for concept relationships in the social sciences or using computational symbolic logic in thinking about social and political discourses, incorporating methods not traditionally used in the social sciences with regularity and using them to further the ends of constructivist and/or critical research agendas.

The chapters in this volume have made this case across a wide variety of theoretical, epistemological, and methodological approaches, using an even wider variety of methods. The chapter authors show that both small tweaks and significant overhauls to traditional uses of quantitative, formal, and computational methods have substantive promise. The chapters fall at different places along the range of methods in IR. Some use methods familiar to the social sciences in service of methodologies with which they are not frequently paired, while others introduce quantitative methods infrequently used in social sciences into the service of constructivist and/or critical research agendas. This concluding chapter looks back at the chapters in this book and forward at the potential futures of interpretive quantification. It reviews the eight substantive chapters in this volume, looking at both the potential and limitations of the specific methods used. It then discusses more broadly the relationship between method and theory, a relationship alluded to but not developed in the introduction to this volume. Finally, it discusses the potential uses of this volume, as well as ways forward from here in the discussion of quantitative methods and constructivist and critical theory.

Methods

The eight substantive chapters of this volume are presented in two parts: the first four use quantitative methods to organize empirical observations, and the second four use (different) quantitative methods to model behavior and/or understand concepts. The first set of chapters includes regression analysis of observed data (Ackerly, and Thies), network analysis of observed data (Hoffmann), and descriptive statistics of survey data (Kowert). The second set includes agent-based modeling (Lustick), conversation analysis (Sylvan), game-theoretical modeling (Barkin), and formal concept analysis (Sjoberg and Knudson).

These different methods all fit broadly under our heading of "quantitative" but have very different applicability that does not map one-to-one to any particular theoretical approach or research agenda, which demonstrates that these methods have little in common methodologically other than that they are (or could be) expressed in numbers and therefore require or lend themselves to quantification. This leads us to ask what commonalities quantification brings. The process of quantification is one of finding a common denominator across the inputs that one brings to bear on a research question, whether those inputs are empirical observations, model actors, texts, or logical postulates. Narrative research, whether inferential, explanatory, or experimental, can focus on either differences or similarities across inputs and has considerable flexibility in structuring the relationships among inputs. The cost of this flexibility is definitional precision, in the identification of what the units of analysis are, in the separation of the units from each other analytically, and in the specification of their relationship to each other.

Quantification, whether done in the service of looking for representation, description, or exploration, entails a loss of information, but the extent of that loss varies with the kind of information in question and the available and/or practical procedures of quantification. Quantitative methods, whether used for theory testing or theory building, thus present the researcher with a trade-off between analytic tractability and informational richness. Whether this trade-off is worthwhile depends on both the kind of information in question, on the cost side, and the utility of the kinds of analytic tractability that quantitative methods offer to the particular research question being asked, on the benefit side. Ideally, this calculation should be made for each research project, with considerations of not only ontology and epistemology but also the *capabilities of methods*. That most research projects do not take this approach is likely due to a combination of sunk cost in methods training, identification of particular research programs with particular sets of methods, and inherited notions of the process by which researchers determine research design. We argue that this tradeoff is sometimes worthwhile in asking and answering the questions that constructivist and critical theorizing asks.

Having said this, it remains useful to examine the methodological potential of specific methods. An interesting place to begin this examination is with the chapters by Ackerly and Thies, who here use very similar methods embedded within very different methodologies. Both use forms of regression analysis to find correlations among variables. In one sense, both are using the method to test hypotheses, inferring (in a broad use of that term) relationships from correlations. But both the kinds of hypotheses Thies and Ackerly are testing and the kinds of inferences they are making are, in one key way, different. Thies, in neopositivist fashion, is using the test to infer broader relationships among the variables, relationships that hold in other cases as well. The hypotheses being tested are about these broader relationships. Ackerly, in critical fashion, is using the test to infer a set of relationships within her case that are not what those relationships are commonly thought to be. The hypotheses being tested are about what is happening in that case, not about general relationships among variables.

As noted in this book's introduction, regression is useful when a research question requires identifying aggregate relationships and when empirics can be reasonably quantified, both situations that clearly apply in Ackerly's chapter. While the trade-off between analytic tractability and informational richness is the same in principle for both Ackerly's critical analysis and Thies's neopositivist one, the need for the latter analysis to compare across discrete cases biases it to analytical tractability. This might partly explain why bias toward the quantification of observed data is greater for neopositivist methodology than for critical methodology, although methodological considerations themselves cannot account for the extent of the bias in practice in most of the social sciences.

More broadly, this comparison suggests that the method of regression analysis is compatible with a broad range of epistemologies. The use of the method in the context of analytical and scientifically realist methodologies would be much like Ackerly's use; it could serve to describe a case and compare that description to a predefined model. The relationship between the model and the description differs across methodologies, however. For analytical models, the role of statistical description is to illuminate the relationship between model and observation. For scientific realisms, it is more likely to be used to find ways to best empirically describe a real but unobservable thing-in-the-world.

The distinction between the use of regression analysis in neopositivist and scientifically realist research points to an interesting tension in Thies's chapter and, through it, in the role of statistical methods in constructivist research. Constructivist theory appears in two very different forms in that chapter, both as the source of a thing to be explained and as the source of hypotheses to be tested against explanatory hypotheses from other theories. Following Alexander Wendt, Thies takes "cultures of anarchy" as real things in the world that are to be explained, but he looks to test "constructivist" variables, such as satisfaction and negotiation, against variables drawn from other theories, to explain movement between cultures. He then uses quantification both to describe the extent of the cultures and to test explanations against the resultant description.

A second useful pairing of chapters pairs those by Hoffmann and Kowert. Both use statistical methods to analyze quantitative empirical data, but data that are different from the sort of observational data used by Ackerly and Thies. In the case of Hoffmann's chapter, these data are different in that they are about relationships rather than individual actors (whether those individuals are people or states). In Kowert's chapter, the data are individual impressions gathered from purpose-designed surveys, used to build a picture of the intersubjective from the subjective, rather than from observed behavior. Both methods are either widely used or, in Kowert's case, modeled on methods widely used elsewhere, within IR for network analysis and in social psychology for personality research. Both share the characteristic that they have rarely appeared in published constructivist research in IR, despite being focused on social relationships.

Both Kowert's and Hoffmann's methods are a little more specialized in focus than generic regression analysis and are therefore more limited in their application in social science generally and in IR in particular. They are appropriate only if one is interested in the structure of social networks or of state identities, respectively. They are more specialized tools that can be used for describing and analyzing specific kinds of quantified data, rather than the more generalized tools used by Ackerly and Thies. In the context of the core argument of this volume, the chapters by Kowert and Hoffmann serve to illustrate the potential of specialized methods to address specific sorts of constructivist and critical research questions relating to network structure and identity in corporate political actors. While both chapters address constructivism, both their topics could well be of interest to critical theorists as well, as could the methods each author uses to address those topics.

Both chapters present the potential of constructivist theory and show some basics of how that method might be applied in the context of that theory. But as Jackson points out in chapter 10, neither Kowert nor Hoffmann embed their examples in full research designs. The methods themselves are tools for describing, in accessible ways, the aggregate form of certain kinds of data (about relationships and identities, respectively). Both chapters leave open the question of what might be done with those descriptions. As Jackson suggests, they can be used in a variety of methodological ways. They can provide the inputs to neopositivist cross-case hypothesis-testing or can be used critically to highlight contradictions in disciplinary interpretations of world politics. They can be used to construct Weberian ideal types or to illuminate scientifically realist understandings of networks or identities. Identifying the way in which a particular method fits within a broader research design was not necessary for the purposes of this volume but is necessary in the use of methods to fully address research questions. In many ways, the variable utility of the descriptions produced in the chapters by Kowert and

Hoffmann demonstrates our argument that methods can be deployed for different theoretical and methodological ends.

A third useful pairing of chapters pairs those by Sylvan and Lustick. Both have in common that they present methods for formalizing certain kinds of data to create models for understanding behavior. Like the first four substantive chapters, the chapters by Sylvan and Lustick quantify observed behavior in some fashion, for the purpose of applying analytical tools that create a description that is different from what would otherwise be clear from the observations. Still, these two chapters differ from the first four in that Sylvan and Lustick focus on ordering the relationships among different kinds of data, rather than isolating relationships among a set of prespecified variables. They both create rules of behavior against which observed behavior can be analyzed and through which it can be explained, rather than focusing on correlation.

Sylvan's method of analyzing conversations seems at first to be a marginal fit for this volume, given that his modeling is computational but not quantitative per se and that the interpretation of data in the method does not follow precise predefined rules. But it serves well as an example of a method that captures the benefits of formalizing analysis without the loss of information that comes with strict quantification. Similar modes of analysis could also be used for written text and visual communication and on popular as well as diplomatic discourse. Such methods might also be able to provide an analytic bridge to literatures on signaling in IR. As Jackson notes, Sylvan does not explicitly provide a broader research design in which the conversations he analyzes as examples fit. But the underlying methodology seems scientifically realist; the conversations have real meaning, and conversational analysis can explore that meaning. One could presumably use a set of such analyses as a basis for neopositivist hypothesis-testing, as one can with most methods. But Sylvan seems to intend the method for exploring (rather than comparing) cases, a task to which the method is well suited. Sylvan's computational discourse work can provide contextualization for the conversations being analyzed, both within the discourses of the conversations and among other conditions in global politics.

Lustick provides an example of agent-based modeling (ABM) that is designed to yield specific predictions of future events. The computational tools he uses are similar in kind to those used by other exercises in ABM in the field, although more sophisticated than most. The goal of prediction, however, makes his methodology different than many such exercises. ABM is often used to generate ideal-typological thought experiments about the interactions of behavioral rules and structural conditions over time. This makes it well suited to the use of the method as a heuristic in the kind of constructivist theorizing that Jackson would call "analyticist," which is how it has tended to be used in explicitly constructivist analyses. These agent-based models used to generate thought experiments, though, simplify to highlight particular rules or structures, whereas Lustick's model complicates to improve predictive power. This makes Lustick's approach, as Jackson notes, methodologically suited to neopositivist prediction rather than analyticist understanding, and it is therefore a somewhat awkward fit with constructivist theory.

At the same time, neither constructivist nor critical theory in IR is *a priori* uninterested in patterns of behavior and potential future behaviors in global politics. Instead, when constructivist and/or critical IR researchers inquire into those issues, they are often interested in patterns and prediction in different ways, for different reasons, and with a different theoretical framework than traditional analysis in IR. In Lustick's work, the *research end* differs from traditional predictive IR theory. Lustick looks not only to understand what might happen but also to explore the ways that manipulating the parameters of heuristic, predictive models might help envision the possibility for alternative, normatively preferable futures. While Lustick's model can be read as an exercise in prediction, it can also be read as an exploration of constitutive social relationships.

Like the chapters by Lustick and Sylvan, the fourth set of chapters that can be paired, the ones that we wrote, use formalizations to explore ideas that are explicitly inspired by constructivist and/or critical IR theorizing. In common with all of the other chapters in the book, they use methods broadly understood as quantitative. With each other, our chapters share the exploration of the *internal* dynamics of a phenomenon or concept in global politics, rather than the *external* dynamics of how that phenomenon or concept relates to other things in the global political arena. As Jackson comments on Barkin's chapter, the goal of the account is not generalizability across cases but an exploration of a case—much like the goal of many qualitative, interpretive case studies that have traditionally been used by constructivist and/or critical IR.

Barkin's account looks to explain how a particular regime, or system of norms, came to be and how it is influenced by intersubjective meaning, symbolic value, and social identities. In so doing, Barkin both applies constructivist theorizing and uses constructivist methodology in creating and implementing a formal model. This endeavor shows the utility of formal models as both heuristic and exploratory—uses that have potential to have a whole host of applications across constructivist and critical theorizing. Here, Barkin is not looking for generalizable results but is analyzing a particular case with a methodology/method combination that could be used to explore explanations for a wide variety of social and/or normative phenomena in global politics.

Sjoberg and Knudson's chapter also proposes a method that is specific to the concept analyzed in their chapter in this book but that could be used for a variety of applications in constructivist and/or critical IR theory. Using formal concept analysis, Sjoberg and Knudson's chapter explores what constitutes "democracy"—in different definitions, operationalizations, and discursive deployments of that term—by looking at locational clusters in extant data descriptive of democratic (or undemocratic) countries around the world. This sort of geometric concept analysis could be used to explore constitutive relationships across constructivist research programs; to manipulate potential changes in concept structures in global politics, in service of emancipatory critical research programs; and to engage relationships between significations, in service of poststructuralist research programs.

Across all eight chapters, we see various quantifications used in service of various strands of constructivist and critical theorizing in IR. Those quantifications are useful for their research programs in a variety of ways, with different methodologies and epistemological assumptions. To fully understand their potential, however, it is necessary to return to the relationship among methods, methodology, epistemology, and ontology discussed in the introduction to this volume and to build into this relationship a discussion of the meaning and purpose of theory.

Theory

In this book's introduction, we invoked theory in a number of ways, without clearly defining what we mean by the term. We claim there that theory need not be tied to specific method but, at the same time, that method is not neutral in relation to theory. We, along with a number of the authors of chapters in this book, have spoken of different sorts of IR theory, as well as of theory building and theory testing. At the same time, theory does not appear in the set of relationships that we illustrate as Ontology ↔ Epistemology ↔ Methodology ↔ Method. That initial mapping looked at the substance of knowledge without attention to the disciplinary sociology of theory and theorizing. What is theorizing? To what end is theorizing done? Where, then, does theory fit into the project of interpretive quantification?

At the outset of this book, we set up the test case of our spectrum Ontology ↔ Epistemology ↔ Methodology ↔ Method as quantitative, computational, and formal methods for critical and/or constructivist IR theory. The implicit assumption in the use of this test case is that critical and/or constructivist IR theorizing is largely, if to varying degrees, interested in interpretive methodologies. The chapters in this book have conformed with this assumption. Still, to understand the full benefits *both* of interpretive quantification and of rethinking the relationships between ontology, epistemology, methodology, and method, it is important to look at what theorizing is and what it does.

In the introduction, we define method as specific techniques and processes for gathering and/or analyzing information, and methodology as what methods are chosen and why—the process of search and research, given certain assumptions. Three types of assumptions are relevant to methodological choices: ontological, epistemological, and theoretical. Ontological assumptions are about the nature of being—*what the world is.* Epistemological assumptions are about the ways that it is possible to know the world—*what knowledge is and how it can be obtained.* Theoretical assumptions are of varying types, depending on the theorists' positions on these other questions.

In other words, different ontologies, different epistemologies, and different methodologies have different relations with theory. These differences become even clearer if one defines methodology broadly, as Jackson does in chapter 10, as philosophical ontology rather than as the particular relationship between question and method in the context of a specific research design. In a deductive-nomological model of science, what Jackson calls "neopositivist methodology," theory is a set of covering laws from which hypotheses can be derived and tested. This is what Marysia Zalewski identifies as "theory as a tool," where "theory is something that is used by those wishing to make sense of events in international politics" and functions as a "framework for understanding the world."[15] This approach assumes separation between theory and theorists (Jackson's dualism), assumes a separation of theory and the real world (Jackson's phenomenalism), and assumes the value of enlightenment rationality (Jackson's neopositivism).[16]

Zalewski appropriately identifies two ways that critical theorists understand theory in social science. The first, considering theory as critique, understands theory as actively interrelated with the "real world" (Jackson's analyticism).[17] Citing Andrew Linklater, Zalewski suggests that those who see theory as critique are interested not just in seeing the world "as it is" but also in tracing how it gets there, with a goal of emancipation.[18] In other words, "theory as critique" is an account of the world intended to facilitate understanding the world in a way other than received wisdom, rather than an attempt at strict correspondence with that world. According to Zalewski, the second way that critical theorists understand theory is as everyday practice.[19] In this view, theory is not a noun (as in "a theory") but a verb (as in "theorizing"). What one does, then, is theorize, rather than use theory (Jackson's reflexivity and then some). This interpretation differs from the interpretation of theory as a tool, not only in the act of theorizing but in who theorizes and how. Considering theory as everyday practice changes the events that are theorized, who is seen as theorists, and what issues are deemed relevant and irrelevant to the category of "theorizing."[20] This approach sees theorizing as "a way of life."[21]

Theory understood as a tool precedes the research project, the goal of which is testing the theory that began outside of that project. Theory understood as critique is an integral part of the performance of the research project, where observation and theorizing are co-constitutive rather than independent and where theorizing is inherently (and intentionally) political. Theory understood as everyday practice is constitutive of a differently envisioned sort of research project, where lived experience and research are co-constituted.

Exploring these three very different understandings of the utility of theory demonstrates that there can be many roles that theory plays in any given social science research project. Particular projects can be designed to build theory, to apply theory, to test theory, to practice theory, or for some combination of these four purposes (recognizing, of course, that terms such as *apply* can mean very different things in different methodological contexts). These different understandings of theory do not make theory indeterminate or irrelevant to thinking about the relationships between ontology, epistemology, methodology, and method. Instead, they differentiate the ideas of theory and the locations at which theory intervenes. Across these differences, it is possible to see that theorizing matters to the ways that methodology and method are paired and that the pairings of methodology/method and epistemology/ontology influence not only the substance of theory but also its place and form.

A statistical model, for example, can be used to test whether predictions drawn from a theory (as a tool) match observations, to test theories (as tools) against each other, to illustrate how a given theory (as a tool or as critique) applies, or to describe a theorization (as critique or as practice). An agent-based model can be used directly in a theory-building exercise and can also be used to help explain a particular case. Critical theorists, scientific realists, and analyticists all theorize, but the role of theorizing in each differs. Weberian analyticists attempt to keep politics and science distinct in their theorizing, recognizing the conceptual difficulty in doing so, while critical theorizing is explicitly and intentionally political. For scientific realists, along with neopositivists, theorizing is an attempt to describe a world that is separate from the scholar. For critical theorists and analyticists, theorizing is an attempt to organize an understanding of the world that is inherently and irreducibly inseparable from the scholar.

While the role of theory varies across epistemologies and methodologies, it also varies within them, along the same lines. A critical theorist theorizes a case but also brings empirical evidence to bear in evaluating the application of that theory to the case. In both scientific realism and analyticism, theory building is a more generalized process than in critical theory, in that generalized models of the world can be built outside of specific cases to be studied (although the process is quite different across the two philosophical ontologies). These theories (models in the case of analyticists, causal claims in the case of scientific realists) are then applied in a variety of ways to explain particular cases. In neopositivism, it is less clear where theory comes from in the context of a particular research design (theory in neopositivist methodology is supposed to be prior to research design, but if this is the case, there is no clear role for theorizing in research design), but theory building, whatever the source, is a clearly distinct process from theory testing.[22]

Where does all this leave us in thinking about theory? In chapter 10, Jackson defines theory as "scientific ontology," assumptions about what there is to be studied, about what things in the world matter. Under this definition, the word *things* refers not just (or, in the case of social sciences, even primarily) to material things but also to social constructions, processes, significations, and so on. In this formulation, for example, evolution as a process is a thing-in-the-world, since we can point to an observed outcome and call it the result of evolution, even if there is no object *per se* that can be pointed to as evolution. Similarly, gender hierarchy and the state are things-in-the-world, even though we can point only to manifestations of them rather than to each essential thing in itself.

At first, this formulation may seem to fit awkwardly with some of the various uses of "theory" discussed above and with some ways in which the term *theory* is used colloquially among scholars. At the same time, we can see that the understandings of theory as a tool, as critique, and as practice all have embedded in them scientific ontologies about what things in the world are important to give attention to and what things in the world are less important. Theory as a tool can be wielded by researchers who see things in the world as independent of the theory and the theorist and as directed toward anything in the world that the theorist sees as important to engage.

Theory as critique can be wielded by researchers who recognize the political nature of knowledge in service of the political ends that those theorists see as important in the world, particularly when looking for emancipation. Theory as practice is a political act of researchers who identify everyday people as theorists and everyday life as theorizing—a "scientific ontology" of attention to the margins of the global political arena.

Understanding theory (and takes on theory) as scientific ontology, with Jackson, can be a useful operating understanding of theory for the purpose of understanding the relationships between theory, epistemology, methodology, and method. Theorizing then becomes the positing of what things matter with respect to a given question or set of questions, in social science more generally or IR specifically. For neopositivists, these things then serve as the basis from which testable hypotheses are drawn; for scientific realists, as claims about real structures in the world; for analyticists, as useful bases for organizing observation; and for critical theorists, as counterclaims to unexamined theoretical assumptions.

Jackson speaks of sets of theories with "family resemblances" that can be organized into paradigms or research programs, of which a classic example in IR is realism. Constructivism also falls into this category, as not a theory but a set of distinct theories with a common affinity for the idea of social construction. Specific assumptions about things in the world, however, can be distinct across different constructivisms—for example, relational networks (as for Hoffmann in this volume) or linguistic structures (as for Sylvan). It is also worth noting in this context that theoretical affinity groups are not mutually exclusive. Hoffmann is simultaneously a constructivist theorist and a network theorist; Barkin is a constructivist theorist and a regime theorist. In constructivism, theory can be either a tool or critique; it analyzes the world either to understand it or to change it.

While constructivism is, according to Jackson's definition, a description of a type of theory, critical theory (ironically, given the name) fits into the category of theory less easily. In Jackson's terms, it might be useful to see critical theorizing as a way of theorizing (where *critical* is an adjective that modifies *theorizing*), or a methodological approach to theorizing. One would then have a "critical theory of *x*" (human rights, class, gender, etc.), where *x* would describe the theory per se, the assumption about things-in-the-world, and "critical theory" would describe the approach to studying *x*. One can quibble with this definition; critical theories, at least in IR, have in common a focus on structures of power, which can, in themselves, be taken as things-in-the-world. But the definition nonetheless highlights a useful point, which is that critical theory comes with methodological commitments in a way that constructivist theory, as an aggregate category, does not. At the same time, as Zalewski argues, there are two distinct sorts of critical theorizing—theorizing as critique (which identifies injustices as the things-in-the-world worth considering) and theory as practice (which sees everyday life *as theory* as a thing in the world).

What, then, are the relationships among theory, methodology, and method? This volume begins with one entry from each of these categories, in bringing together constructivism, critical theory, and quantitative methods. The framing of the volume, around the use of quantitative methods in constructivism and critical theory, focuses on two of these relationships, between method, on the one side, and theory and methodology, on the other. We have discussed, in principle, both the possibilities of and limits to these relationships, and the substantive chapters provide examples. In chapter 10, Jackson looks at the third of the relationships, between theory and methodology, and makes the claim that there is no necessary relationship there either. He uses the example of (political) realism and notes that realist theory has been approached from "wildly divergent methodologies."

But realism is an affinity group of theories, made up of some clearly distinct assumptions about things-in-the-world. The question therefore still remains of whether there is a necessary relationship between specific theories and methodology. Even at the level of specific theory by Jackson's definition, there is not a necessary relationship. A theory of human rights, for example, can be matched either with a test of correlations of human rights legislation with other political variables or with an examination, as Ackerly's chapter shows, of rights enjoyment in a specific context. Both uses can begin with similar understandings of what human rights are, how important they are, and even how to measure them in any specific instance, yet each builds on a very different set of methodological claims. By Zalewski's definition, each is using a different form of theory.

One ramification of the understandings of theory engaged here is that, according to them, theory cannot, even in principle, be tested. Neopositivists can test hypotheses derived from theories, but if the tests prove negative, it cannot be conclusively determined if the error lies in the theory or the derivation. Empirical evidence can suggest that scientifically realist theory is more or less likely to be accurate, but that evidence cannot show the theory to be false. Analyticist and critical theory can be more or less useful in explaining any given case (useful analytically in the first instance and politically in the second), but being useful is quite a different thing from being right or wrong. Understood as assumptions about things-in-the-world, theory is inherently untestable within a given research project; one cannot test one's own assumptions (if one does so, they are, by definition, not assumptions). Theory, then, is evaluated by research communities rather than by scholars, on the basis of utility rather than accuracy. What counts as utility may well differ across methodologies and across research communities, but the success of particular theories, understood as assumptions about what matters in the world, is likely best indicated by the extent to which they are taken up by other scholars.

By this definition, constructivism is a set of theories that have in common the assumption that social constructions, understood as constitutive of political relationships rather than reflective of them, matter in IR. We agree with Jackson that Lustick's chapter fits unconventionally, if at all, in this category (which does not, of course, mean that the methods Lustick outlines in his chapter could not be useful in the context of a constructivist theory). Thies's chapter, however, has a more complicated relationship with constructivism. It invokes constructivism in two different ways, although both are based on theory (in Zalewski's terms) as a tool. At one level, it engages in constructivist theory, by assuming the existence of Wendtian cultures of anarchy and taking them as its object of study. These are not tested for; rather, they are taken as ontological givens. At another level, it tests what Thies calls "constructivist variables" (which are operationalized as legitimacy) against realist and liberal ones. Constructivist theory is thus both assumed and "tested" in the same research design.

The research design presented in Thies's chapter does not, in a meaningful way, provide a test of constructivist theory, because the realist and liberal variables are themselves socially constructed. Parts of the chapter can be read as a neopositivist test of the correlation of legitimacy variables with certain kinds of conflict behavior in the context of dyadic conflict theory, and other parts as a scientifically realist discussion of the nature of zones of peace as social constructions. In trying to have it both ways, Thies brings together both the methods and the language of two distinct research communities, at the expense of a methodological grounding that risks internal contradiction. This risk is one that we are likely to face frequently in the sort of exercise we are promoting in this book, which generally takes scholars out of their comfort zones in terms of either method or theory (or both).

How It All Fits Together

The field of IR, as is the case with many of the social sciences, often disciplines itself in the first instance epistemologically and methodologically and subsumes method to these. The primary goal of this volume is to argue against this reflex, using the relationship between quantitative methods, on the one hand, and critical and constructivist theory, on the other, as an example of an underused combination, to illustrate the potential for a more creative relationship among method, methodology, epistemology, and ontology. In the introduction, we presented this relationship as linear and argued for a move from a unidirectional relationship to bidirectional relationships.

But this representation still has method connecting to epistemology through methodology, methodology connecting to ontology through epistemology, and so on. In response, Patrick Thaddeus Jackson argues, in chapter 10, for a two-dimensional (rather than one-dimensional) representation, with three nodes instead of the four presented in the introduction. This two-dimensionality allows each node to be shown as connecting to each of the others directly. The representation in the introduction is a useful heuristic for making the case against unidirectional relationships. The representation in chapter 10 is a useful heuristic for demonstrating the dangers of a neopositivist disciplining of quantitative methods used interpretively.

The traditional disciplining function of methodology and method in IR has the effect not only of reducing the tools available to scholars in designing and carrying out research but also of reducing communication across both methodologies and methods. Thinking in terms of Jackson's two-dimensional relationships can help provide channels for increasing this communication. In particular, communication across both methods and methodologies by scholars who begin with compatible theoretical assumptions can improve our ability to address the political concerns that brought us to the field in the first place. A greater focus on communication within theory can also serve as a useful point of entry for better understanding the utility of both methods and methodologies with mechanics unfamiliar to us.

At the same time, we see the triad that Jackson presents as incomplete for our purposes. We worry about the implications for research design of conflating theory/ontology and methodology/epistemology in order to collapse the five nodes of our original linear diagram (including theory) into a triad. While Jackson's point that the ordered line presented in the introduction is too limited in terms of the directionality of interaction is well taken, we suggest that Jackson's triad is too limited in the parts of the research process that it considers. Both our initial diagram and Jackson's, we believe, go a reasonable distance toward expressing the critique of the methodological straitjacketing that happens across disciplinary IR and in the social sciences more generally. Still, we think it is possible to suggest a more complex configuration.

At the end of the day, rather than Jackson's triad, we see a pentagon, where all five vertices (method, methodology, epistemology, ontology, and theory) have bidirectional relationships with each of the others. This incorporates Jackson's suggestion that our initial model lacks the dimensionality that would allow us to imagine each concept interacting with all of the others, while preserving the importance and distinction of all five concepts, particularly distinguishing methodology and epistemology. We argue that whether we diagram the relationships among ontology, epistemology, theory, method, and methodology as a pentagon, a triad, or a string of bidirectional relationships going forward, it is crucial to *stop seeing* them in a unidirectional, trickle-down relationship—which, we are arguing, is how much of the field of IR specifically and much of social science generally treats not only method selection but also methods training and substantive engagement.

This volume hopefully serves as a first step in this effort. It gives several examples of the potential for creative use of different methods across theoretical settings that can all be loosely described as constructivist and/or critical and across philosophical ontologies ranging from the neopositivist to the critical. This volume does not provide a template for how to do interpretive quantification or even for how to do either interpretive research or quantitative research. Instead, it provides a number of different experiments in and possible pathways for interpretive quantification. Each "interpretive," like each "quantification," is unique. It was never our intention to provide an ontologically, epistemologically, or methodologically *unified* volume. Our intention is twofold: to break down (false) assumptions that cause the tethering of methodology and method and to demonstrate the underutilized potential of quantitative, formal, and computational methods for constructivist and/or critical IR to do so.

Still, interpretive quantification is not easy to practice. The chapters in this volume suggest several potential pitfalls. For example, there is a danger of neopositivist disciplining of quantitative methods when alternative interpretive methodologies are not clearly specified and detailed. The reflex toward neopositivist hypothesis-testing in the discipline of IR, particularly when numbers are involved, is strong enough that it can easily co-opt research beginning from constructivist theory, when a path is left open for it to do so. This is the essence of Jackson's critique of this volume's chapters by Hoffmann, Kowert, Sylvan, and Sjoberg and Knudson. This is the sort of path dependence that we are trying to break in the discipline. It can be broken by theoretical analysis that explores the ways in which neopositivism is an awkward fit for constructivist theory; whereas the former assumes continuity across cases (this is the basis for inferences that correlations are relevant beyond the cases studied), the idea that social constructions need not be the way they are and need not remain so is inherent in the latter. The assumption of continuity, in other words, does not hold for constructivism. This does not mean that neopositivist constructivist work is impossible, but it rather that it must be undertaken with care, and purposefully rather than by default. It is more difficult to imagine a successful marriage between neopositivism and critical theorizing. At the same time, as Jackson's critique of the descriptive nature of some of the self-identified critical chapters in this volume shows, the difference between neopositivist and critical theorizing is not the data that is used *or* the methods being used to analyze that data but the purpose for which that analysis is being done and the analytical purchase taken from it.

Quantitative, formal, and computational methods can be useful for some critical and/or constructivist research projects. Deconstructing the tethering of method and methodology to epistemology and ontology, a restraint that currently dominates our discipline, is a necessary first step to realizing the potential of this combination, along with other underused combinations in social science research. Still, we do not want to suggest interpretive quantification as a new norm of social science research generally or interpretive IR research specifically. As we noted in this book's introduction, we are not interested in contributing to or feeding trends of method-driven research, and we certainly are not interested in contributing to the popularity of the assumption (increasingly visible in our field) that quantitative work is better because it is quantitative. Judging different research programs by the standards appropriate not only to their methods but to their methodologies and epistemologies is much more likely to be useful in helping us to understand the social world than is the fetishization of the quantitative for its own sake, inside or outside of constructivism and/or critical theory. We mean this volume to be a source of methodological freedom—freedom from the constrained ontology/epistemology/methodology/method combinations that have too long hampered creativity in quantitative research and limited the methods available for constructivists and critical theorists. We hope that the methods in this book, along with other quantitative, computational, and even experimental methods, become more frequently seen as potential tools for critical and/or constructivist IR work and that the deployment of those tools in that work creates space for creativity in the use of quantitative methods in IR.

Notes

1. Albert Einstein, *Sidelights on Relativity (Geometry and Experience) (1920/1921; reprint,* New York: Merchant Books, 2010), 28.

2. Alexander Wendt, *Quantum Mind and Social Science (*Cambridge: Cambridge University Press, 2015).

3. Einstein, *Sidelights*, 28.

4. Ibid.

5. Ibid.

6. See, e.g., J. Samuel Barkin, "Qualitative Methods?," in *Qualitative Methods in International Relations*, eds. Audie Klotz and Deepa Prakash (New York: Palgrave, 2008); Salvatore Babones, "Interpretive Quantitative Methods for the Social Sciences," *Sociology*, forthcoming, doi:10.1177/0038038515583637; Michael A. Westerman and Stephen C. Yanchar, "Changing the Terms of the Debate: Quantitative Methods in Explicitly Interpretive Research," *Theory Psychology* 21, no. 2 (2011): 139–54.

7. Gary King, Robert Keohane, and Sidney Verba, *Designing Social Inquiry: Scientific Interference in Qualitative Research* (Princeton, NJ: Princeton University Press, 1994), 6.

8. Patrick Thaddeus Jackson, *The Conduct of Inquiry in International Relations* (New York: Routledge, 2010), 67.

9. Ibid.

10. King, Keohane, and Verba, *Designing Social Inquiry*, 4.

11. Jackson, *Conduct of Inquiry*, 67.

12. Cynthia Enloe, *Does Khaki Become You? The International Politics of Militarizing Women's Lives* (London: Pluto, 1983).

13. Laura Sjoberg and Caron Gentry, *Mothers, Monsters, Whores: Women's Violence in Global Politics* (London: Zed Books, 2007); Caron Gentry and Laura Sjoberg, *Beyond Mothers, Monsters, Whores* (London: Zed Books, 2015).

14. See, e.g., Laura Sjoberg and Jeffrey Horowitz, "Quantitative Methods in Critical Security Studies," in *Critical Approaches to Security: Introduction to Theories and Methods*, ed. Laura J. Shepherd (London: Routledge, 2013), 103–17, gaming a critical argument about ontological security and economic sanctions.

15. Marysia Zalewski, "'All These Theories and the Bodies Keep Piling Up': Theories, Theorists, Theorizing," *International Relations Theory: Positivism and Beyond,* ed. Steve Smith, Ken Booth, and Marysia Zalewski (Cambridge: Cambridge University Press, 1995), 340–53, citing, as an example of this position, James Rosenau, "Probing Puzzles Persistently: A Desirable but Improbable Future for IR Theory," from the same volume, 318–27.

16. See Zalewski, "All These Theories," 342–43, for descriptions of these assumptions.

17. See ibid.

18. Ibid., citing Andrew Linklater, "The Achievements of Critical Theory," in Smith, Booth, and Zalewski, *International Relations Theory*, 279–300.

19. See ibid., 346.

20. See ibid., 347–49.

21. See ibid., 346.

22. The material in this paragraph and the preceding one was developed with input from Matthew Hoffmann, although errors of interpretation are the authors', of course.

Contributors

Brooke Ackerly's research interests include democratic theory, feminist methodologies, human rights, and social and environmental justice. She is currently working on the intersection of global economic, environmental, and gender justice. She integrates into her theoretical work empirical research on activism. Her publications include *Political Theory and Feminist Social Criticism* (2000), *Universal Human Rights in a World of Difference* (2008), and *Doing Feminist Research* (coauthored with Jacqui True, 2010, second edition forthcoming). She advises academics and donors on evaluation, methodology, and the ethics of research and serves the profession through committees in her professional associations. She has been a member of the editorial board for *Politics and Gender* (journal of the APSA, Women and Politics Section) and is currently a member of the editorial boards of the *Journal of Politics* and *Politics, Gender, and Identities.*

J. Samuel Barkin is Professor of Global Governance and Human Security at the McCormack Graduate School of Policy and Global Studies at the University of Massachusetts Boston. He received his PhD and MPhil in Political Science from Columbia University. He is author or editor of several books, most recently *Saving Global Fisheries: Reducing Capacity to Promote Sustainability* (coauthored with Elizabeth DeSombre, 2013) and *Realist Constructivism: Rethinking International Relations Theory* (2010). His work has been published in *International Organization*, *International Studies Quarterly*, the *International Studies Review*, *Foreign Policy Analysis*, *Global Environmental Politics*, *Global Governance*, *Millennium*, and *Environmental Politics*, among other journals, as well as in numerous edited volumes.

Matthew Hoffmann is a Professor in the Department of Political Science at the University of Toronto and at the University of Toronto, Scarborough. He is also Co-Director of the Environmental Governance Lab at the Munk School of Global Affairs. His research and teaching interests include global governance, climate change politics, complexity theory, and international relations theory. In addition to a number of articles and book chapters on climate politics, carbon markets, and global governance, he is the author of *Climate Governance at the Crossroads: Experimenting with a Global Response after Kyoto* (2011) and *Ozone Depletion and Climate Change: Constructing a Global Response* (2005). He also is a coauthor on a recent collaborative book, *Transnational Climate Change Governance* (2014).

Patrick Thaddeus Jackson is currently Associate Dean for Undergraduate Education and Professor of International Relations in the School of International Service. He previously taught at Columbia University and New York University. He received his PhD in political science from Columbia University in 2001. In 2003–4 and again in 2012–13, he served as president of the International Studies Association–Northeast. He was formerly editor in chief of the *Journal of International Relations and Development* and is currently series editor of the University of Michigan Press book series Configurations: Critical Studies of World Politics and coeditor of ISQ Online. He was recently named the 2012 US Professor of the Year for the District of Columbia by the Carnegie Foundation for the Advancement of Teaching.

Kevin Knudson is Professor of Mathematics at the University of Florida. He is an expert in computational topology and is the author of two monographs, *Homology of Linear Groups* and *Morse Theory: Smooth and Discrete,* in addition to several journal articles. He writes about math for Forbes, teaches a lot of calculus, plays the guitar, and watches too much baseball.

Paul A. Kowert is Associate Professor of Political Science at the University of Massachusetts Boston. He teaches undergraduate and graduate courses on foreign policy making, international relations theory, national security, political psychology, US-Japan relations, and research design. His research explores the way leaders differ in their use of information and advice, the way they incorporate normative principles into their policy choices, and the way people form perceptions of other countries. He is the recipient of research and teaching grants from the National Science Foundation, the Social Science Research Council, the Japan Society for the Promotion of Science, the Fulbright Foundation, and the International Studies Association. He is the author of numerous scholarly articles and the author, coauthor, or editor of four books, including *Groupthink or Deadlock: When Do Leaders Learn from Their Advisors* (2002), *Cultures of Order: Leadership, Language, and Social Reconstruction in Germany and Japan* (coauthored with Katja Weber, 2007), and *Psychology and Constructivism in International Relations: An Ideational Alliance* (coedited with Vaughn P. Shannon, 2011).

Ian S. Lustick is Professor of Political Science at the University of Pennsylvania, where he holds the Bess W. Heyman Chair. He has published widely on issues in comparative and Middle East politics and is a pioneer in applying agent-based computer simulation techniques to problems in intelligence and social science theory. Lustick's writings on Arab-Israeli relations, American foreign policy, ethnic conflict, social science methodology, and agent-based modeling have appeared in *Foreign Affairs, Foreign Policy, World Politics, the American Political Science Review, Polity, the Middle East Journal, Middle East Policy, Critical Review, International Organization,* and *Comparative Politics.* His books include *Unsettled States, Disputed Lands: Britain and Ireland, France and Algeria, Israel and the West Bank–Gaza (1993)* and *Trapped in the War on Terror* (2006). His current research focuses on explaining Israel's failure to pursue a two-state solution to the Palestinian problem while it was available and on explaining political cascades and the impact of violence on processes that generate or prevent them.

Laura Sjoberg is Associate Professor of Political Science at the University of Florida, with an affiliation with the Center for Women's Studies and Gender Research. She holds a PhD from the University of Southern California and a JD from Boston College Law School. She is author or editor of several books, including, most recently, *Women as Wartime Rapists* (2016), *Beyond Mothers Monsters, Whores* (coauthored with Caron Gentry, 2015), *Gender, War, and Conflict* (2014), and *Gendering Global Conflict: Toward a Feminist Theory of War* (2013). Her work has been published in more than two dozen journals in international relations and gender studies, and she currently serves as the homebase editor for the *International Feminist Journal of Politics* and as coeditor of the *International Studies Review.*

David Sylvan is Professor of International Relations and Political Science at the Graduate Institute of International and Development Studies in Geneva. He is the coauthor of *A Rationalist Methodology for the Social Sciences* and *U.S. Foreign Policy in Perspective: Clients, Enemies, and Empire* and has published journal articles on numerous topics in the social sciences. His current research is on the sociology of international relations, the garrison state and republicanism, and sequences in social life.

Cameron G. Thies is Professor and Director of the School of Politics and Global Studies at Arizona State University. His research interests are varied and span traditional subfields of conflict processes, international political economy, and foreign policy analysis, as well as international relations theory more broadly. In particular, his recent work has focused on state building in the developing world, trade and conflict, and role theory and foreign policy. His books have been published by Stanford University Press and Routledge. His journal articles appear in such outlets as the *American Journal of Political Science*, the *Journal of Politics*, *World Politics*, *International Studies Quarterly*, and the *European Journal of International Relations*.

Index